THE POWER OF
LOVE

HOW KENNETH JERNIGAN CHANGED
THE WORLD FOR THE BLIND

THE POWER OF
LOVE

HOW KENNETH JERNIGAN CHANGED
THE WORLD FOR THE BLIND

NATIONAL FEDERATION
OF THE BLIND

THE POWER OF LOVE
How Kenneth Jernigan Changed the World for the Blind

Edited by Ramona Walhof

iUniverse books may be ordered through booksellers or by contacting:

iUniverse
1663 Liberty Drive
Bloomington, IN 47403
www.iuniverse.com
1-800-Authors (1-800-288-4677)

ISBN: 978-1-4917-8451-8 (sc)
ISBN: 978-1-4917-8450-1 (e)

Library of Congress Control Number: 2016900427

Print information available on the last page.

iUniverse rev. date: 1/22/2016

CONTENTS

INTRODUCTION

by Ramona Walhof

Kenneth Jernigan (1926 to 1998) was truly one of the great men of the twentieth century. I was one of the fortunate people to be his student and his friend. I feel it both an obligation and a privilege to do what I can to share with those who did not know him personally a picture of greatness that continues (more than a decade after his death) to guide and inspire people around the world. His wisdom, his methods, and his actions will do this as long as people are aware of what he said and did. His words and his actions will be blended with those of his students and colleagues and will reach ahead to guide yet other generations.

Blind throughout his life, Kenneth Jernigan led the National Federation of the Blind for almost twenty years as its President and far longer as one of its principal leaders. During that time this organization grew to become the leading force for acceptance and change for the disabled in the United States and beyond. While his emphasis was blindness, all of the disabled learned about and benefited from the philosophical positions and progress of the blind. Sighted associates in work with the blind, in government, and in business were also guided and influenced greatly by him. Most of all he left a large number of speeches, articles, and books expressing his keen wit, his brilliant thinking, his decisive leadership, and his compassion.

As a young child in Tennessee, Kenneth Jernigan felt restricted by his family. There is no doubt that they loved him, but because he was blind, they wished to protect him from harm. They worried about snakes and falls and getting lost. His parents were farmers and had no knowledge about blindness or about techniques he could use to reduce the lack of vision to the level of a mere nuisance. It became his work, his struggle, and his joy to find ways to assist the blind to be integrated into the mainstream of society and to help the general population itself to accept blind persons as productive and interesting citizens. Tens of thousands of blind people around the world and teachers and leaders of the blind have learned from him and put his ideas together with their own to make a different climate for the blind.

Influence may be a hard thing to measure. Yet this is a story as exciting and dramatic for the blind as the development of computers or space exploration. It is as significant for the blind and other disabled Americans as the life and work of Dr. Martin Luther King, Jr. was to racial minorities.

Kenneth Jernigan was wise enough and dynamic enough to combine his abilities with those of others through the National Federation of the Blind and the World Blind Union in order to reach, not only throughout the U.S., but also into every continent and most countries. He encouraged the people he touched to make their own contributions and insisted they could. Many wished to help, and the momentum grew. He was the leader, but hundreds (perhaps thousands) of others became leaders carrying his message of hope and confidence for the blind far and wide. His message became their own message, and it continues to grow and bloom today with more new ideas and more people to carry on. Individuals with different kinds of disabilities learned from the blind. To some degree their needs were different, but they followed the pattern of seeking legislation, understanding, and legal decisions to make their lives better.

Because blind people do not live in isolation, Kenneth Jernigan touched and changed the lives of sighted people as well. This is a story of change for the blind—but the story cannot be told without the involvement of sighted colleagues and friends. When he found a kindred spirit with knowledge and ability that were helpful, he would build and maintain a relationship with that person, who would frequently become a partner in his work and his friend, often a life-long friend.

Dr. Jernigan's articles and speeches are read and reread by tens of thousands still today. The generations of blind leaders who learned from him and moved forward along with him continue his work. Many are well-known in their own right and have continued to advance the integration of the blind into society. It is not surprising, but noteworthy, how many of today's blind leaders were students of the master, Kenneth Jernigan. His blind students became professionals in work with the blind: engineers, lawyers, businessmen and women, and more. His sighted colleagues are as diverse.

The chapters of this book were written by twenty-nine of Dr. Jernigan's students and colleagues and will introduce readers to the methods and creativity of their teacher and mentor. Certain techniques were used repeatedly, but always effectively and frequently in a new application. He always hoped to keep people guessing. He told me that he felt responsible to entertain and surprise those he worked with—and he did. The people, both sighted and blind, who have written chapters in this book tell how they applied the lessons learned in their own work and lives. All looked to Dr. Jernigan as the primary leader as long as he lived. However, he expected each to carry a share of the work. And this we have done cheerfully, sometimes with fear, but always with the wish to accomplish the goals set forth by our teacher. Both blind and sighted colleagues continue to join in the work now led by our current president, Mark Riccobono.

There are those who say the blind led the emancipation of the disabled during the latter part of the twentieth century. For many, blindness is the most emotional of the physical disabilities. The techniques used by the blind (Braille, talking computers, white canes and guide dogs for independent travel) are not used by any other group. These techniques require specialized instruction for blind children and adults. The day has not yet arrived when blind people universally receive the training they need, but progress has been immense. Kenneth Jernigan taught that: With these special techniques, blind people can be competitive in the workplace, at home, and in their communities, as long as they are offered the opportunity to do so. He and his colleagues and students taught and demonstrated that this is not just an intellectual thesis. Rather, it is a philosophical basis for life and work. Its truth and his leadership made it possible for tens of thousands of blind people to become productive and prosperous individuals. Dr. Jernigan proclaimed proudly that blind people are a cross section of society and can be integrated as such. He led the trend which continues to accelerate.

Beginning in 1958 when Kenneth Jernigan became director of the Iowa Commission for the Blind, he used his ideas and techniques to assist the blind to learn to be independent. He taught the philosophy and demonstrated repeatedly that it worked and how. This was his work and his goal, and it continues today to be the goal of his students and colleagues through the National Federation of the Blind and beyond. As he predicted, it will continue on until blindness is reduced to the level of an inconvenience or nuisance, a simple characteristic. There is no wish to ignore or forget about blindness, only to make it respectable in every sense of the word. The goal has not yet been attained, but today there are thousands who understand and pursue it.

In the words of some of his students and colleagues, describing some of the experiences they shared with their teacher and what they went on to do, I hope to show the man and his work in a way only those who lived it have previously known.

Many more of Dr. Jernigan's students and associates could tell their stories. To be included in this book, first an individual had to write and submit something. Each story can stand on its own but complements the others selected. Although some activities are referred to by more than one writer, I have cut out lengthy repetition of activities. Some approaches were repeated with literally hundreds of students and staff members. Anyone who wishes more information can find it in Kenneth Jernigan's own papers, in the *Braille Monitor*, in the Kernel books, and on the NFB website.

Dr. Jernigan told much of his own life through stories in the Kernel Books—a series he began in 1991 and edited for eight years, which were distributed by the National Federation of the Blind. Dr. Marc Maurer edited similar books for another seven years. These are available today from the National Federation of the Blind, 200 East Wells Street *at Jernigan Place*, Baltimore, Maryland 21230 and on the internet at www.nfb.org under publications. His own Kernel Book chapters relate personal experiences from his childhood and mature life.

Many speeches and articles are published in *Walking Alone and Marching Together* by Dr. Floyd Matson, published in 1990, and in the *Braille Monitor,* the monthly magazine of the NFB. *Kenneth Jernigan: The Master, The Mission, The Movement* edited by Marc Maurer is a compilation of Dr. Jernigan's writings during the last decade of his life. The present book draws from previously printed material a little and includes a number of new accounts.

The story of Kenneth Jernigan would not be what it is without those he taught and led. It is the story of the emergence of a significant portion of population from dependence to freedom; from sympathy and pity to competence and admiration. It is the story of the work and joy of Kenneth Jernigan, his teachings, and his students and colleagues.

If I and the others who have contributed to this book have succeeded in bringing to life the true personality and wisdom of Kenneth Jernigan, the message of this book will inspire and educate all who read it. We have seen the impact of the man and his life. I hope to pass the gifts he gave on to those who wish to learn and be inspired by one of the greatest thinkers and doers of the twentieth century.

And Kenneth Jernigan would not wish to have this story told without giving credit to his mentor and founder of the NFB, Dr. Jacobus tenBroek, who served as President for most of the first twenty-five years of the National Federation of the Blind. He was loved and revered as Professor at the University of California, and he wrote hundreds of articles and five full-length books. Dr. tenBroek's writing on Constitutional Law is still read and quoted extensively today.

In 2008 the NFB began holding the Jacobus tenBroek Disability Law Symposium annually. The symposium gathers attorneys, judges, and professors who are experts in constitutional law and the law as it affects the disabled throughout the country. The 2015 symposium was attended by more than 200 of the nation's leading disability rights legal scholars and experts. Dr. tenBroek was a giant in his own time. Dr. Jernigan built upon the work of Jacobus tenBroek. His successor Marc Maurer has done likewise. Dr. Maurer, himself an accomplished attorney, has led the Federation's legal efforts with passion and focused legal strategy to major victories in the courts, which will have far-reaching effects for generations to come.

At the time of his death Dr. Jernigan (as most of us called him) was planning the construction of the new National Research and Training Institute for the Blind to be created and operated by the blind themselves and located at the headquarters of the National Federation of the Blind in Baltimore, Maryland. Dr. Marc Maurer, who had succeeded Kenneth Jernigan as president of the organization, spearheaded a campaign to raise the funds to build the Institute, which upon completion was named the National Federation of the Blind Jernigan Institute. Over the next fourteen years President Maurer led the development of state-of-the-art programs, which have made the Institute the focal point of the nation's most innovative work with blind children, youth, and adults. It is fair to say that the promise of the Institute Dr. Jernigan dreamed of has, under Marc Maurer's leadership, come to full realization and more. To say that Kenneth Jernigan had identified and trained his successor takes nothing away from the leadership, originality, persuasiveness, and wisdom that Marc Maurer came to exercise throughout his presidency.

In 2014 Dr. Maurer retired after serving and leading the Federation for twenty-eight years. For nearly ten years he had been training and mentoring Mark Riccobono as an up-and-coming young leader. Just as Dr. Jernigan had done earlier, President Maurer had decided that the time was right for him to step aside, and Mark Riccobono was elected to lead the organization. Mr. Riccobono's readiness for the presidency can be attributed in no small way to the mentoring he had received from President Maurer. Later in this book Mr. Riccobono writes movingly about his relationship with Dr. Maurer and his gratitude for all that he has received from him.

The National Federation of the Blind has been amazingly fortunate to have had three outstanding long-term presidents—Jacobus tenBroek, Kenneth Jernigan, and Marc Maurer. What is perhaps even more amazing is that each of them has sought out and mentored another leader fully capable of providing the same caliber of leadership. The tradition of our presidents has been not merely to continue the legacy of their predecessors, but to solve the challenges facing blind individuals in their own times using their own unique capacities to carry the work of the Federation forward to ever new levels. Although this book focuses primarily upon Kenneth Jernigan's legacy, it should be noted here that he himself expressed great satisfaction with Marc Maurer's presidency, regarding his leadership as firm, kind, creative in its own right, and filled with energy. The very substantial accomplishments of the Maurer presidency confirm that assessment.

The first year of the Riccobono presidency gives every indication that we have again found the right leader—one possessing the characteristics of his three predecessors—energy, commitment, passion, intellect, and, above all, love. In short, we believe President Riccobono will lead the blind into a future bright with promise. Tens of thousands of members and friends are counting on it.

CHAPTER 1

MEET KENNETH JERNIGAN

by Mary Ellen Jernigan

Note: Mrs. Mary Ellen Jernigan was recruited as a cane travel instructor for the Iowa Commission for the Blind shortly after she graduated Phi Beta Kappa from Drake University in Des Moines. Dr. Jernigan was looking for young individuals with ability whom he could train to do the work he was pursuing. She became deputy director of the Iowa agency and then chief assistant to the president when Dr. Jernigan moved NFB headquarters to Baltimore. She became Mrs. Jernigan in 1986. Together, Dr. and Mrs. Jernigan were an unbeatable team. How could I find a better person than his loving wife to introduce this extraordinary man?

KENNETH JERNIGAN WAS BORN IN 1926 ON A FARM IN middle Tennessee. It was an isolated existence in a four-room house on a gravel road. It was an unusual thing for an automobile to drive by. There was no indoor plumbing or electricity. There were no radios, telephones, or newspapers.

1

His parents were good people, and they loved him, but they had no idea what to do with a blind child.

Young Kenneth and Lloyd Jernigan on the family farm in Tennessee, circa 1930.

Nobody in the neighborhood had ever known a blind person. His parents feared for his safety. Mostly that meant he was forbidden to leave the porch. His mother told his older brother Lloyd that, after she and his father were gone, it would be his responsibility to care for Kenneth.

The isolation of his childhood years gave Kenneth Jernigan time to do a lot of thinking. He was determined not to spend the rest of his life as a prisoner on the porch of that four-room house on the farm or as a ward of his older brother Lloyd.

At six he was sent to the school for the blind in Nashville. He got an "F" in Braille that first quarter, but that was only because he had had to wait until January to start since he was not yet six in September when the others had started. He quickly caught up to his classmates.

Soon he realized that going to college would be his ticket off the farm. From that point on he read every Braille and audio book he could get his hands on.

When he was a senior in high school, he had an experience that shaped—not only his own life, but the lives of blind individuals for generations to come. Here is how he describes that pivotal experience:

> "In 1945 I had my first contact with a rehabilitation official. A counselor came to the School for the Blind, and he and I sat down for a chat. When we got past the niceties, the counselor asked me what I wanted to major in when I went to college. I told him I wanted to be a lawyer. He replied by

asking me to tell him three or four things I might like to do.

I told him I didn't need to give him three or four. I wanted to be a lawyer. He was not an unkind man, but what he said was clear. I could be a lawyer and pay for it myself, or I could be something else, and the rehabilitation agency would help pay.

Since I didn't have the money, I went to college and was something else. The counselor undoubtedly thought he was acting in my best interest; but I know now he was wrong."

The "something else" as far as college was concerned turned out to be degrees in English literature and history and a job offer to become a professor at a Midwestern college.

But in the bigger picture, the "something else" quite directly became the foundation for this reflection and the essays that comprise this book. Here is what happened. Although the college professorship was tempting, he did not accept it. Instead, he took the job he was offered to teach English at the Tennessee School for the Blind.

I suspect that that misguided rehabilitation counselor never knew the immense gift he gave to future generations of blind people when he told a brash teenager that he couldn't study law. For his action had helped Kenneth Jernigan come to the decision to work to create a world where blind people can live the lives they want—not the world of the low expectations of the rehab counselor, not the world where the blind person settles for "something else."

He met Jacobus tenBroek, the founder of the National Federation of the Blind, in 1952. Soon after, he moved to California and spent the next several years working closely with Dr. tenBroek, where he continued to develop his ideas about the true nature and consequences of blindness—what those consequences really were, and equally important, what they were not. Never far from his mind was the misguided rehabilitation counselor who had emphatically insisted that there was no possibility he could ever become a lawyer and had used his power to prevent him from even trying.

He and Dr. tenBroek soon devised a plan. The plan was to find a state program for the blind with a vacancy for director—one that was terrible; one where no one else wanted the job; one that might hire a blind person with radically different ideas about blindness; in short, a place where Kenneth Jernigan could put his ideas to the test.

The perfect chance came in 1958. The Iowa Commission for the Blind was looking for a director. This state agency fit the bill almost perfectly: the budget was minuscule, $20,000; the staff numbered six; the office consisted of three small rooms in a condemned building; it ranked last in the nation in rehabilitation; and, most importantly, there was no long line of candidates seeking the job—exactly the right profile Kenneth Jernigan and Dr. tenBroek were looking for.

Dr. Kenneth Jernigan sits at his desk at the National Center for the Blind, 1990.

Perhaps the remarks made in connection with the presentation of a citation from the President of the United States in 1968, just ten years later, best sum up the significance of what came to be known as the Iowa Experiment: "If a person must be blind, it is better to be blind in Iowa than in any other place in the nation, or the world."

While the presidential citation recognizes what happened to the programs of the Iowa Commission for the Blind, it sheds no real light on how it is that so many of his students there continue to be utterly convinced that their own lives were transformed in some fundamental way by his. Nor does it speak to the same effect in the lives of many of us who are not blind. For that explanation one must look far beyond the subject of blindness.

But first, let me sum up briefly what he believed and taught about blindness. It begins and ends with a startlingly simple belief system. The central element of which is that the characteristic of blindness is merely one of the thousands of attributes that define an individual; that blindness does not in and of itself limit an individual in ways that are more significant than those imposed by other characteristics. These notions and the hope implicit in them were forged from his own lived experience sifted in with the experience of other blind people. They were at the root of an unshakeable article of faith that given training and opportunity, the average blind person could compete on terms of equality with the average sighted person similarly situated, and that blindness could be reduced to the level of a physical nuisance.

Looking beyond anything relating to blindness, one quickly notes that Kenneth Jernigan had a brilliant intellect apparent to all who knew him, even casually. That he was well educated was also clear. His strong and resonant voice with just an occasional remaining tinge of the south was easy to listen to. Precision, neatness, and order hung about him like a cloak. Courtesy was ever present. It would have been hard to be unaware of his love of good food. Were his eyes not mostly closed because of long-atrophied facial muscles, one would frequently have observed a twinkle.

Mary Ellen and Kenneth Jernigan, in their home, 1986.

A stellar combination of attributes to be sure; yet not, I believe, the crucial factor explaining the fundamental, permanent transformation so many credit him with bringing about in their lives. Like his breakthrough thought about blindness, his life-changing capacity to transform lives was rooted in the simplicity of an unshakeable belief system. It was this belief system that he ceaselessly radiated and thus was able to transmit to those of us—blind and sighted alike—who were fortunate enough to be his students.

I would paraphrase the transmission we received in the following way:

> You have within yourself all that you need to make the world a better place for yourself and those around you. I care about you. Tell me what you would like to do, and I will help you do it. Alone, things are hard to get done, but together all of us have lots of power, and we can change the world, making a difference for ourselves and others. You can do this. Don't settle for less than you want. Work to get it. Find and help build the mechanisms that make these things come true. You are going to live anyway, so you might as well live with joy. Do so, and you will transform your hope into something real.

Through this, what he taught us was a particular way of seeing, of reflecting, and of responding to life that can transform every experience and every event (whether good or bad) into a significant encounter with reality to be consciously considered and woven into the fabric of a purposely constructed life. We learned that this particular way of seeing and responding did not come about by chance—that it was a technique to be learned and a discipline to be practiced, not on the way to somewhere else, but as the heart of life itself.

When Kenneth Jernigan was a teenager in the 1930s he wanted to work in the fields making hay with his father and the neighboring farmers. They worked from dawn to sundown in blistering heat. Not believing there was any task a blind boy could do that would truly help the effort, they told him there was no place for him on their crew.

So instead, he designed and built tables and lamps. Having no power tools, he scoured the neighborhood asking for empty wooden sewing spools. He collected old automobile steering wheels from the local junkyard. The spools, which would otherwise have been thrown in the trash, he strung on iron rods to make table legs since he had no lathe. The junked steering wheels formed the bases for his lamps. He made many tables and lamps that summer. The men who had rejected his offer to help make hay only made $1.25 for a day's work. He made $8.25 a day making and selling furniture.

Kenneth Jernigan died in 1998. When it came time to plan the monument for his grave, I gave much thought as to how to capture the vibrancy of his life in a cold slab of granite stone. For many months no thought came. Then in a flash, I knew. The granite slab came to life when I envisioned a six-foot tall replica of a wooden sewing spool carved on each side. What more fitting symbol could there be for a man who spent his life transforming lives believed to be without value—lives destined for the trash bin, now solid as granite. A man who loved deeply and who, in return, was deeply loved.

CHAPTER 2

THE JERNIGAN INSTITUTE: THE EXPRESSION OF A MAN

by Dr. Marc Maurer

Note: Here Marc Maurer tells his own story, giving credit to Dr. Jernigan as so many do.

I MET DR. KENNETH JERNIGAN IN THE SUMMER OF 1969 shortly before the commencement of the convention of the National Federation of the Blind. Within a very short time he became my teacher, my mentor, my friend, and my trusted superior in the National Federation of the Blind. I had just graduated from high school, and although I had been blind for all of my life, I had come to the state rehabilitation program for the blind in Iowa, a program directed by Dr. Jernigan, to learn about blindness. I wondered what I didn't already know. I had, after all, been blind all of my life. Though I was only eighteen years of age, I thought my experience gave me substantial understanding of what blindness was like. I learned from Dr. Jernigan that my concept of the nature of blindness was dramatically inadequate.

In 1998, Dr. Jernigan died after fighting cancer for a year. I was in the room with him when his life came to a close. Although observing his struggle with cancer was one of the most painful experiences I have encountered, I was glad to be with him, and I was honored. The intervening twenty-nine years had changed my prospects, shaped me into a being with possibilities I could never have imagined, and brought to me a kind of fulfillment that many human beings can only hope to achieve. An enormous element in this transformation is the influence and the support of Dr. Kenneth Jernigan. He was a magnificent man, and he cared for me and thousands of others. It is hard to put into words what his life meant to us.

I became a student in the rehabilitation training program directed by Dr. Jernigan in 1969. I had successfully graduated from high school in the top part of my class, but I had no idea what future might be available to me. I had a vague notion that I might be able to attend college, but I knew this to be expensive, and I did not know where I would find the money. My older brother had departed the family home for college two years earlier. During the summer months he earned money, which he used for tuition and other college expenses when he returned to school in the fall. I had attempted to get employment myself, but the people with the jobs didn't want me. I was a blind kid, and they had businesses to run. They took it for granted that I wouldn't be of any value, and although I found this distressing, I knew of no way to challenge this assumption. At one level, I wondered whether their categorization of me as less capable than others was fair. When Dr. Jernigan got hold of me, he expressed the view that my imagination had been too narrow, and he backed up this idea with concrete examples.

The first dramatic example of the instruction I received from him involved barbecuing hamburger. First, he asked me to form hamburger patties out of ground beef. He criticized my effort, saying that my hamburgers were skimpy. When he put his hands on the burgers, they grew to about a third of a pound apiece—or bigger. Then, he said, it was time to build a fire. He showed me a charcoal grill, and he asked me to put charcoal into it. The size of the pile of briquettes never seemed to be quite enough until the apparatus was almost full. Then, he wanted me to add charcoal fluid. Once again, the quantity was expected to be substantial. "Light the fire," he said and handed me a match. The flame came boiling out of the grill—it seemed to me to be an inferno.

He handed me a pair of gloves, telling me that these were welding gloves. When I had them on, he said, "Now, put your hand in the fire."

What! I thought? You want me to put my hand in that great big towering blaze? Dr. Jernigan said quietly, "When you are wearing welding gloves, you can stir the fire with your fingers. Here, let me show you." Dr. Jernigan had his hand in the fire; I put mine into the blaze and stirred the charcoal briefly. We put the raw hamburgers into a barbecuing rack, and we cooked them over the fire. When we had finished eating the results, Dr. Jernigan pointed out that an imaginative approach can make it practical to perform many, many activities previously thought impossible for the blind. Besides, the hamburgers were excellent.

The schedule for the class day established for me in the program operated by Dr. Jernigan commenced with gym class at 5:30 in the morning. After gym class, we were expected to get cleaned up, to prepare ourselves for the day, and to locate breakfast. At 8:00 a.m. my class schedule required me to be prepared to learn to travel with a white cane. At 10:00 a.m. industrial arts began. At 12:30 I was expected to be in home economics unless the class included preparing food for lunch. If lunch was a part of the class activity, I was expected to arrive in home economics at noon. At 2:30 the Braille class began, and at 3:30 typing occurred. At 4:30 I was expected to be in the philosophy class which lasted an hour. In this class we considered what blindness meant and what it did not. Many people have chuckle-headed notions about the nature of blindness, and this class was conducted to demystify the topic. At 5:30 we were free to set our own schedules and do our own thing unless we were invited to participate in special events. One of these was a class in grammar taught by Dr. Jernigan. This class was available by invitation only. Those who succeeded in the class learned a great deal about the grammar of the English language, but they also learned about logic and the ability to think.

During my growing-up years, I had heard about how blind people might succeed in many different endeavors. My teachers wanted to lift my spirits about the fact that I am blind. However, despite their brave words, I was perfectly certain that these people knew very little about the topic they were discussing. However, Dr. Jernigan knew a thing or two about blindness, and he spoke to me with authority. He was blind himself, and he had interacted with many thousands of blind people all over the United States and in other parts of the world. He demanded that those of us receiving instruction from him be prepared to work and be productive in what we did. Other people accepted excuses from blind individuals for the failure to accomplish extraordinary activities, but Dr. Jernigan did not. He expected excellence, and he was willing to help us find the methods to get it.

One snowy day in the fall, Dr. Jernigan sent us on an expedition to cut wood. He said that blind people could cut down trees, and he supplied us with a couple of five-foot two-man crosscut saws and a teacher. Before we were finished, I (along with another student) had felled a tree three feet in diameter. Unfortunately, it was the wrong tree. The farmer who owned the land had not imagined that we would tackle one of that size, so he hadn't told us that we were prohibited from cutting it. Although this event occurred decades in the past, it remains impressive to me still.

As part of the rehabilitation process, each of the students who took industrial arts (in those days the men took shop, and the women took sewing) were expected to build something as a graduation project. It might be the case for a clock, the frame for a bed, a cedar chest, or something else. One student built an octagon-shaped poker table with a felt top and places for chips for each player. When the shop instructor (who was a friend of mine) asked me what I wanted to build, I told him I didn't want to build anything. "So," he said, what do you want to do?"

"I want to overhaul an automobile engine," I said.

"Do you have an automobile?" he asked me.

"No," I responded.

"Can you get an automobile?" he wanted to know.

"Certainly," I said. I was without a job and without money. I had no idea where to get an automobile.

A few days later the shop teacher told me that we were going shopping. This did not ordinarily happen during shop class. Never before had we taken the time during class to shop. When we got to the hardware store, the shop teacher said that we would need wrenches if we were going to overhaul an automobile engine. I agreed. Then he said, "We'll need a hoist, I guess."

"Yes, indeed, we'll definitely need that!" I said.

"We will probably need some pullers, don't you think?" asked the teacher.

I had never heard of a puller. "Yes," I said, "We will certainly need them!" Then, I thought to myself, I had better get an automobile. I called a friend of mine from high school, and I asked him if I could overhaul an automobile engine for him. Within a few days he loaned me a 1963 Ford Galaxy 500 with a 352-inch V-8 engine in it. I pulled the engine from the car, and under the direction of the shop instructor, I tore it apart completely, and I rebuilt it. By the time I had completed the work, that engine was ready for another 100,000 miles.

Dr. Jernigan wanted me to do what I wanted to do. He wanted to help me have experience that I might not ever get without his assistance. When I asked to overhaul an engine, he created the program to make it happen.

Dr. Jernigan thought that I was college material, and he urged me to apply. He also said that he would help me find the money to pay for it through the rehabilitation program. I had been contemplating attending a Catholic college in Minnesota. Dr. Jernigan said to me, "Why don't you go to the University of Notre Dame? That's a Catholic college." This thought had never occurred to me. My application was accepted; I headed for the University in 1970 intending to become an engineer. A few months into this study, I was talking with Dr. Jernigan. He said that engineers were useful to humanity. Those who became engineers built products and systems—airplanes, missiles, bridges, and the like. Those who built society needed to understand human beings and the ways policies came into being. They needed to know history, literature, philosophy, and public policy. I shifted my course of study to focus on these things. After graduating with a bachelor's degree, I entered law school at Indiana University, and I took a degree in law in 1977.

When I first met Dr. Jernigan in 1969, he was serving as President of the National Federation of the Blind. One of my first exposures to him occurred at the convention of the Federation which took place during the first week of July that year. Dr. Jernigan stood on the platform at the national convention, and he said to those who participated in the program that blind people were important and that programs for the blind had to be conducted effectively. When failures in such programs occurred, he challenged the administrators of them to make the improvements that the blind of the nation needed. It was a demonstration that working together blind people could have more effectiveness and more power than any one of us could have individually. This understanding made me want to be part of the Federation. I joined the Des Moines chapter of the organization, and I have remained active in the Federation ever since.

An incident at my first convention indicates a bit about Dr. Jernigan's character. I was heading for the meeting room one morning, and I happened to meet him in the elevator. He had earlier urged me to attend the convention. Part of the justification for my being there was that we who were knowledgeable about blindness should tell others what they needed to know. Dr. Jernigan had expressed this sentiment to me, and I had been flattered by the notion.

When I met Dr. Jernigan in the elevator, he asked me, "Are you learning anything at this convention?"

I had learned quite a lot, and I admitted as much. Then he asked me, "Are you teaching anybody anything at this convention?"

Inasmuch as I had been urged to come to the convention partly to help others learn what they needed to know, it seemed the prudent thing for me to say that I had been teaching. I probably had taught some people some things, but I doubt that I had taught very much.

Dr. Jernigan asked me, "Have you been learning more, or teaching more?"

I thought it would be presumptuous of me to say that I had been teaching more than I had been learning. Besides, I had been learning more than I had been teaching. I said this to our Federation President.

Then, he asked his final question. He put it this way, "So, why have you been taking more than you've been giving?"

The question startled me. I could not imagine what to do with it. I am sure that he meant to startle me and that he meant to stimulate my imagination. He accomplished both.

When I graduated from law school in 1977, I began looking for full-time employment, and I landed a job with a public interest law firm in Toledo, Ohio. Dr. Jernigan, who had been President of the National Federation of the Blind since 1968, had been having substantial medical problems. He resigned from the Presidency of the National Federation of the Blind in the summer of 1977, but he continued his work as the director of programs for the blind in Iowa. His reputation for excellence was outstanding. Rehabilitation programs for the blind in Iowa were regarded by the federal government and by the blind of the nation as the best in the world. Each year visitors from throughout the United States and from a number of foreign countries would come to Iowa to learn the secret. Rehabilitation in the state of Iowa was producing better results than similar programs in any other place.

While Dr. Jernigan was directing programs for the blind in Iowa, he was also continuing to build activity within the National Federation of the Blind. In many states and on the national level rehabilitation practices that belittled the blind or damaged them economically were being challenged. Programs that paid blind people subminimum wages were threatened with reorganization because blind people were taking their case for equality of opportunity to the newspapers and to public officials. Some of the directors in these substandard programs for the blind were looking for a way to fight back, and they wanted to challenge the reputation of Dr. Jernigan as a mechanism for stopping the progress of the Federation. The plan was to make the President look bad so that the organization itself would look bad. One of these public officials had become friends with the editor of the newspaper in Iowa.

Because of the enormous reputation Dr. Jernigan had achieved, a newspaper reporter in Iowa decided to try to gain reputation for himself and his paper by exposing the "seamy side" of Dr. Jernigan's character. The reporter felt that all human beings make mistakes, and all human beings succumb to temptation now and then. All he had to do was look long enough and hard enough, and he would "get the goods" on Dr. Jernigan. He discovered a disgruntled former employee of the agency for the blind who told fantastic tales about Dr.

Jernigan. The information appeared in the newspaper, and the reporter asked the United States Attorney what she was planning to do about it. The U.S. Attorney had been planning to run for governor, and she was looking for a case that would help her to gain recognition in the state. With the newspaper posing questions and the U.S. Attorney planning to run for governor, the story was magnified. Dr. Jernigan was soon under investigation.

Some of the newspaper reports did not seem obviously irrational, but some did. One story reported that at the agency Dr. Jernigan was directing, there were anti-aircraft guns on the roof and a troop carrier in the basement. A brief examination at either place would have demonstrated the idiocy of such claims, but they were reported as fact regardless of their fantastic nature and complete falsehood. Some of the other claims were less obviously false, such as those asserting that Dr. Jernigan was diverting rehabilitation funds into charitable organizations.

Because I had come to know some of the members of the legislature in Iowa, and because I had come to know Dr. Jernigan and the magnificent work he was doing, I quit my job in Ohio to return to Iowa to try to help. Because I had only recently become a lawyer, I could not practice law in Iowa unless I passed the Iowa Bar Exam. I gathered material and began to study. One morning when I was at the library, my wife called me to say that an agent from the FBI had been to our apartment to look for me. I had become part of the investigation of Dr. Jernigan. When I asked Dr. Jernigan what he wanted me to do, he advised me to wait patiently until he had found a lawyer to represent me. The FBI wanted to know if I had documents that I could share with them regarding the programs that Dr. Jernigan had been conducting. We provided the documents, and the FBI checked them thoroughly. Later, when we reviewed FBI files, we discovered that the FBI investigators reported to the U.S. Attorney that there was absolutely nothing to find. This report was made in about ninety days after the beginning of the investigation, but the newspaper was still interested. The U.S. Attorney continued the investigation without help from the FBI for about two more years. In 1980 the U.S. Attorney wrote to say that the investigation had been closed. Nothing had been discovered that violated the law. Dr. Jernigan had conducted his business throughout his public and private careers in the most scrupulous and upright fashion.

Dr. Jernigan resigned his position as director of programs for the blind in Iowa in 1978. He moved to Baltimore to establish what has now become the preeminent center for the blind in the United States. The National Center for the Blind has since been renamed the National Federation of the Blind Jernigan Institute. The work pursued and completed in this Institute has enhanced opportunities for the blind in the nation and has provided inspiration for the blind from throughout the world.

I asked Dr. Jernigan one time why he had not sued the newspaper in Iowa. He told me that he had checked with the lawyers and that they had been confident that he would win. However, they also said that the fight would probably take at least five years and that the newspaper could report about him everyday while the argument lasted. Beyond that, they said that he would have time to do nothing except work on a constant basis to pursue his legal claims. Dr. Jernigan did not want to give up the opportunity of pursuing his goals in the Federation. He did not want to give the newspaper the chance to write negative stories about him and other blind people for a period of many years. Although in doing so he released claims against people who deserved to face the hardships of the courts, he decided that blind people would be served better if he built programs that would create opportunity rather than seeking to demonstrate the disreputable character and evil intent of those who were trying to belittle and injure the blind.

At the end of the 1970s and into the 1980s, Dr. Jernigan began the difficult work of bringing cooperation and harmony to entities within the field of work for the blind. Employees of some blindness programs were being paid less than the federal minimum wage. Dr. Jernigan sent me and others to help these employees form into unions for the purpose of bargaining collectively for better wages and working conditions. In a workshop operated by the state of Utah, blind employees who spoke up for themselves or others were attacked and physically beaten by their supervisors. We visited the governor of Utah to demand recompense and reorganization of such programs. The Department of Education of Utah was responsible for conditions in the workshop for the blind, and officials from the Department were irate that the governor should be informed and the incidents reported to the press. This is but one of the many actions that caused hostility in the field of work for the blind.

Dr. Jernigan caused a committee of executives of major entities in the blindness sphere to come together to talk about creating improvements for the blind. One of the changes in law that occurred as a result of these meetings was a provision in the Copyright Act which states that books and materials for the blind may be created in formats other than print without requiring permission from copyright holders. A second change in law is the provision of the Individuals with Disabilities Education Act declaring that blind children have a right to learn to read Braille. That such a provision of law was required is an indication of just how dismal programs of education for the blind had become. Nevertheless, the level of harmony and cooperation in the field of blindness had increased dramatically because of Dr. Jernigan's efforts.

In 1984, I was practicing law in Baltimore. Some of my clients were blind people who are members of the National Federation of the Blind. Dr. Jernigan had promised these people that the Federation would help them with cases of discrimination, and he had asked me to do the work. After one particularly strenuous period of effort, I came to visit with Dr. Jernigan about policy matters dealing with blindness in various parts of the United States. He had resumed the Presidency of the National Federation of the Blind after a one-year absence. Nevertheless, the health troubles that had caused his earlier resignation had continued. He was quite ill. I spent some time trying to discuss legal and policy issues with him, but he was not able to give such matters his full attention. He was sick enough that I wondered if he would live.

When he had recovered, I urged him to contemplate the future for the Federation. In his Presidency, Dr. Jernigan had demonstrated extraordinary leadership, and I wanted him to continue to do so. However, when he had resigned in 1977, the person who had become President was quite ineffective, and I wanted Dr. Jernigan to make it clear that he would not be supporting that ineffective person to return to office. He asked me if I was prepared to serve as President myself, and I indicated that I was.

In 1985, Dr. Jernigan expressed his view to the convention of the National Federation of the Blind that he would not be running for the Presidency of the organization in 1986 and that he would be supporting me for it. Somebody complained to him, saying that we should have an open election in 1986. Dr. Jernigan responded to this criticism by pointing out that he had expressed his view of the matter a year before the election was to take place. If anybody else had a candidate to suggest, a whole year was available for planning.

In 1986, I ran for the Presidency of the National Federation of the Blind, and I was elected unanimously. Dr. Jernigan was a dramatically good leader and a dramatically effective President. He loved the work of directing the National Federation of the Blind. For him not to run for the Presidency is a testament to his great love for the Federation. He did not run because he wanted the organization to survive him. He and I worked closely with one another for the next twelve years until his death in 1998.

Marc Maurer and Kenneth Jernigan celebrate
Maurer's election to NFB Presidency at the 1986 NFB
National Convention in Kansas City, Missouri.

In 1990, Dr. Jernigan created the International Braille and Technology Center for the Blind. For him, this was not difficult.

He said that we would collect all technology, all computer programs, and all peripheral devices that could be used by the blind to manage information. He decided that we would put all of these things in one place and that we would make this technology laboratory available to inventors, to blind people, to public officials, and to anybody else who needed information about the technology used by blind people. Within a few weeks, what he said would happen did happen.

In 1991, Dr. Jernigan began editing a series of publications denominated "The Kernel Books," which describe the details of the effort of individual blind people to achieve independence in their own lives. Thirty of these would be published before the series came to a close. He created them because he was convinced that the blind need a literature that reflects the reality of our lives as we live them.

In 1994, Dr. Jernigan created NFB-NEWSLINE®, a service which makes newspapers and magazines available to the blind. Each morning more than 370 newspapers are available by telephone or by computer. Almost fifty magazines are distributed in the same way so that the blind can receive the information they contain at the same time that it becomes available to sighted readers—or earlier.

In 1998, Dr. Jernigan began to work on plans for the expansion of our Baltimore headquarters. The National Federation of the Blind Jernigan Institute was constructed beginning in 2001, and it has been in operation since 2004. In the Jernigan Institute we are conducting programs that expand educational opportunities for blind children and extend research on the subject of bringing independence to blind people. We have taught blind students to build payloads for rockets that have flown more than 5,000 feet into the atmosphere, we have devised control mechanisms for automobiles that the blind can use independently, and we have conducted dozens of other programs.

Each of these efforts is a tribute to the inspiration, imagination, and drive of this extraordinary human being. Each of these efforts is an extension of the philosophical understanding Dr. Jernigan possessed about the nature of blindness and the importance of blind people. Blind people are normal human beings who cannot see. Blind people have capacity similar to that possessed by the sighted, and they want to use it to build productive lives. Blindness is not a badge of inferiority, and blind people are as respectable as anybody else. Programs to encourage and support blind people can incorporate such thoughts and will produce better results than others if they do. Such is the living expression of Dr. Kenneth Jernigan.

CHAPTER 3

OPPORTUNITIES

by Tom Bickford

Note: Tom Bickford met Kenneth Jernigan at a young age when Dr. Jernigan was the supervisor of the training center for blind adults in Northern California. Tom continued to work with him in different ways for more than four decades. In the following account, he describes the relationship and mentions many experiences and responsibilities that developed in whole or in part from Dr. Jernigan's instruction and the relationship that followed. Although Kenneth Jernigan did not do all of the things his students did, he encouraged them to develop skills and pursue new ideas and experiences. Tom Bickford did just that.

MY INTRODUCTION TO KENNETH JERNIGAN WAS AS A debater and teacher. He outworked me on both accounts. I was a beginning student at the California Orientation Center for Blind Adults, and he was the first staff member to interview me. We talked about the things I might learn in my time there. He worked the conversation around to independent travel. I finally asked,

"Do you mean you would take your white cane and fly to Japan?" He said simply, "Yes." I didn't believe him, but I didn't say it. My silence said it for me. In training he led me to believe in myself. Kenneth Jernigan helped me to learn, not just to travel, but to go wherever and whenever I wanted to go. And I have traveled by almost every mode of modern transportation across the United States and around Europe from Paris to Moscow and back.

Tom Bickford, 1997

Kenneth Jernigan was not the chief administrator of the Orientation Center program, but he was the philosophical and spiritual leader. He had many talents, and his activities were diverse. He read us short stories and led discussions about them. We learned parliamentary procedure. We worked out in morning gym classes that he led, and the word "worked" was taken seriously. By the time I left, I was in the best physical shape I have ever been. More than fifty years later, I still use some of the exercise routines that I learned there.

The most important class was called "Business Methods and Procedures." Ken—we were quite informal then—had started a discussion group on that subject. As time went on, the class evolved into discussions about all aspects of blindness. We talked about everything from how to eat peas to how to think of ourselves and meet the rest of the world.

Ken gave of himself in any way he could. He organized an occasional weekend picnic in the park and brought the food himself. From time to time, he would select two compatible dinner guests and invite them to go with him and his wife to one of his favorite restaurants, nice restaurants. He didn't talk about it; he just did it.

The class on parliamentary procedure met in the evening. One evening one of the students—just for the sake of making a motion—moved that we should adjourn and go for a round of Coke. Someone else amended the motion to make the drink Pepsi. At that point Ken called his wife and asked her to make some popcorn, lots of it. We got the sodas and adjourned to his apartment, which was across the street, for pop and popcorn.

Ken was not the "outdoorsy" type. But when the students decided to have a weekend in one of the state parks, he came along and led one of the hikes over hill and dale and across a creek. We removed shoes and socks and rolled up our pants above the knees to cross the creek. "A good time was had by all," as Ken would say. This is an example of how he gave of himself in many ways to help blind people learn to believe in themselves. The classes and activities were opportunities to practice. We would find the skills useful. The philosophy we learned needed, not only to penetrate into our heads, but also to be absorbed into our emotions and reactions. Center students were a cross section of the community; we just happened to be blind. The training was mental, technical, physical, and social. It has stayed with me and has become one of the great influences in my life.

A couple of years later, Kenneth Jernigan applied for the directorship of the Iowa Commission for the Blind. It must have been just what fate had in store. Mr. Jernigan—things were on a more formal basis by then—worked hard to get the job and got it. I was between jobs at that time, and he offered me a position as a rehabilitation counselor. Both Mr. Jernigan and I were too idealistic about it. I had the right philosophy, but I am not the right kind of person to be a rehab counselor. He helped me move on to another phase of my life, and we parted company with cordial feelings on both sides.

During my eight months on the staff, I saw his ambitions for the agency. He made friends wherever he went: local blind people in their homes; members of the Jewish Sisterhood; state legislators and the governor; members of civic organizations and more. He organized poker games with legislators in the evening. He told me once, "I have never worked so hard in my life." He worked sixteen-hour days and more from his office as director. The need for all that work was his realization that he was "under the gun to succeed." The NFB philosophy was on trial. All around the country, rehab directors and their staff members were watching. Mr. Jernigan expected that training blind people would pay for itself by saving taxpayer money; those who went to work would no longer be on welfare. He told the legislature and the governor this was the goal. The governor was sensible enough to recognize the need for the "startup" time. After that first year, Mr. Jernigan made his prediction come true. All around the country those rehabilitation directors who had been sharpening their knives preparing for the Kenneth Jernigan roast dinner, had to back off and watch his accomplishments. The success of the Iowa Commission for the Blind could not be denied. Some rehabilitation personnel were slow to change, but all rehab for the blind has been influenced by the work led by Mr. Jernigan in Iowa.

As I have said, Kenneth Jernigan gave of himself for the people he served. During that first year in Iowa, one of the clients got a professional-level job, but he did not have the clothes he needed. Mr. Jernigan took from his own closet three business suits and gave them to the client so he could make the right appearance on the job. That was just the way he operated. That was also the way he led the National Federation of the Blind. He never had much to say about that kind of leadership, but the people and the organization flourished because of his generosity.

Washington, DC. In 1962 I qualified for a program to study the Russian language at Georgetown University. There were thirty blind students who came from almost as many states. Six students studied German while the rest of us studied Russian.

When I was preparing to move to Washington, DC, I got a map and went over it with a sighted friend. Anyone who has been to Washington first learns that there is a grid of numbered streets running north and south and lettered streets running east and west. That is simple enough, but there are also avenues drawn on various angles, most of which are named for states. Where the avenues cross, there is a traffic circle. You have to learn them one at a time because no two are alike. When my friend and I were studying the map, I realized that all these streets were running at different angles and commented that there must be some rather strange shapes formed by the streets. The reply was a very definite yes.

Thanks to my thorough training in cane travel, I caught on sooner than most of the other students. Only the students from Iowa and one young man from California had received the travel training I had, and it was very noticeable. Even so, I had opportunities to become disoriented at first. That means that I got lost and turned around more than once.

When I arrived in Washington, I found that our language classes were held in a building just a block from DuPont Circle, quite a large circle with a fountain and park area in the middle. Connecticut Avenue runs through a tunnel underneath; Massachusetts Avenue crosses at a different angle; P Street and 19th Street come into the Circle from both sides; and New Hampshire Avenue crosses at still another angle. There are a few traffic islands dropped around the edge like decorations on a cake. That is just the circle itself, and the irregularities have their effect for blocks around. Some changes have occurred since I arrived nearly fifty years ago, but the patterns are still similar. My first apartment was on one side of DuPont Circle, and our classes were on the opposite side. Therefore, I crossed it at least twice a day, and that helped me learn to travel in Washington, DC, traffic.

One Saturday a friend and I went shopping downtown. We went by bus, but when it was time to return home, she said she wanted to walk back. I asked if she really meant it, and she said she did. I realized later that I had just accepted a friendly challenge to walk an area for the first time. I decided that I could follow the grid and aim for Massachusetts Avenue, which would take us home. We encountered two unexpected traffic circles. It is fortunate that Washington is a tourist town with local people always willing to help those who aren't sure how to get to their next destination. We got back with only a few extensions off the direct route. Actually, driving in Washington, DC is worse than walking. Some streets are one-way, and when the traffic light changes, you must move even though you don't want to turn that way. Pedestrians don't have this disadvantage. Once you learn the basic patterns and rules, the city is workable. I have directed many people, sighted and blind, because I now know the way.

I studied Russian intensively for four years and learned a lot of it. I was looking for a job, but another opportunity came along.

Background. My parents were missionaries, and my sisters and I were all born in China. We lived there until I was seven. I have lived in the U.S. since then with visits to China and Europe. We discovered my glaucoma when I was in the ninth grade. I became blind in the eleventh grade, finished high school in Pasadena, and completed college in Los Angeles. At the suggestion of my rehab counselor, I enrolled at the Orientation Center, which was then located in Oakland, and that's when I met Dr. Jernigan. I spent three and a half years in Iowa before I moved to Washington, DC.

Europe and Russia. When I moved to Washington, I moved there to stay. But I still enjoyed traveling. In 1966 I was one of four people who made a five-week auto trip around Western Europe. After four years of Russian studies, I decided that I would extend the trip on my own to explore the part of the world I had been studying. I parted from my friends in Paris. I took the opportunity to visit the Louis Braille home in Coupvray, France. I was shown the whole house. Upstairs was the family one-room home. Downstairs was Louis Braille's father's cobbler shop. Since the guide spoke French, and I had studied French for only one year, I had to think hard to understand him. My tour of Louis Braille's home was several years before it was "prettied up" and turned into the museum that it now is.

I stayed in Paris to arrange my hoped-for trip to Russia, but the arrangements did not come together. So I took the overnight train to Brussels. Then I started my trip to Russia from Brussels and had a connection in Achen, Germany. On these international trips, I discovered something about communicating with people. When you cross a border and you know the language, it is a new country. When you cross a border and you do not know the language, it is a foreign country. I knew enough German to help me get through arrangements there. At the Polish border, the passport officer greeted us in Polish. The rule is that you should answer in the language in which you want to continue. Polish and Russian are close enough that I understood the lady officer, so I replied in Russian and gave her my stack of tickets, visas, and passport. All were satisfactory.

At the Russian border, I was greeted by an "In-tourist" host who spoke to me in French. I had started from a French-speaking country, after all. When they discovered that I spoke passable Russian, we continued in the local tongue.

One evening in Moscow, I had a couple of hours of free time and decided to go out for a walk just to find out what the city was like. I found the main street and walked along, enjoying the early fall weather and listening to the light car traffic and the groups of friends who met each other. Two boys, perhaps fourteen years old, greeted me and asked, "Where are you going, uncle?" "Nowhere," I replied. "I'm just out for a stroll." A little later I heard someone mention a candy store, so I thought I would go in to find out what they had to offer. There was a juice counter and a candy counter. I was offered prune juice or tomato juice. I took the prune. As I stood there and drank it, a couple came in with their two children, probably under ten. The father gave them their choice, and they took tomato. Since there was a candy counter, I bought a small piece of chocolate. I must have seemed a glutton because I stood there and ate it. I later found that chocolate was considered a rare treat.

I asked about visiting the school for the blind, but I had arrived on a Friday, and it could not be arranged over the weekend. The In-tourist desk suggested that when I arrived in Leningrad (now St. Petersburg), I should ask at the earliest opportunity to visit the school for the blind there.

My local guide and I were shown around the school for the blind in St. Petersburg. We visited an English language class, a science lab, the wood shop, and the dormitory. It seemed to me the school was run efficiently, and the children were very polite, standing to show respect as their principal came in and greeted them. My only disappointment was when I asked what kind of employment the students found after graduation. I was told that a few went on to higher education without specified goals, but most of the rest took work as typists or masseurs at health resorts. I had hoped for higher ambitions, although things had not been much different for the blind in Paris or Brussels.

The flight to Kiev was not too much different from flights in the U.S. The air hostess made the same kinds of announcements about the length of the trip and how high and fast we were traveling. They did not have a loud speaker system though, which surprised me. Because I was a foreigner, the hostess asked if I had understood her. I assured her that I had.

A friend who had been to Kiev the previous year referred me to someone there. It turned out that this person lived in what we would consider lower class public housing with halls strewn with newspapers. The people, however, were hospitable and pleasant.

On my return trip, I had another transfer in Prague. I was able to speak Russian with the younger people and German with the older folks. Railroad staff was helpful, if brusque. Helping blind passengers was not their assigned duty. I caught the train to Luxemburg and made my connection back to New York.

Working for the Library of Congress. I was hired by the Division for the Blind and Physically Handicapped (now National Library Service or NLS) to do quality control for recorded books (known as talking books). This program has produced more books for the blind than any other program I know of. After the books were recorded, I was one of the people who gave the books one last listen. We made sure that the opening and closing announcements were correct, that the sound track was clear, that the reading matched the book, and the pronunciations were correct. I had always liked to read, so this was an ideal job for me. One of the few drawbacks was that I only made spot checks, and I am sure that occasional errors were missed. However, we found enough corrections to improve the quality of the recorded books and to make the work worthwhile.

There were often funny or thought-provoking short passages that caught my attention. During the last half of my thirty-nine years in this employment, I decided to share some quotes with the rest of the staff. I made very few rules for myself. The passages had to be short enough for the Braille to fit on a five-by-eight-inch card. Then I typed the same text for sighted staff members. I taped these cards to the hallway partition outside my office. Occasionally, I found contrasting views on the same subject and put them up side by side. No topic was excluded. It just had to catch my interest at the moment. Some quotes were happy; some sad; some thoughtful; some serious; some profound; and some silly. I put up a new quote each day and gave each of them a serial number and a date before filing. From 1980 until I retired in 2006, I collected more than 1,700 quotes. Now I have a project for my retirement years. I am keying the quotes into the computer, sorting them into thirty subject groups, and editing them to make the collection more usable. Someday I may try to publish them as a book, but I have to get them ready first.

When I joined the staff at the Library, books were just beginning to be recorded on cassette tapes. At first the only touch-legible identification on each cassette shell was a small square of plastic tape with a Braille number and a raised Arabic number. Several times I asked if we could make Braille labels, which would include the book titles. I knew many readers would find labels helpful. The answer always was: There isn't enough space.

One day my workroom was being painted, and I couldn't use the equipment until the paint dried. I decided to put my time to some practical use. I found a standard Braille slate and stylus, a micro Braille slate and stylus, and some blank cassette labels with adhesive backing. I carefully placed the labels on the slates and wrote full Braille cells just to show that there was enough space to use words on the cassette labels. I stuck the labels on a sheet of paper, typed an explanation of what I was demonstrating above each label, and gave it to the assistant director.

I am sure that you have heard the quotation from Thomas Edison: Genius is 1 percent inspiration and 99 percent perspiration. Perhaps determination is included in perspiration. I think I proved that Braille could fit on cassettes, but other staff members still had to design and produce the labels. My contribution was small, but that was the beginning of complete Braille labels on National Library Service cassettes. This was an opportunity, and I was glad to make the demonstration. It is the kind of thing that I learned more than a decade earlier from Kenneth Jernigan in California and in Iowa.

Care and Feeding of the Long White Cane. During my years in high school, I knew that my sight was getting gradually worse. I decided to get some help. I bought a Braille watch and a white cane. Using the watch was and is easy. Just snap the top open, feel the hands lightly, and follow them out to the edge of the dial to where they point.

The cane was a different matter. I asked the lady at the agency who sold it to me: "How do I use it?" She answered: "Anyway you like." That was no help at all. Mostly, I held it in front of me to find step-ups, and the lower end of the cane bumped the step. It didn't do any good on step-downs, and you can guess what happened.

After college when I attended the training center in California where I met Dr. Jernigan, there was an excellent travel teacher named Larry Lewis. In fact, he became a legend in his own right, and he recommended a longer cane. That cane came up to my chin.

From time to time, people would ask me about independent travel. The things to know and do are fairly simple. It takes time to practice until it feels natural. You tap the cane from side to side in front of you to be sure that the space is clear and to find landmarks. One day when a friend asked me about this, I thought about writing it down. I broke up the cane travel instructions into several short chapters. Then I wrote the name of each chapter on an index card and spread them out on a table to decide the right order.

I wrote a few chapters and sent that much to Dr. Jernigan. I asked if he would be interested. I don't remember his words, but the basic message was to go ahead. It probably took me about nine months to write the text. I had to find an hour or two several times a week. I was working full time and had a wife, one daughter in high school, another in college, and participated in church and community activities. The first draft of the composition was written on the Braille writer, a totally mechanical device which is still in use. I could not have completed the work without my friends, Lloyd and Judy Rasmussen. Together, they transcribed the text into electronic format and ran off a Braille copy on paper. I took it to a state NFB convention and showed it to Dr. Jernigan, and he read it. When he gave it back to me, he said: The next time you give this to me, I want a copy in Braille, a copy in print, and one in electronic form. I did a little more writing, rearranged the chapters, gave it to a friend for more editing, and then the Rasmussens gave it another run. They produced the three media requested, and I sent them to Dr. Jernigan. Dr. Jernigan had arranged for a cover to be designed, and then the Federation published the book. I received a case of forty-eight print copies the day after Thanksgiving in 1993. After reading the book, a friend asked if I had a section on attitudes. I said, "It begins and ends with attitudes."

Most people think it is a shame to be blind. They say, "Oh, look at that poor blind man over there with his white cane." My blindness is a natural thing with me, and I find no shame in it. I use my cane as a bumper and a probe. It is long enough (now up to my cheekbone) to find step-downs, landmarks, and obstacles. I use the cane, my ears, and my brain to keep on track, and I have traveled very much the same way for the last fifty years. My booklet *Care and Feeding of the Long White Cane* turned out to be only sixty pages. So far 30,000 copies have been distributed. If only half or fewer of those readers have used it to improve their travel techniques, I am glad to have helped my fellow blind.

The story above is only one side of my life. During my first year of employment, I met a pleasant lady, Virginia Flasche, who accepted my proposal to be my wife. We have had a good life together. We raised two daughters and now have four grandchildren. We have taken active roles in our community and joined tours around the United States and abroad. There are still things I would like to do: more travel, perhaps publish a book of quotes, and who knows what other opportunities may come along.

Were it not for the Federation as first personified by Kenneth Jernigan, my life would have been flat and empty. He helped me become an ordinary person with my share of good and bad qualities. I changed a lot during that training in California and continued to grow because of the opportunities I found. Without the Federation, I am not sure I would have been worthy of work, marriage, parenthood, and other roles in society. What I learned from Kenneth Jernigan about blindness changed the way I see myself and the way others see me. What I learned from Kenneth Jernigan about living is impossible to quantify, but just as important. In a real sense, I owe my quality of life to Kenneth Jernigan and the NFB.

CHAPTER 4

OF GATES AND GOOD INTENTIONS

by Joyce Scanlan

Note: Joyce Scanlan was elected and reelected president of the National Federation of the Blind of Minnesota for thirty-four years. She describes the years of her presidency and the valuable education she received from Dr. Jernigan. She became a strong president and is well known in Minnesota and throughout the country for her tough and determined positions when necessary. She also learned loving. Joyce served on the NFB Board of Directors for thirty-two years and was elected secretary and first vice president several times.

Joyce found it necessary to confront the agency for the blind, which was funded by the government, on more than one occasion because services the agency provided to blind Minnesotans were not what they needed. Then Joyce founded Blindness: Learning in New Dimensions (BLIND), Incorporated, a private training center, in 1986 and directed it for sixteen years. This excellent program was modeled after the training center in Iowa, established and directed for twenty years by Kenneth Jernigan.

Below she describes some of her experiences as she grew in the National Federation of the Blind and benefited from Dr. Jernigan's coaching. She became his close associate and friend.

Joyce Scanlan speaks during the Roll Call of States at the 1987 NFB National Convention.

"Lift up your heads, O ye gates; and be lifted up, ye everlasting doors." These are lines from the Twenty-fourth Psalm, which for many years were code words between Dr. Jernigan and me to signal our memories of an incident in which he, the consummate teacher, helped me to understand more fully how to be a leader in the organized blind movement.

In 1973, when I was a fairly new member of the National Federation of the Blind, by some fluke of fate I was elected president of our Minnesota affiliate. Now, if we all remember our history—and there are many who will never let me forget that history—Minnesota had the dubious distinction of having two Federation affiliates, the only state with such a distinction, and the group of which I was elected president had the additional notable feature of owning and operating a residential home for the blind.

This home had gates at the tops of the stairways—you know, to protect the blind people from falling down the stairs and being hurt. Well, this was a situation in which Dr. Jernigan helped me to get out of a potential mess. Shortly after I became president, some of our new Federationists in the student division prevailed upon me to take the gates off the stairs because, they argued, having the gates wasn't consistent with Federation philosophy. The gates should be removed so the residents could learn to be independent. Most of the residents were elderly, and they were used to having the gates. Of course they were most unhappy when the gates were taken away. Someone called Dr. Jernigan to complain about what had been done, and he called me to discuss the matter.

He began the telephone conversation by telling me about Alexander Hamilton and Thomas Jefferson and how one had a philosophy but no army, while the other had a large army and didn't worry much about philosophy. Dr. Jernigan then said that if I was to accomplish all that we hoped for in the Federation, I would need an army of people to do it, and the philosophy would come second. He said the gates weren't that important and should be put back on. He also cautioned me that it should be done with good grace, not grudgingly. I conceded that he was right and returned the gates to their proper spot at the top of the stairs. The residents of the home were again happy, and I was prevented from being a very short-term state president.

Dr. Jernigan hadn't been at all harsh with me. He was very gentle in explaining why it had been a mistake to tamper with something the older people had come to depend upon. He said I needed those people as part of an army as much as they needed the gates. Any philosophical conflict between the gates and Federation thinking could be worked out. Having the gates for a little longer wouldn't hurt, and eventually, he said, the people at the home would ask for the gates to be removed. The home was sold in 1980, and I have always regretted that I didn't keep one of those gates as a memento of that most valuable educational experience.

Over the years Dr. Jernigan and I often spoke of that incident. It was a wonderful lesson for me. In fact, this single incident made up an entire textbook of Federation instruction, which has often served as a guide along the way as I have wrestled with our philosophy and how it can be applied to real life and how the National Federation of the Blind functions. "Remember the gates," Dr. Jernigan would often say. The incident of the gates set down a firm foundation for me in how the Federation values people. We love one another, and we treat each other with fairness and respect.

Dr. Jernigan taught me many more lessons. I had always envied those who had learned from him as students at the Iowa Commission for the Blind. They benefited from ongoing contact with him over a period of many months. However, my contacts with him at national and some state conventions, Thanksgiving Board meetings, leadership seminars, and a few other meetings here and there made each and every encounter so special and so memorable that I can appreciate my good fortune for having had the benefit of knowing him and working with him for many years.

I'll never forget having dinner with him at the Waikiki Room restaurant at the Leamington Hotel in Minneapolis where we both enjoyed sampling every hors d'oeuvre on the menu while sharing a Sidewinder's Fang. Then there was the time we sat down for breakfast at a restaurant in Madison, Wisconsin, early in April and he asked the waitress, "Do you have any fresh figs?" The answer was a definite "No." When in his presence, one could never be sure what to expect; one could only anticipate surprise, humor, challenge, gentle persuasion. No matter what the subject under consideration might be, he was able to draw the full attention of everyone around as he offered insightful gems of wisdom. He gave me guidance, support, and counsel throughout all these years, through good times and difficult times.

As a new state president I had much to learn about political strategizing. There were times when I might be discouraged by the burdens of a state presidential election when the older members of the Minnesota affiliate would campaign hard and seem to gain strength. I would call Dr. Jernigan and whine about the tactics being used by the opposition. Political organizing was all new to me. The old folks had long experience fighting everything and everybody, including each other. My supporters were mainly college students, who had neither skills nor experience in political scrapping.

I made so many stupid errors in chairing state conventions that I marvel at how Dr. Jernigan could sit there patiently and watch me struggle with the tough old guys winning on most points. Then Dr. Jernigan would call me the following week to review my performance. Although it seemed to me that I had done just about everything wrong, and he told me what errors I had made, he somehow always found some good in what I had done. He talked to me about doing my homework. The old folks had done theirs, and they had won. Dr. Jernigan guided me through these difficulties and showed me how to take chairing conventions and weathering elections in stride. He would say when I complained, "Now, Joyce, you don't expect your opponent to stand up before you and salute you and say, 'Shoot me first,' do you?" He taught me to pay heed to the votes. He would also say, "When you have the votes, you can afford to be nice to your opponent; when you don't have the votes, you *must* be nice." His deep personal integrity set a high example for all of us to follow. I have always tried very hard.

There were many fun times too. He gave my husband Tom and me a lesson in making NFB tea one Sunday afternoon after a Board meeting. At that time, and probably still today, there was no recipe for NFB tea. He had a whole shelf full of liquid spices, and he would take each one in turn, uncap it, tip it over the mixing bowl of tea, and say, "Now listen, this is how much you put in," as the spice trickled into the mixture. There was no formal measurement, only the auditory method, listening to the trickle. It was great fun, but how could anyone repeat such a performance and come out with fine NFB tea? No one really understands that.

I thank Dr. Jernigan for giving me a meaningful life. When I came into the National Federation of the Blind in 1970, I had lost everything: my eyesight certainly, but also my livelihood, my confidence and self-esteem, any hope for a successful career. I had just come through a period of abject poverty and total misery. Life for a blind person in North Dakota was very bleak—no opportunity, no hope for change. I was in the proverbial shipwreck at sea and had never learned to swim.

Then Dr. Jernigan and the Federation came along, and everything began to change. Blindness might bring problems, but there are definite solutions to those problems. Blind people have the right to equal treatment and opportunity, and blind people can dream of how life can be made better. Blind people can turn dreams into reality. Working together, blind people have the power to change what it means to be blind. We have a united voice; we have a firm philosophy; we have a common purpose. All of this meant a great deal to me. But it was all very different from everything I had known during the early years of my life. It also meant that I had to change my whole approach to life—no more hiding out, no more excuses, no more shirking responsibility.

The model set for us by Dr. Jernigan challenges all of us to a high standard of conduct. I remember well his guidance and teaching during the Minneapolis Society for the Blind lawsuit and proxy fight. This type of litigation and corporate warfare was totally new to all of us. During the trial, when Dr. Jernigan came to testify, the Society's lawyer asked him if the Federation was funding the lawsuit. Dr. Jernigan's response was, "Well I don't know if we have put any money into it or not, but let me say that, if we didn't, we should have." That floored the attorney, who had expected an outright denial. How strong and decisive Dr. Jernigan was in answering unfriendly questions. He took the Society attorneys completely off-guard by being so definite and giving specific reasons to support what he said. Dr. Jernigan always knew what to do. He was always ready with ideas for what should be done. Of course we won the lawsuit against the Society.

None of us had ever before been involved in a proxy battle either. It was a time of vicious attacks, threatening phone calls, character assassinations where our people were employed, high-priced, hostile ads attacking the Federation and its leaders circulated far and wide. When the troops would seem to waver and begin to wonder whether the whole battle was worth all the trouble, Dr. Jernigan would say, "We are in this battle now, and even if we fight and lose, we will be better off for having fought than if we had never tried at all." He told us that we were fighting for a worthy cause, and at the best we would all know the triumph of high achievement; and at the worst, if we failed, we would at least fail while daring bravely. Once again he was there; he listened to our mournful complaints and lent his words of wisdom and support. During that difficult time, I came to appreciate his daily phone calls to check on our progress and above all to lend his highly-valued counsel.

All this time Dr. Jernigan was being attacked from every direction. Our opponents were very busy attempting to destroy our leaders and the Federation. I tried to give to him the same support he had given me, but I know I received far more than I gave. Hopefully we will never again be called upon to engage in such battles, for today, again thanks to Dr. Jernigan's powers of persuasion and charisma, the field of blindness is experiencing unprecedented harmony. Agencies which once opposed us are no longer viable. But the National Federation of the Blind is stronger today than ever before.

In my early life, I had been a teacher of secondary English, history, and Latin for six years. My long-range goal had always been to become a college English professor. The possibility of ever administering a rehabilitation training program had never entered my mind. However, as a state president I became heavily involved with advocacy issues on behalf of blind individuals experiencing problems with public and private rehabilitation programs. Terms such as consumer representative, orientation to blindness, self-advocacy, and alternative techniques came to have greater significance. Several customers of our state rehab agency were being denied college funding when their grade point averages were below a B level but were still acceptable to remain in college. Others were threatened with loss of Social Security benefits because they were reported as being "uncooperative" by the state agency. Many young blind people wanted orientation training but were not willing to settle for the one training center available in Minnesota. We were quite active in dealing with these and many other advocacy issues.

Personally, my one and only positive rehab lesson was taught me by Dr. Jernigan. I was a member of the "First" Federation leadership seminar over Labor Day weekend in 1973, just three months after becoming a state president. The first evening when we were all going out to dinner together, someone suggested we go to a place called the Charcoal Pit. We were told that we would be able to select and grill our own steaks. Somehow I had had the impression that in the Federation we should speak up about how we felt. So I did. I said I didn't like the idea, because I had never before grilled a steak to my liking. Dr. Jernigan very calmly said, "Oh, well, we'll help you." I was suddenly terrified. I prayed that by the time we arrived at the Charcoal Pit, he would have forgotten what I had said. Of course, that didn't happen.

He immediately escorted me to the refrigerators where all the steaks were kept. We began examining all the shapes and sizes of steaks and ultimately made a selection for which one to grill. He was so enthusiastic and seemed to be having such fun that I began to enjoy the venture myself. With the steak we had selected, a plate, and a long fork, we approached the big pit. He said, "Now, throw your steak out there; just toss it out there." I did, thinking about losing the steak forever in the fire. After a short while, Dr. Jernigan said, "All right, reach out with your fork and find the steak and put it on the plate." I did. Then he showed me how to turn the steak over. I was so glad he had done it so I wouldn't have to touch that hot meat. However, he flipped the steak back and said to me, "Now you do it." I should have known he wouldn't let me off the hook. Then we grilled the steak on the other side, and I became more comfortable handling it. Then I ate the steak and found it very tasty, too. Everyone was having such a good time, and for the first time, I actually enjoyed a steak. Dr. Jernigan asked me to grill a second steak for him. It must have been o.k., because he ate it without complaint. That was my best rehab lesson—the only one I ever had. Dr. Jernigan was a teacher to me; yet he treated me as an equal. I learned so much about myself and about dealing with blindness just from that one experience.

In 1986 Minnesota Federationists learned that we might have an opportunity to create a consumer-directed orientation-to-blindness training center. After much soul-searching and extensive and cautious planning, we decided to move forward with the establishment of Blindness: Learning in New Dimensions (BLIND), Incorporated—more new territory for us. Again, Dr. Jernigan gave us valuable counsel and support. He provided training for our staff numerous times; his experience and wisdom were greatly appreciated. Frankly, I'm certain he saved us from numerous blunders by his emphasis on the Center environment being consistently positive—no conflicting messages to confuse students. The staff serves as strong role models. When he asked us to give one word that characterized the atmosphere of a Center, his own word was "salt," indicating how the correct seasoning was important. He would challenge us to explain how operating a Center was like handling crystal. He really made us think deeply about what we were launching into. Everything he said was both inspirational and frightening.

When he visited our Center in 1989 and toured and held a seminar for students and staff, he expressed approval of our newly-remodeled Center. Students were delighted to meet him, and all of us felt proud and honored to participate in one of his philosophical discussions and learn from this warm and awesome teacher. He inspired the BLIND, Incorporated students and uplifted the spirits of the Center staff.

During later years I'm sure I benefited from the extensive mentoring I received from Dr. Jernigan to move forward with greater independence and self-confidence than I had in my early years as a Federationist and certainly as a state president. As our BLIND, Incorporated programs strengthened and expanded, hopefully my skill as a leader and as an administrator continued to develop and improve. I always knew Dr. Jernigan was available to me whenever needed; however, regular contact with him or ongoing reliance upon him for direction or support was no longer as necessary as it had been in previous years. I was at last competent to take on the role of the teacher and leader.

For example, after BLIND, Incorporated had been in operation for about four or five years, we were in a position to purchase our own building. We visited sixteen properties before deciding upon the appropriate facility to meet our needs. Our next struggle was dealing with the panic-stricken neighborhood into which we hoped to move. We settled into the building, and the neighborhood ultimately calmed down. This all occurred over a period of more than two years during the mid-nineties, and I did not have any contact with Dr. Jernigan on the matter during that entire time. As I think about all that today, it's almost unbelievable to me that I could manage that entire project without seeking counsel from my tried-and-true mentor, Dr. Jernigan. Yet I know that it is true.

Challenges were constantly on the horizon for a state president. We in Minnesota were occasionally faced with an unfriendly administrator of the department in which our state rehabilitation agency was located. By that time, Dr. Jernigan was no longer with us, and I found myself faced with the necessity of writing a forceful letter to that hostile administrator outlining our opposition to his policies without the possibility of conferring with my mentor. A few years later, we dealt with a difficult director of our rehab agency serving blind people. This person suddenly abolished a major group-model program for seniors losing eyesight, as well as a six-week training program for newly-hired agency staff. Also, this person closed a store which had made available blindness-related items not readily available elsewhere in our area. We felt compelled to hold a march in front of the agency building to inform the public of what had been done and of the harmful effects on blind Minnesotans of those actions. I felt confident that Dr. Jernigan would have given heartfelt approval to everything we did.

My thirty-four years as a state president of a National Federation of the Blind affiliate and my sixteen years as executive director of BLIND, Incorporated were made far more successful with the leadership and guidance of one person, Dr. Kenneth Jernigan. From 1970, when I went reluctantly to a national convention of the NFB in Minneapolis (my city of residence) and sat spellbound in the audience as he chaired the crowd so competently and efficiently, until August 1998 (less than two months before he died), he gave me the greatest in-depth education on life in general and helped me to understand the meaningful role I could play in the drama of life. He was there for me when my need was greatest and stayed with me until I had learned to fly on my own.

The best of all I know and believe about blindness and about life I learned from Dr. Jernigan. He taught me to dream of a better world for blind people and how to work hard or fight—if that was necessary—to make that dream come true. All of us today who knew him consider what his loss means to the National Federation of the Blind and to blind people everywhere. Yet within each of us lies the very best that we have been given by a most generous and loving person.

Although he has passed from our midst in one sense, he will always be with us in spirit to guide, to persuade, to mentor, to support, to teach. All of us have better lives because of the organization he built. If we all live our lives as Dr. Jernigan lived his, we know the organized blind movement will thrive in years to come. We can make it happen, and, Dr. Jernigan, we will make it happen. We will all follow the legacy you have set and march together to continue the work of the National Federation of the Blind. And whatever my personal role in the Federation may be in the future, I promise, Dr. Jernigan, I will always remember the gates.

CHAPTER 5

THE SOUTH CAROLINA STORY

by Donald C. Capps

Note: Don Capps and Kenneth Jernigan were friends and colleagues in the NFB from the mid 1950s until Dr. Jernigan's death. Dr. Capps describes the relationship and work they did together in this article taken from the *Braille Monitor* January/February 1999 issue.

Donald Capps served as second vice president and then first vice president of the National Federation of the Blind from 1959 to 1984. After a year's sabbatical for health reasons, he served on the Board of Directors from 1985 to 2007 thus serving longer than any other board member.

He had a long career, first as a claims examiner and later as staff manager of the Claims Department for the Colonial Life and Accident Insurance Company, retiring in 1985. As president of the National Federation of the Blind of South Carolina, Dr. Capps backed thirty-six pieces of legislation affecting the blind, which passed the South Carolina legislature and became law. He describes below the efforts to create the Commission for the Blind in South Carolina, one of his proudest accomplishments.

He also led the effort first to construct and then to expand the Education and Recreation Center of the National Federation of the Blind of South Carolina, and he supervised its operation for decades.

Dr. Capps received the Order of the Palmetto, the highest honor conferred by the state of South Carolina, as well as awards from his employer and the National Federation of the Blind.

Betty Capps has been an active Federationist as long as her husband has. The Cappses and the Jernigans worked together and sometimes were able to relax together as well.

Don and Betty Capps, 2003

OVER THE YEARS, DR. JERNIGAN MADE MANY TRIPS to South Carolina and always seemed to enjoy his visits in the Palmetto State. In the 1960s, Dr. Jernigan and his parents spent several Thanksgivings with Betty and me at our home in Columbia.

He was very observant. Before his Thanksgiving visits, Betty would give the house a good cleaning, dusting everything, since she knew Dr. Jernigan would check out things while visiting us. He not only relied upon his great intellect but also his hands to learn, and learn he did. Using his long white cane, Dr. Jernigan, who enjoyed the out-of-doors, identified every tree in our yard.

He also loved children. During his Thanksgiving visits with us in the 1960s, our two children, Beth and Craig, were small, but they still remember the good times they had with Dr. Jernigan, who would always accompany them to the nearby city park. He would ride on the swings and the see-saw with them.

Betty and I always enjoyed Dr. Jernigan's visits. We knew he enjoyed good food, and he especially liked Betty's fried chicken. We would always have two elderly sisters, Aunt Lelia and Aunt Mattie, who babysat for Beth and Craig, bake a nine-layer chocolate cake for Dr. Jernigan and his parents.

Growing up in rural Tennessee, Dr. Jernigan understood and appreciated Southern culture and down-home cooking. In the 1970s, Columbians were introduced to Lizard's Thicket, considered by most to be the premiere restaurant in the area for down-home cooking. Each time Dr. Jernigan visited with us, we made sure to dine at Lizard's Thicket. Though the entrée included three vegetables, Dr. Jernigan always ordered at least six and ate them all. We cherish these memories.

Dr. Jernigan had a tremendous impact upon state programs for the blind in South Carolina. At our 1964 state convention in Charleston, we adopted a resolution calling for the creation of a Commission for the Blind. When this legislation was introduced in 1965, it set off a storm of opposition from the sheltered workshop and the Division for the Blind of the South Carolina Department of Public Welfare. In 1965 our state organization was small and not very strong. We had our work cut out for us. However, we knew that Dr. Jernigan was an expert on commissions for the blind since he had been appointed executive director of the Iowa Commission for the Blind in 1958. In 1965 the legislature could not agree upon the merits of creating a Commission in South Carolina. However, it did establish a nine-member legislative study committee to consider the advisability and feasibility of establishing one.

Our longtime friend, Earle E. Morris, Jr., was then a member of the South Carolina Senate and was elected chairman of the study committee. Senator Morris held several hearings across the state concerning the commission bill. Ultimately the committee invited Dr. Jernigan to testify. In November of 1965 he traveled to Columbia and made an outstanding presentation to the legislative study committee, after which the nine members voted unanimously to recommend the creation of the S.C. Commission for the Blind. Several of the members told me directly that Dr. Jernigan had absolutely convinced them. Incidentally, two committee members were invited to visit the Iowa Commission for the Blind and did so. This was also highly influential in the committee's recommendation to establish a Commission.

Dr. Jernigan was NFB president in 1969 when the NFB convention was held in Columbia. He demonstrated his care for South Carolina and its leaders. One nationally known speaker on the convention agenda informed Dr. Jernigan before he made his presentation that he planned to attack Senator Strom Thurmond, primarily because the two held different political views. Since the legislative issues important to blind people have been supported by political figures with widely differing political views, Dr. Jernigan quickly and clearly advised the speaker that such a presentation would not be appropriate, and he withdrew the individual's invitation to address the convention.

During that same convention a reception was given at the governor's mansion with a receiving line headed by Governor Robert E. McNair. It was the first time that any governor had given a reception at the official residence for an NFB convention, and Dr. Jernigan was very proud of that occurrence. Shortly after the 1969 convention we traveled with Dr. Jernigan to Washington to seek Senator Thurmond's assistance. In the 1960s the NFB's primary fundraising involved unordered merchandise, such as greeting cards and neckties, which was sent through the mail to prospective contributors. Several officials of the IRS wanted to tax this project by making a ruling, a ruling that we believed was inappropriate and illegal.

We discussed this situation with Senator Thurmond, who requested that Dr. Jernigan write an appropriate letter. He would then place it on his official letterhead and send it to the commissioner of the IRS. Senator Thurmond was as good as his word, and he did not change a single word of the letter Dr. Jernigan drafted for him. The IRS commissioner, who was from Greenville, South Carolina, never gave the NFB any further trouble.

Betty and I were fortunate enough to travel abroad with Dr. Jernigan on several occasions. In 1988 and 1992 we traveled with Dr. Jernigan to World Blind Union conferences held in Madrid and Cairo. In 1989 Betty and I joined Dr. and Mrs. Jernigan for a voyage on the Queen Elizabeth II to England in celebration of our fortieth wedding anniversary. During this trip we traveled with Dr. and Mrs. Jernigan to Suffolk, England, where we visited Dr. Jernigan's ancestral home at Somerleyton Hall, which is actually a castle. A member of the British House of Lords now resides there. He gave a delightful luncheon in Dr. Jernigan's honor at Somerleyton Hall. We also visited the church where several of Dr. Jernigan's ancestors are entombed.

Our last trip with Dr. Jernigan occurred in October 1997 as we once again boarded the QE2 in New York City for a voyage back to England. Unfortunately, during that trip Dr. Jernigan became seriously ill and was hospitalized for several days in Paris. The first of November, Dr. Jernigan, Mrs. Jernigan, Betty, and I boarded the Concorde in London and flew back to New York City in slightly more than three hours.

Dr. Jernigan was both thoughtful and caring about others. He was especially fond of Betty. When we visited him in Baltimore, at national conventions, or other places, he always had a music box for Betty's collection. He would say to her, "I have a pretty for you." Betty proudly displays many of these music boxes in our home. When we visited with Dr. Jernigan in Banner Elk, North Carolina, while he was receiving alternative treatment, he once again said to Betty, "I have a pretty for you." When he had heard that we were coming, he had his secretary send him a music box for Betty. The last music box he gave her was at the 1998 Dallas convention. He was also generous to me. He often remembered me with a gift when he traveled abroad. One treasured gift is beautiful cuff links, which I wear on special occasions.

Sometimes when we visited Dr. Jernigan, especially in his National Center office, he would say to us, "I have squirreled away some goodies." He would then serve us chocolates or macadamia nuts.

Dr. Jernigan was sensitive to the special needs of people. When Hurricane Hugo caused tremendous damage in 1989, several blind families were victims. Upon learning of this Dr. Jernigan arranged for a contribution of $10,000 to assist the blind people who had suffered from the hurricane.

Even in moments of distress Dr. Jernigan could be humorous. While attending the 1988 Thanksgiving meeting of the NFB Board of Directors in Baltimore, our new 1988 Cadillac was stolen from in front of the National Center. Learning of this, Dr. Jernigan quipped, "Well Don, whoever stole it had good taste." Shortly after telling him that we could replace the car but not the several cases of cassette tapes of music we had recorded, we received copies of most of his favorite cassette tapes featuring Bing Crosby, our favorite, and others. Dr. Jernigan also knew when to respond without being asked. In May 1997, when Betty had a serious fall while visiting our son Craig in New York City, Dr. Jernigan found an individual who was able to come to New York City to drive us back to Columbia as soon as Betty was able to travel. You don't forget that kind of kindness.

Dr. Jernigan had many rare qualities including tremendous charisma and a magnetic personality. Never have I seen anyone with better and more ideas than he demonstrated throughout his life. He was very creative and was an intellectual giant. The book of life will require many chapters to cover the innumerable accomplishments of Dr. Kenneth Jernigan. His life made our lives much better.

CHAPTER 6

THE BEGINNINGS IN IOWA

by James Valliant

Note: Jim Valliant was Kenneth Jernigan's top assistant for more than a decade as they worked to build the Iowa Commission for the Blind from a tiny state agency into the most renowned program for the blind in the world. Jim Valliant participated fully in everything from poker playing with Iowa officials to hiring staff and planning budgets and winning legislative support for them. Then he returned to his home state of Maryland where he established a very successful import business. After his departure, he kept in touch with Dr. Jernigan and continued to support the NFB, even attending some national conventions. Here he attempts to give the flavor of the feverish work he and Kenneth Jernigan did in order to create the kind of service program for the blind that had never before existed anywhere.

SOME TIME AGO MRS. JERNIGAN AND MRS. WALHOF visited me to ask if I could write a short article about the impact that Dr. Jernigan had on my life. I've been very dilatory in preparing this article because of the limitations of language. I'm told that English is more precise and more expansive than any known language. But even Shakespeare would have difficulty explaining fully the complexities, the passions, and the effectiveness of Dr. Jernigan. I have chosen a few snippets of our time together and hope they reveal a little of the effect he had on work with the blind as well as the impact he had on the sighted that worked with him.

Jim Valliant speaks from the floor at the
1971 NFB National Convention.

In 1958 on a sparkling early September day, I sat on a low brick wall reading Hardy's _The Mayor of Casterbridge,_ wondering what had gone wrong. I was just outside the Iowa City airport entrance, almost 1,000 miles from home, with no phone number to call should plans go awry. It was already 2:30 pm; he said he would pick me up at 1:00.

At exactly 3:00 one of the biggest, blobbiest, yellow-tannish autos I had ever seen came to a stop on the drive in front of me. The passenger window lowered, and Kenneth Jernigan said, "Good afternoon Mr. Valliant. Sorry to be late. I had delays. Get in the driver's seat. You can take over the driving. We are on our way to Louisville, Kentucky, for our annual meeting of the NFB of Kentucky." Short, to the point, and almost incomprehensible. Why fly west to Iowa only to drive immediately east to Kentucky?

That was my introduction to Dr. Kenneth Jernigan who was to be my boss for most of the next thirteen years, during which I realized there was always a method to his madness.

Of course, he wanted time with me to impart knowledge of the history and meaning of the NFB and how it had practical use for the Iowa Commission for the Blind. I was to learn in exhausting detail what he meant when he said, "Without a philosophy no bread can be baked."

To relate all the anecdotes that describe the effect Dr. Jernigan had on me, on Iowa, and on his students is not possible in this short article. Rather, I will primarily tell of only one segment of his wide-ranging life's work: how he established an orientation center for training blind adults to live and work competitively. I knew from our first meeting that the Center was his special dream and passion.

In mid-1958, Kenneth Jernigan became director of the Iowa Commission for the Blind primarily because over the years he had developed a serious correspondence with Mrs. Dorothy Kirsner, a volunteer Braille transcriber in Des Moines who had interest and time to Braille books he requested. The Iowa governor had recently appointed her to the Board of the Commission, an infinitesimally small, independent agency with but six employees and which spent very little money and caused no waves politically. Many state legislators did not know it even existed.

Soon after Dr. Jernigan arrived to take control, he had to leave for Boston for the 1958 NFB annual convention, which by total chance I had also attended and casually met Dr. Jernigan. Two months later I was driving to Louisville, listening intently to his philosophy of blindness, his ideas about its implementation in the real world, the NFB and its Civil War, and how that affected what "we" were going to do in Iowa.

I was not asked to be on the team. It was obviously assumed that, of course, I would be a player. That really irritated me. But the arguments were so cogent and persuasive that by the time we drove back to Des Moines I was willing and eager.

Dr. Jernigan simply had no time to waste to argue about what I wanted. And I had no time—he told me—even to look for an apartment. I could live at his house until an apartment would somehow appear deus ex machina. As if he had almost willed it, the apartment did appear across the street six months later.

Since its creation in 1925, the Commission had done little work and, with so few employees, had no effective programs to supervise. It would have taken "the Boss" about one-half hour a month to supervise the programs of the pre-Jernigan era. Eventually that was the time he gave them. But the other thirty-nine and one-half hours each week (or more properly, sixty-nine hours minimum) Dr. Jernigan used to cultivate the land and plant the seed to grow his dream, like a farmer prepares his ground for planting.

He penned his vision for an effective program for the Commission and sent copies to members of the state's administration, legislature, and to important leaders of Iowa Lions and Iowa Federation of Women Clubs. I became his assistant and one of his principal drivers. He personally crisscrossed the state to visit as many of those people as possible in shot-gun fashion, for he was not even aware which of those were part of the power structure. We even visited some legislators who were to lose seats in the upcoming November elections.

We spent much time with Howard Benshoof, the director of the office of federal rehab programs in Kansas City, who had formerly been Director of the Vocational Rehabilitation Department in Iowa and spent weekends at his farm just south of Des Moines. It was important not only to gain his support but to gain an understanding of the use of federal matching funds available for rehabilitation. Many an evening was also spent with Don Overbeay, superintendent of the Iowa Braille and Sight Saving School, who was also on the board of the Commission.

As I look back to those days, I now realize what Dr. Jernigan was doing. He was going back to his roots. After all, he had been a teacher—not an administrator. He was, in effect, teaching Iowa about blindness—equality, security, and opportunity.

He was the Socrates of Iowa, expounding Federation beliefs to the people of power who could agree to whatever was necessary to accomplish his goals. If his teaching was valid, they would also believe—and they would produce the funds to accomplish those goals.

Plans often had to be rearranged. The Commission was housed in the old Amos Hyatt Building, which had lots of empty space. His plans to use it as an orientation center fell apart when he found out it was a condemned building. (The fact that the government housed the Commission in a condemned building shows the esteem in which the Commission was held.)

Not only did state officials hold the Commission in low esteem, but so did the Commission employees themselves. Dr. Jernigan knew that for a person or agency to be held worthwhile by his or its peers, he or it needed self-esteem. He put into effect a very simple rule: this agency will use last names only. Heretofore, if a phone rang and someone asked for the home teacher, the secretary would say, "I'll put you through to Ruth." Now the secretary would say, "May I ask who is calling please?" and "I'll connect you with Miss Brackney." And should Miss Brackney come into the secretary's office, she would no longer say, "Ann, I have a question." Rather, she would say, "Mrs. Maher, I have a question." It may sound silly today, but in 1958 the staff learned that Mr. Jernigan valued them and they, in turn, learned to value themselves.

As he had with the Iowa public, legislators, and government administrators, he taught NFB philosophy to the expanding Commission staff. He would speak with us individually, in staff meetings, or at hamburger cookouts at his home. (If sighted people want to learn to cook the perfect hamburger every time, they should learn the Jernigan method.) His scholarly approach toward his own staff convinced all of us (blind and sighted) of the value of the work upon which we were embarking.

Looking back at those days, I now realize that, to a man, the staff never worked for Dr. Jernigan—they worked with him. That distinction is as important as the difference between an organization of the blind and an organization for the blind.

After a decade of Dr. Jernigan's leadership, I truly believe that there was no staff in Iowa government (indeed, in all the United States) that was as eager and willing to do its appointed work as that of the Iowa Commission for the Blind.

A real plus at the opening of the legislative session in January 1959 was that his budget request for state funding seemed small compared to other agencies. But he had studied the federal law with Mr. Benshoof and found that for every state dollar used, the federal government could potentially match with nine dollars—something the previous administrator had ignored. We seemed to be on our way to a program that would form a basis for future opportunities for the blind.

Suddenly, the bombshell. The Des Moines YMCA wanted to sell its building—a solid six stories with full basement (and pool) taking up over one-quarter of a large block in downtown Des Moines.

Immediately Dr. Jernigan acted. He toured the building the day after the news article appeared and found it perfect for his vision. It even had enough space for a library, something he thought would take years to accomplish—space for offices aplenty and space for his dream, classrooms and residence rooms for his beloved training center. And it was right where he wanted it—in the middle of Iowa's capital and largest city where the public could see the progress of students traversing busy streets.

Well before the legislative session convened, Dr. Jernigan had hired the first instructor for the orientation center that, itself, was still a dream. Mr. Jim Witte joined us as the travel instructor. Even with a skeletal staff Dr. Jernigan began working with a few students, and Jim Witte had students learning to travel around the capital building amid the heavy snows of January 1959. Arriving legislators could see a few blind students using the long cane successfully to travel a few blocks around the capital building and overcome even the difficulties presented by the snow. Arriving legislators were going to be impressed. That was the will of Jim Witte and Dr. Jernigan.

All the support gained came to fruition when the legislature reached an agreement for the state to purchase the old YMCA and for subsequent funds to remodel the building. It was not chance or luck that it all came about, although the actual opportunity to buy the building was serendipitous. Dr. Jernigan had the vision of the proper program and had worked hard to teach Iowa about the worth of the cause.

Now he could create his dream of a total program—a school to show blind adults and the entire state that it is respectable to be blind; a library to impart knowledge; and a rehabilitation and placement program to make jobs available to those he loved the most, his students. The rest is history.

But the history was Dr. Jernigan's creation. He gave Iowa a moral compass based on a philosophy of logic, effectiveness, and worthiness. When opportunities arose, the ground had already been planted. The land bore fruit.

The lesson he taught was not just for the blind. Rather it is for all. To base an action on what is right and proper, not for self or gain, is eventually the unassailable method of achieving a lasting result. Either solve tangential issues quickly or toss them aside. Always focus on the objective.

I moved on to head the largest company of its kind in the nation (even if it was in a small industry) by using Jernigan methods: respect the worth of people; teach them honesty of purpose; ground one's efforts in a proper philosophy so staff would work with you, not for you; and direct your work toward those goals that establish the keystone of what you want to build.

Dr. Jernigan was the epitome of what President John Quincy Adams once said: "If your actions inspire others to dream more, learn more, do more, and become more, you are a leader."

CHAPTER 7

WHAT A LUCKY DAY!

by Jan Omvig Gawith

Note: When Dr. Jernigan moved to Iowa as director of the Commission for the Blind, Jan Gawith was one of the very early students to enroll in the Orientation and Adjustment Center. After her training, she was employed as a medical transcriber for the Veteran's Hospital, worked as a secretary for a member of the Iowa legislature, was hired as one of the first staff members of the Idaho Commission for the Blind, and the last twenty-two years of her career she was in business. She credits Kenneth Jernigan with assisting her to turn her life into the productive one it has been. Clearly, the relationship became a close friendship, as happened with so many others.

WHEN I FIRST MET KENNETH JERNIGAN I WAS ALMOST twenty-eight years old and had just been fired from a job. Little did I know that this was the day that my new, better life was about to begin. It was around seven o'clock in the evening, and he was still at work. "Are you blind, Jan?" he asked. Truthfully, I didn't know. Nearly ten years earlier I had been denied services at the Commission for the Blind; I was told I was not blind enough (without an eye exam). Mr. Jernigan pronounced me blind after I had difficulty finding his hand to count fingers.

Jan Omvig Gawith, 2004

Growing Up in the 1940s. My early years were spent on acreage outside the small Iowa town where I was born. The admonishment to "stand up straight" was usually followed by "watch where you are going." Lots of skinned knees and elbows! When I was five, my grandfather took me to an eye specialist, and I was fitted with thick, heavy glasses. They cleared up the fuzziness but falls continued. School did not enchant me; the halls were dark and the blackboards hard to see. And I may be the only person to have failed art! My eye condition caused my field of vision to be very narrow and continue to shrink.

In the small town of Slater where we lived when I was a teenager, the superintendent was also the school coach. He seems to have been the first to recognize that my poor vision was at the root of my "clumsiness." He suggested that we consider the Iowa School for the Blind for my last years of high school. My parents were very good about it, leaving the decision up to me. Of course, the term "blind" was not applied to me, and a great deal was made of the "sight-saving" large print books when we visited at the school. My insecurities and low self- esteem made change somehow seem like a good thing. So at sixteen, off I went.

Many of the lessons I learned were not part of the curriculum. For example, I learned that as a person with a little vision, I was able to help the totally blind students so that they could go to town. It was policy that no totally blind student could leave campus unless accompanied by a student with some vision. Why I didn't get us killed is beyond me. Also, only students with some vision were allowed to serve meals to the young students in the Children's Cottage. This policy probably also gave the little ones quite a negative message. Totally and partially blind students were paired to make the trip to the dining room. Many pages could be written about this negative aspect of my "education" at the School for the Blind.

Struggling with Poor Vision. Ethel Towne Holmes, director of the Commission for the Blind, visited the students at the school to discuss possibilities after graduation. Although my family did not have the funds for me to go to college, it seemed there might be hope that I could. I was shuffled around from one agency to another, but no financial assistance was offered. After reaching several dead ends, I was referred to a company that was hiring and got a job as a clerk.

In some respects this was one of the most difficult jobs I ever had. We had to skip around the documents to find those coded items to fit into the eighty spaces on the punch cards. I was bedeviled with eye strain and headaches and could not be efficient. After a year and a half, I resigned and moved to Kansas City to live with a friend. One thing I did learn at the School for the Blind was to be a good typist. In Kansas City, I worked for about eighteen months as a Dictaphone typist. Then my mother wrote to say that she had received a small inheritance and, if I would commute to Des Moines to school and stay at home, she thought she could swing the other college expenses. By this time, my younger brother Jim, who had less vision than I, had graduated from high school. He was "blind enough" to receive some financial assistance from the Commission for the Blind. He hired me as his reader. Poor guy! My reading was so slow and laborious that I literally put him to sleep.

After two years and lots of hard work, I had sixty-seven credits and received my A.A. degree and a teaching certificate. I found a job in a small town near Des Moines. I had found some ways to hide my vision loss. For example, I assigned seating and memorized the arrangement. I identified the students by the sound of their voices and by where they sat. One parent told me that her son said that I had eyes in the back of my head.

After two years, I was off to the University of Iowa for another year of college; the general rehab agency helped with tuition and books. Before Christmas, I began having severe double vision and could only read for two or three minutes. My housemates read my assignments for those classes that I did not drop. My parents joined me for a visit to the eye clinic at the University of Iowa. After failing their field test, they prescribed blocking one lens and reading with one eye. I struggled through the remainder of the year. I went to California and taught for a year. It is good that there is a strong work ethic in our family. It was often tempting to throw in the towel. And, after one year, I headed back to Iowa to regroup. I played and put off getting a job. With the help of a friend, I finally got a job in 1960. The president of the company hired me, and I told him that I had a lot of difficulty seeing and wanted a position as a Dictaphone typist. He went out of town, and the vice president fired me. What a lucky day!

Yes, I was upset, frightened, and a lot of other descriptive terms. I called Mrs. Heffner, the mother of a blind friend, who worked at the Commission for the Blind. She told me that I must go to the training center there. I explained that I had not previously qualified for services. She informed me that Mrs. Holmes was no longer the director, and things were very different. What an understatement! She made me an appointment for the interview that resulted in my meeting Kenneth Jernigan.

Mr. Jernigan gave me his own personal eye exam saying, "How many fingers am I holding up?" I murmured, "I have to find your hand." His immediate response was "You're blind." Interestingly enough, it was exactly the right thing to say to me, and it has never been as hard to be "blind" since. After discussing dates for my entry into the training center, Mr. Jernigan offered me a ride home. After that interview, I was drained, scared and excited.

Training. One of the first things I learned was that I would be expected to wear blindfolds, which we called sleep shades during my classes. The reasoning was: if I learned the skills using no vision, I would not have to struggle with my limited vision. If I believed I could be independent and competitive as a totally blind person, my bad eyesight might sometimes be useful, but it would not make me more or less successful. Knowing what the sleep shades were for was not the same as putting them on and walking down the street with a long white cane! With my travel teacher holding his hand over mine and helping arc the cane, I was shaking like a leaf but turtled to the end of the block. Then the travel teacher had the audacity to tell me to walk back on my own. My cane hit several parking meters and dropped off the curb three or four times, but it finally dawned on me that I hadn't bumped the meters nor had I fallen off the curb. This was indeed progress! The second day the travel teacher sent me around the block, alone. Although I wandered into a parking lot, I made it.

While I was a student, the Iowa Commission for the Blind building was being remodeled. With our white canes in hand, we students skirted jack hammers in the halls, painters on ladders in the stairwells, and other construction activities. We cooked wearing blindfolds and using electrical appliances. The home ec teacher, Ruth, and Mr. Jernigan expected us to cook luncheon for the Chairman of the Board of the agency! And we did.

In discussion classes, we were expected to think, express ourselves, and defend our positions. I particularly remember when all the students agreed with each other repeatedly about a certain point. After inviting a change several times, Mr. Jernigan slapped the flat of his hand on the desk making a sound like a shot and said "You Sheep! You're all wrong!" I got the message! THINK!

One morning I came to class, and my travel instructor told me that I would be followed by a newspaper man and his photographer on my route. It was rather daunting, but I was beginning to get used to the unexpected. That day, a pedestrian decided to walk with me and generally make a nuisance of himself. Finally I told him that I was being followed by a newspaperman, and he should look and see if he could see him. Thankfully, that did the trick; he scurried off. The next day our program was featured on the entire back page of the Des Moines evening *Tribune*.

It might be noted here that training was treated like a job. We were expected to be on time and fully participate in all activities. My parents were taking a two week trip to visit relatives in Montana in late June. When I discussed taking the time off, I was told I could have one week. Since they were traveling by car, I said I needed two weeks. It was strongly "suggested" that I return on the train or bus. I had a great train trip.

One day when I was on travel in downtown Des Moines a gentleman stopped me and asked if it would be all right to talk with me while I was wearing the blindfold. I thought I recognized the voice. He introduced himself; it was the president of the company from which I had been fired just before beginning my training. He said he had planned to hire me back, but when he learned from my friend what I was doing, he felt that it was a great opportunity for me. How right he was—and what a boost for my ego. Sometime later I learned that the vice president who fired me had also been fired.

Students often went with Mr. Jernigan or one of the staff to speaking engagements and were asked to say a few words. Later, students would be asked to make the presentations. What an excellent experience!

When my skills in Braille, cane travel, etc. were developing well, I was given the opportunity to learn to operate the switchboard and serve as receptionist. I also helped with new students.

Further, on Friday evenings sometimes there were meetings of the Des Moines chapter of the National Federation of the Blind (NFB). Other Friday evenings we read *Hope Deferred: Public Welfare and the Blind* by Dr. Jacobus tenBroek, President of the NFB, and we discussed it. During the winter, we had an opportunity to get wood for the fireplace. We cut limbs off the trees, sawed them into appropriate lengths, loaded them into the truck, stacked them behind the Commission building, and then burned them in the fireplace—always wearing our sleep shades. Mr. Jernigan built big fires because he wanted the next group of students to have the same experience chopping wood.

We baked for a fair, and we learned about legislation. Before the remodeling of the building was quite complete, Mr. Jernigan would go over to the Statehouse and invite legislators to lunch. We only learned at the last minute whether we would be serving one or thirty-five guests. As soon as lunch was finished, we would all hurry off to other classes to demonstrate what we were learning there. After the guests were gone, we students would go back to the kitchen and clean up. It was hectic and also exciting. We had no idea just how much confidence we were gaining. Although shy and frightened at first, I was right in the middle, grabbing hold of confidence and self-esteem. Thank you, thank you, Kenneth Jernigan!

We students were often invited to the Jernigan home or that of one of the other teachers for dinner or a cookout. We were learning all the time. At people's homes, we were assigned jobs, and we wanted to help. We did not have time to worry about whether we might make a mess or break something. We would go in large or small groups to restaurants, plain or fancy, sometimes out of town.

When I finished training, Mr. Jernigan offered me the opportunity to manage the grill in the Commission building. The temptation was great, as I would be in daily contact with people that I truly liked and admired. However, I felt that it would be best if I could get out into the business community and demonstrate my ability with the new skills. I took tests for various positions in Des Moines and throughout the state. One of these was with the Veterans Administration. I was able to get a position as a medical transcriber at the VA Hospital.

VA Days. My class time at the orientation center ended on a Friday in the middle of April 1961. The following Monday, I began work at the VA Hospital as a medical transcriber. I took a class in medical transcription at a local hospital. My supervisor was a terrific person and taught me much more than the class. I had no accessible lists of names of medications and began making my own using dark ink and large print. After about two weeks, it occurred to me that I should be doing the list in Braille, so I went about the business of copying it. How lucky. Exactly four weeks to the day after starting work, I discovered most of my remaining vision was gone. I finished the morning at work and left at noon to participate in the wedding of my roommate. No time for self-pity and really no reason.

While at the center, my typing teacher and I developed a method of erasing errors, including carbon copies. Upon arrival at the hospital, I learned that they all used a product called Correct-a-Type. So it goes. What a difference today. Medical terminology and medications are probably available through a built-in dictionary in the computer.

While at the VA, I continued to be involved with students and activities at the Commission. One weekend we all went water-skiing; another camping and learning to shoot pistols.

Iowa Legislature. During my tenure at the hospital, I was invited by a state legislator to be his secretary. My leave was approved when recommended by a member of congress on Veterans Affairs Committee.

My first day at the legislature, we secretaries were told in no uncertain terms that we would be fired if we did any lobbying. Fortunately for me, I did not need to open my mouth to lobby successfully in support of the Commission for the Blind programs. I only needed to do my job, walking the stairs, going for the mail, taking notes at hearings, and the myriad of jobs done by all—without computers. We had a system called cut-and-paste (hard copy) to add amendments to original bills. This was really not possible for me, but a friend was working in a comparable job. She taped for me, and I babysat for her. It was a great trade.

Working in the legislature was a terrific experience, and one which I would never have dreamed possible before going through the Commission training program. Yes, I learned cane travel and Braille and learned alternative methods in typing and homemaking activities, but most of all I learned to dream, reach for those dreams, and to work for them. Kenneth Jernigan and the staff with whom he surrounded us taught us to take the *can't* out of our ideas and replace it with *can, how,* and *why not?*

Just for the record, I did not lobby in the way that would have caused me to lose my position. Nothing prevented me from answering questions posed by legislators, including those on the Appropriations Committee. I was there conveniently, and they did ask questions. Mr. Jernigan requested two capital improvement appropriations which had not made it into the governor's budget. He talked with the governor to clear going after the funds. The governor agreed that we should try. When asked by legislators about different budget or program questions pertaining to the Commission for the Blind, my responses were either that I would get the information for them, which I did, or that the Commission was a wonderful program and growing. Almost the full $93,000 was approved. Now remember, I did say that I was a shy, frightened young woman. By training me, believing in me, challenging me, encouraging me, and providing me with speaking opportunities, Mr. Jernigan gave me a life which I had only dreamed of.

More Change. While my VA hospital job paid well, it was rather boring. After six and one-half years, I was ready to move on. My hope was to work with other blind people. Most good jobs in this field required at least a BA degree, and I did not have it.

Mr. Jernigan had instituted what was referred to as College Days for blind students being assisted by the Commission for the Blind to get higher education. I asked if I might sit in, and he agreed. There were many questions from students and staff about how to accomplish various tasks and why not opt out of classes such as physical education and science labs, etc. Before lunch, I began to scheme and dream. I cornered Mr. Jernigan and asked him if I would be eligible to go back to college. That very day, a Saturday, he assigned me to a rehabilitation counselor, and we began planning. This was the Saturday before classes at Drake University began on Wednesday. On Monday morning, I resigned my position at the VA and went to Drake to register for classes. Then I went back to work for another day and a half. I began classes at Drake on Wednesday morning. I moved to an apartment within walking distance of the University in September. How I loved school!

But there was more change coming. In late October I received a phone call from the newly-hired director of the Idaho Commission for the Blind, who had also been Dr. Jernigan's student, offering me a job. I turned him down flat. I discussed this matter with Mr. Jernigan and others. I wanted to work with the blind, but I had just quit a good job and was happy in college. The offer was repeated, but this time I would be able to finish the semester and then move to Idaho, and I was told to expect to be able to continue to work on my degree. I caved. Finals, packing, and parties kept me busy. Because of fog, my flight out of Des Moines was cancelled. I took the bus to Omaha, and landed in Boise at midnight in order to work the next day.

Idaho. The Idaho Commission for the Blind was a brand new agency with its office in a very small house. The bathroom was bigger than my office. The boss's office was equally cramped. It was the only place for our three students to meet with him for discussion class, but they could barely fit in. I taught home economics and typing out of my apartment, and Braille and cane travel out of the office. In the beginning I worked with orientation students in the morning. In the afternoon I changed hats and was a rehab counselor and home instructor. Some weeks I boarded a plane and did counseling and home instruction for several days in another part of the state. A short week was sixty hours or more. While it was exhausting, it was also invigorating and satisfying.

In Idaho we had an opportunity to offer to blind adults the kind of training that changed my life in Iowa. Although I did not yet have a BA degree, I felt privileged to pass along my experience, as did the other staff members in this brand new agency. Sometimes I helped train sighted staff members who knew nothing about blindness and needed to rid themselves of the old fashioned ideas so embedded in the thinking of society.

My return to college did not occur until the summer of 1974 when I enrolled at Boise State University. In 1975 I graduated with a BA in elementary education. I took nine and twelve credits per semester, but I was determined to get that degree. After all, I had first enrolled in college twenty-two years earlier.

Harry. One activity I had always enjoyed was bowling. One of the sighted teachers at the Commission for the Blind, Harry Gawith, and I joined a league in the fall of 1975; Harry and I were married the following May. We bowled league together for thirty years and often had other blind persons on our team.

For a period of about four and one-half years, Harry and I served as resident staff living in the Commission building. Working with students after hours and on weekends was often great fun and sometimes extremely challenging.

When I was about sixty, Harry had become an avid golfer and most of the family had taken up golf. My initial participation was driving the cart, not always safely. My brother-in-law coaxed me into trying to play golf; I have progressed from extremely awful to pretty bad. However, there is not much like early morning outdoors where it is quiet with wildlife all around and the freedom to run or walk quickly through the grass to the green. Usually I use my golf club to give me ground information. Before Kenneth Jernigan and the training at the Iowa Commission I would never have tried golf. But I continued playing far into my seventies.

Cafeteria. In the fall of 1981 I decided to quit work; boredom set in rather quickly. In 1983 there was a vacancy in the business enterprise program for blind clients of the Commission for the Blind. By this time, the Commission fully occupied a five-story building in downtown Boise. The cafeteria in that building was available for a new operator. I had to take some training in business and food service, but I applied for and was assigned to this facility. Talk about full circle. It had been just about twenty-two years since Mr. Jernigan offered me a similar facility at the Iowa Commission for the Blind headquarters building!

While at the Commission cafeteria in Idaho, I often had occasion to work with the students who were in training at the Center on such things as carrying trays loaded with food, serving themselves both hot and cold beverages, and dealing with currency. After eight and one-half years at the Commission cafeteria, I moved to a larger location at the state office building nearest the Capitol, and we called it "Jan's Cafeteria." I did everything from taking money at the cash register to washing dishes to planning menus and hiring staff. Harry did much of the cooking and bookkeeping. I continued at that cafeteria until I was nearly seventy-four years old. My customers were state employees, elected officials, visitors to the capital, and others. After I retired, I missed working with the public. Seldom do I now go shopping or out to eat when I do not run into a former customer. They became my friends, and I love to hear about their families and activities.

National Federation of the Blind. From the 1962 NFB convention through 1975, I attended all national conventions and made many business trips around the country, traveling alone. That changed in 1976 when I married Harry who has attended conventions with me. He is also a committed Federationist.

For a number of years, it was possible to spot Iowa-trained persons by the assured way they traveled with their long white canes through the convention. In 2011 at my fiftieth convention I commented to my husband that it is no longer possible to ascertain the state where a person was trained. There are many great cane travelers from many states. The occupations that blind persons hold include many we were afraid to dream of before Kenneth Jernigan began to direct the Iowa training center. Other state agencies for the blind and private training centers have adopted as much of Dr. Jernigan's approach as they think they can. Dr. Jernigan had guts, tenacity, brains, and belief in the basic normalcy of blind persons, and he put his all into helping us make our individual dreams come true. Wonderful as he was, Dr. Jernigan could not have accomplished what he did without the National Federation of the Blind. He knew that and invited blind people to join and participate whenever he could.

Mr. Jernigan received two honorary doctorates in the 1960s in Iowa. He received several more from other universities in other parts of the country since that time. One of the techniques he used for helping blind people and the public at large understand and feel that it is respectable to be blind was using last names with other staff members at the Iowa Commission for the Blind. I never used his first name but called him Mr. Jernigan. After he received so many honorary doctorates, he is thought of by most Federationists as Dr. Jernigan, and I often use that form of his name. Whatever title is used, Kenneth Jernigan should be and is remembered as a man of determination, passion, imagination, and brilliance.

It is now more than fifty years since that fateful night I met Dr. Jernigan at the Commission in Des Moines. The influence of his work and thinking still impacts the beliefs and thinking of one Jan Omvig Gawith. And just for the record, I continue to use what I learned from him about blindness constantly, especially when I meet with newly blind persons.

CHAPTER 8

A GOOD LIFE
KENNETH JERNIGAN
WAS RIGHT!

by James H. Omvig, Sr.

Note: Jim Omvig has used the training he received as a young adult at the Iowa Commission for the Blind to pursue a long and productive career. As an attorney, he has helped with legal issues. As an administrator, he has worked for better opportunities. As a caring member of the NFB, he has reached out to blind members and professionals in work for the blind. He has been both persistent and innovative. He tells his story below.

THE BIG CHALLENGE. "IT IS PERFECTLY RESPECTABLE to be blind, and you can come to realize that. I and the others here at the Center will help you!" So said Kenneth Jernigan to me when we first met in his office in Des Moines, Iowa, in November of 1960. As I recall it now, he was very persuasive, but at that time I didn't understand or believe a single word he said. I was twenty-five years old, and for heaven's sake, I was blind! I knew that blind people were mostly rug weavers or beggars on the streets and that I couldn't do anything worthwhile.

Jim and Sharon Omvig, Norway, 2006.

Going Blind. I was born on February 12, 1935, and grew up in Slater near Des Moines. Those years were pretty ordinary, except that I wasn't good at baseball or basketball, which was a major pastime of young boys in Iowa farming towns.

We learned the reason for the poor performance when I was ten or eleven. My school decided to do some simple medical testing. The nurse said to me in the gymnasium, "Just stand here on the free-throw line and read that eye chart on the wall over there." I stood on the line, scanned the wall carefully, and asked, "What chart?" Testing revealed that I had

Retinitis Pigmentosa (RP)—a hereditary, degenerative disease of the retina. I was told by the doctors that I would be totally blind one day. What fear! What a distressing prognosis, not only for me but also for my family.

The next few years were difficult. Reading became a nightmare, but the teachers did what they could to accommodate my needs. They had me sit in the front row so I could try to see writing on the blackboard, and some handed me their notes. This singled me out and made me "different." Kids often are not kind to someone who is different. I didn't deal at all well with the vision loss; I was embarrassed and ashamed. Fear and shame can cause one to do extraordinary and stupid things in order to hide from the truth. Perhaps the most outrageous thing I did had to do with my taking the Iowa Basic Skills exam. It was black lettering on dark blue paper. I couldn't read a single word, but I was too ashamed to say so. I went through the entire test marking answers randomly.

By the middle of my ninth grade year, it was decided that I should go to Iowa's residential School for the Blind in Vinton. This was my very first encounter with what some refer to as "the blindness system" of sixty years ago. My parents were excited. They assumed that I would be dealing with professionals who would be able to help me handle my blindness effectively. Sadly, they were wrong!

I learned to weave baskets, rag rugs, and cane chairs. In that era, it was incorrectly assumed by School officials that these were the jobs the blind could do. I was introduced to and assimilated the prevailing belief system about blindness:

blind people are inferior to sighted people; the more blind you are, the more helpless and useless you are; blind people are victims, and a blind person can never expect to be happy, competitive, successful, or to lead a normal and productive life. Now, please understand, school teachers or other staff never said these damaging and damning words out loud. No, we students learned their "defined philosophy of blindness" from what they did, not what they said.

Totally blind students were led from class to class by those with a little vision. Totally blind students could not leave the campus alone in the evenings and on weekends; they had to get one of the "partially sighted" students to lead them. When visitors to the School needed a student tour guide, only students with a little vision were pulled out of class to do it.

Through the years I have learned just how critical good role models are in the life of an impressionable blind person. There was only one male teacher who was blind at the School. He taught me how to weave rugs and baskets and to cane chairs. He was regarded as totally incompetent and was a laughingstock among the students because of his helplessness and inability to function well. Much later I learned, to my amazement, that this teacher and his totally blind brother had built a house and that he traveled independently to and from work with a white cane. I simply did not know this when I was in School. At that time all white canes that were available were very short, and the techniques for using them had not been refined. Further, white canes were regarded as a badge of inferiority, not a tool for independence, and independent cane travel was not understood or taught at the School. And because I had a little vision, I did not learn Braille.

At the time of my high school graduation in 1953, I felt that blindness was a terrible tragedy, and that a person must have sight in order to be successful and happy. I returned to my parents' home in Slater where I lived for the next eight years. Occasionally, I had a part-time job moving butter in the local creamery, and I began to play some music in a couple of combos. I did not date, since I knew I could not support a family. In the silence of the night in my bedroom, I wondered what would ever become of me. My single hope was that I would find a way to restore my eyesight, and my mother totally supported this futile hope. We contacted doctors and clinics repeatedly with the same discouraging response—there was nothing that could be done medically for me.

Dr. Jernigan Comes to Iowa. The Iowa Commission for the Blind was created by the legislature in 1925. In 1957 the federal Office of Vocational Rehabilitation survey and study found that the Iowa program for the blind was the worst in America. This agency would have set me up with a loom to weave rugs or equipment to make baskets for the rest of my life, but I rejected this possibility.

However, in 1958, Kenneth Jernigan became the Director of the Iowa Commission for the Blind.

One Sunday night, probably in 1958, Dr. Jernigan appeared on an interview show. I can recall even now the seething anger I felt when he told the interviewer the often-repeated Federation line, "Blind people are nothing more than normal people who cannot see. Given proper training and opportunity, the average blind person can do the average job in the average place of business and do it as well as his or her sighted neighbor." I was angry because my experience taught me that blind people could not do what sighted people do. I simply could not accept what this man said.

I just happened to be in the right place at the right time. One of my favorite sayings is, "Coincidence is God's way of remaining anonymous." What I know for certain is that my life was changed completely and forever by what I learned from Kenneth Jernigan and the National Federation of the Blind through the Iowa Commission for the Blind!

It was in November 1960 that we finally went to meet this man. My rehabilitation counselor and my sister Janet Omvig Gawith persuaded me. I was in his office for about one minute, sitting across his desk from him, when he asked pointedly and painfully, "Are you blind?" "Oh, no sir," I said, "I'm just a little hard of seeing." This was the cutesy way I had learned to avoid the painful and ugly word "blind." "I see," he said thoughtfully. "How many fingers am I holding up?" I couldn't see his fingers or his face or his body, but I was still ashamed to be truthful, so I guessed. Obviously I guessed incorrectly. "You are blind, Mr. Omvig," he said. "You have to learn how to deal with it." This response cut deeply and stung bitterly.

After we chatted for a while and he described his philosophy of blindness to me, he asked, "How old are you?" Another zinger! After I told him I was twenty-five years old, he said, "My, my, a man your age can expect to live for another fifty years. What are you going to do for those fifty years?"

Needless to say, I was sick at heart and had no answer. Then we talked. Eventually, he took me on a tour of the Orientation Center, introduced me to students and teachers, and we returned to his office for more talk. After an hour or so, I agreed that I would become an orientation center student, and he gave me a start date of March 15, 1961. But deep-seated emotions and feelings of abject inferiority cannot be erased in a day. During the next four months, my mother and I continued to try to find a way for me to regain my eyesight.

But I did show up at the Iowa Commission for the Blind on March 15. My life was changed forever! I learned rather quickly that "Kenneth Jernigan was right!" He was right in his beliefs about blindness and the normality of blind people, and I took full advantage of the doors opened by this new thinking.

My life at the training center was difficult, tiring, exciting, challenging, and rewarding. My training day began with men's gym class at 5:30 a.m. and, after practicing Braille for a couple of hours with two of my friends, ended at around 11:00 p.m. Classes included independent cane travel, shop, home ec, Braille, group discussions, and other activities from time to time. I did all these things wearing a blindfold, so there could be no lingering doubt in my mind about whether any vision would be desirable or necessary in order to do what I needed to do to be successful and happy. There were confidence-building activities, such as chopping down trees in the snow to get wood for the fireplace, water skiing in the summer, etc.

Dr. Jernigan, it seemed, worked night and day seven days a week. He taught the early morning men's gym class and a grammar class on Monday evenings. No matter what the activity, he was teaching us much more about blindness than anything else. I didn't totally understand that until many years later. In one of those grammar classes, he delved deeply into the topic of "giving back." He quoted the Bible to us saying, "To whom much is given, much will be required." In time, I accepted that I had a responsibility to give back to other blind people and to help society in general.

In another grammar class, Dr. Jernigan gave me yet another life lesson. He asked, "What do you think you might like to do for your future?" I replied, full of new-found confidence and joy, "I love what you're doing here. I think I'd like to go into work with the blind and run an orientation center for the blind someday." With his usual insight, Dr. Jernigan asked me casually, "And do you want to go into work with the blind and run a center because you think you would truly love it and be good at it, or because you really believe you can't succeed at anything else, and that getting into work with the blind would be easy?" When I replied that I couldn't answer the question honestly, Dr. Jernigan said, "Then I think you should do something else"—and so I did.

Although I had learned to believe that blind people could compete and succeed in the world, the majority of society did not yet understand what I had learned. I would be reminded of this fact many times in many ways as I proceeded to get an education and pursue a career.

I decided to go to college and then on to law school. I was the first blind student ever to attend and graduate from the Loyola University of Chicago's School of Law. Even that wasn't without civil rights problems because of blindness. The Law School Admissions Test (LSAT) was not available to blind students at that time. I spoke with Mr. Jernigan and Dr. tenBroek, and we agreed that I should try some other method of getting into the school. We could sue the testing service for discrimination, but that would take years out of my life, and I was already too many years behind.

I arranged a meeting with the dean of the Law School, and he agreed that if I would submit a paper to him on a topic he would assign, and if it were done well enough, and if I would also give my prior grades and recommendations to him, he would consider me for enrollment without the LSAT score. I did so, and I started law school classes in the fall of 1963.

I graduated from Loyola Law School in June 1966, took the Illinois Bar, and then became the first blind attorney ever hired by the National Labor Relations Board (NLRB). But that wasn't easy. I had something like 150 interviews before I received a job offer, and some political intervention was involved even then.

I worked for the NLRB in Washington, DC and then later in New York City. I got myself transferred from Washington to New York to realize my dream to work with courtrooms and people, not to be locked away in some back office doing administrative research and paperwork. While I was working and living in New York City with my wife and small son, I developed a passion for justice for the blind, and it has driven what I have tried to do ever since.

My first National Federation of the Blind convention speech was in 1967 in Los Angeles. I was given the opportunity by President tenBroek to tell the story of how the National Federation of the Blind had changed my life.

Learning about Programs for the Blind. In 1968 Dr. tenBroek died and Dr. Jernigan became President of the National Federation of the Blind. Dr. Jernigan asked me to begin traveling as a volunteer to NFB state conventions as one of the Federation's national representatives. I continued to do this for the next eighteen years.

It was not long before I realized that there was no other state in the Union where blind people were receiving the kind of training I had received in Iowa. In fact, I came to understand that in many states, blind people were actually being hurt by the very schools and vocational rehabilitation agencies which had been created to help them, much as I had been at the Iowa School for the Blind. I wanted the blind people I met to have the opportunity to learn Braille, travel independently, get a good education, and work in competitive employment. It was not happening, and I wanted to help.

I was living the American Dream, but I still wanted to help blind people. I called Kenneth Jernigan and said, "I've done 'something else.' I'd like to get into work with the blind for the right reason. My honest answer to your question you asked long ago is that I would love to run a program for the blind, and I know I will be good at it! I want to learn from you how to provide proper training to blind people and to administer an agency."

Dr. Jernigan agreed with the suggested life change. I left my job in New York City in June 1969 and joined the staff of the Iowa Commission for the Blind, where I remained for the next nine years. I also continued to work as a volunteer and travel for the National Federation of the Blind as much as I could.

I have worked hard in and out of the National Federation of the Blind. I have made a lot of friends and had a lot of fun. I have been active in Lions Clubs and in church wherever I have lived. I cannot tell about all my activities, but one is worth including.

In 1971 the NFB convention was in Houston, Texas, and there were news reporters looking for stories. I was in the swimming pool with some of the students from the Iowa Commission for the Blind, and some of my colleagues were with the reporters. One of the reporters said, "I see the blind swimming around the pool safely and easily, but a blind person couldn't climb that ten-meter diving tower over there and actually dive into the pool." Without the slightest hesitation, the NFB PR men said, "Absolutely! Why not? We've got just the guy here who can do it!"

I accepted the assignment (giving back you know). I used my long white cane to climb the circular staircase to the platform on top. I moved to the top edge and put the cane down, paused, and dived. The news clip, along with my voice-over interview about the blind civil rights movement in America, aired on all of the Houston TV channels that evening. There is also a still picture in which I appear to have dived from the top of the Houston convention hotel.

In January 1974, I married Sharon Lewis. From that day to the present, it is a buttons-bursting joy of mine that when achievements are made by either one or the other of us, people generally simply think of "the Omvigs."

In 1976 I participated in the filming and production of the Iowa Commission for the Blind's movie, "We Know Who We Are." The segment of the film in which I'm teaching a blind female student how to water-ski later aired nationally on the NBC "Today" show, and the film received high honors in a film festival. Also in 1976 I was asked by Board members of the American Brotherhood for the Blind (now the American Action Fund for Blind Children and Adults) if I would be willing to seek election to that Board. I agreed, was elected, and serve on this organization's Board to this day as its treasurer.

Social Security. The Social Security Administration had been hiring blind persons but refusing to promote them. With urging from Dr. Jernigan and Jim Gashel, I moved to Baltimore in 1978 to work at Social Security headquarters to help correct this problem. In July 1981, I was able to hand the new Reagan-appointed SSA Commissioner a policy statement which he used completely, and he said "I am committed not only to providing equal employment opportunity for blind persons, but also for all qualified, handicapped individuals." This SSA policy has resulted through the years in countless promotional opportunities for blind employees moving on up into the ranks of supervision and management. At that time, SSA became the model for other federal agencies to follow.

Separate Agencies for the Blind. One of the things that was proven at the Iowa Commission for the Blind when Dr. Jernigan was its director was that rehabilitation agencies for the blind can be most effective when they are a separate unit of government, not mixed in with other services. I first worked on this issue in 1973 in Nebraska. I worked extensively with Nebraska Services for the Blind and Nebraska legislative officials on the issue of making revolutionary improvements in the nature of adult services for the blind there. The blind of Nebraska knew well of "The Miracle of Iowa," and they wanted decent services for the blind in their own state. At the urging of the blind, Nebraska officials had made many trips to Iowa where I and others worked with them to show them what a quality rehabilitation agency for the blind should be. Eventually they decided to hire a Federationist to help establish the "Iowa Model" of adult services for the blind in the Cornhusker State. In the fall of 1973, the Nebraska directorship was offered to me, but I had to turn it down.

In the 1980s, I decided to put in writing the key issues in making a rehabilitation agency for the blind provide the kinds of services that lead to success for their clients or customers. Three articles which appeared in the *Braille Monitor* seemed to be helpful at the time and are still referred to when this issue is discussed today. They are "What We Can Expect from a Commission for the Blind, Viewpoint from the Consumers;" "Are We Blind, or Something Else? What's in a Word?;" and "Who are the Experts Who Should Counsel the Professionals: Comments on Pregnant Women and Blind Consumers." I have continued writing on freedom and empowerment for the blind to this day. My three books are entitled: *Freedom for the Blind; The Blindness Revolution: Jernigan in His Own Words;* and *Education and Rehabilitation for Empowerment* (co-authored with Dr. C. Edwin Vaughan). All of these were published in the twenty-first century long after my retirement. Altogether I have published more than sixty articles, monograms, and books.

I still wanted to run an orientation and adjustment center for the blind. After I had completed my mission at the Social Security Administration, I applied for the directorship of the Sensory Impairment Center, a nonprofit training agency for the blind and deaf, in Anchorage, Alaska, and was selected for the position. Sharon and I, along with our son Jamie, headed for Alaska in October1984.

As I expected, there was a lot of building to do. I flew to Juneau to meet with Governor Bill Sheffield and members of the legislature, and funds were found to double the agency's operating budget. I hired staff and found an apartment building in order to establish a residential training center for the adult blind. We leased a separate building to use as a training center for the deaf. The city of Anchorage rezoned the property for our use, and many Lions clubs provided funds to buy furnishings. By spring 1986 we had dedicated our new facilities, and services at the Alaska Center for Blind Adults had improved exponentially. Now I could run an "attitude-factory" and teach skills to blind students as I had dreamed for so long.

Other Federation Projects: Through the years I have worked on many NFB projects to improve opportunities for the blind. I worked with employees of the Chicago Lighthouse for the Blind and the Cincinnati Association for the Blind to help them organize labor unions in order to obtain fair wages. Although we made progress in these cases and others, the Federation is still working to eliminate pay to blind workers which is less than the required federal minimum wage.

After I was refused the opportunity to buy life insurance when I was traveling, I worked with Herbert Anderson, the Iowa Insurance Commissioner, to eliminate this kind of discrimination against the blind. I worked with insurance regulators to research practices and write a model law which could be adopted by states. I helped blind people make contacts and work for change. As a result of our work, I believe that this kind of discrimination has largely been eliminated.

tenBroek Award: At its 1986 national convention in Kansas City, the National Federation of the Blind recognized me and my work by presenting me with its highest honor for members, The Jacobus tenBroek Award. The presenter mentioned my work in Alaska, airline discrimination, sheltered shop discrimination, insurance discrimination and more. For me, receiving the tenBroek Award (presented from the blind of America—my own colleagues) is my highest honor.

Retirement. At the end of 1987 I was forced to retire for health reasons, and Sharon and I moved to Tucson, Arizona. Of course my heart was still in work with the blind, and I continued to write and work with members of the NFB of Arizona to improve programs there. As I could, I traveled to other states to evaluate their programs, recommend improvement, and provide staff training.

Three NFB state affiliates—Louisiana, Colorado, and Minnesota—were operating private, nonprofit orientation and adjustment centers based on the model Dr. Jernigan started in Iowa. Graduates of these centers became the envy of blind people across the nation because similar training was not available anywhere else. By 1992 a provision called "Informed Choice" had been amended to the Rehabilitation Act by Congress making it possible for blind clients to choose to attend an out-of-state training center with financial support from the Vocational Rehabilitation Agency in their home state. When this "choice" was not supported by the agencies, hearings were necessary, and I was one of the representatives who helped blind people in these fair hearings when they sought to get proper training at the new high-quality centers.

Also in the early 1990s, Joanne Wilson, founder and director of the Louisiana Center for the Blind, and I began to dream about a college program that would train teachers and counselors to have better attitudes about the abilities of the blind. Even the word "blind" seemed to be offensive to some of them. They began to call themselves "vision teachers." They were encouraging parents, children, and blind adults to deny blindness, instead of to live productive happy lives. Joanne Wilson contacted the president of Louisiana Tech University and others and established the Professional Development and Research Institute on Blindness in Rustin in 1996. I had the pleasure of serving on its advisory committee.

Joanne and I discussed the need for fair certification with other Federation leaders, and we decided to start the new professional certification, which would take into consideration the attitudes of professionals in work with the blind. I was the first president of the National Blindness Professional Certification Board (NBPCB) which was established in 2001. So I wrote the Board's Code of Professional Ethics and got it accepted by VR programs in most states. To be on the scene, Sharon and I moved to Ruston, Louisiana, in August 2001. The NBPCB continues to flourish, and I continue to serve on its board of directors as the program expands and adds new areas of special competencies.

Presidential Appointment. When I first met Dr. Jernigan, I could not have dreamed of doing the things I have done, helping to change laws, administering agencies, writing books and all the rest. As I reflect, most amazing of all is an assignment I received from President George W. Bush in 2003 to serve as a member on the President's Committee for

Purchase from People Who Are Blind or Severely Disabled. I was reappointed in 2007 for another five years. Receiving a Presidential appointment requires support from public officials and others in the field. I was encouraged to seek this appointment by Federation leaders, and members contacted their Senators to support this appointment. This gives me the opportunity to continue to work from the "inside" for better wages, benefits, and working conditions for blind workers in sheltered workshops.

Gratitude. As long as I am able, I will continue to do what I can to promote better opportunities for the blind wherever it is possible. My wife Sharon has been my soul mate for the past thirty-six years. I am still surprised and pleased at what I have been able to do. Dr. Jernigan changed my life more than most people can imagine. I regard Dr. Jernigan as a "Hero in History." The effect he had on my life and on thousands of other lives is incalculable. I learned "giving back," and I learned to respect myself and others as blind people. I have tried my very best to do justice to what he taught me and asked me to do. As he smiles warmly down from above, I can only hope and pray that he is well pleased.

CHAPTER 9

I AM A BLIND ELECTRICAL ENGINEER

by D. Curtis Willoughby

Note: Immediately after high school graduation, Curtis Willoughby enrolled as a student in the Orientation and Adjustment Center at the Iowa Commission for the Blind. Although his formal training there continued for less than three months, Curtis began a relationship with Dr. Jernigan that continued as long as Kenneth Jernigan lived. Because Curtis's interests were so different from Dr. Jernigan's, one might wonder how this could be. Curtis says he was not always aware when Dr. Jernigan took actions that made a difference to him, although Curtis saw the evidence that help had been given.

Curtis Willoughby also joined the National Federation of the Blind and found ways to contribute, ways which show his overwhelming interest in electronics and technology. But these are not his only interests. Dr. Jernigan and Curtis Willoughby also had philosophical discussions, which so many students learned from and loved.

Curtis Willoughby, 2007.

AS FAR BACK AS I CAN REMEMBER, I HAVE BEEN interested in mechanical things. When I was three years old, my dad opened a machine repair shop for farm equipment, and our family moved into a house adjacent to it in a small town in southwest Iowa called Griswold. By the time I was six, I was spending time in the shop asking questions and getting my hands on whatever was permitted. Before long I was putting away tools, so I learned to identify wrenches, hammers, screwdrivers of all types and sizes, pliers, etc. Later I learned to use power tools and larger machines. In my teenage years, I often did portions of projects for customers using machines such as the band saw, hydraulic shears and presses, drill presses, and the metal lathe.

When I was seven, Santa Claus brought me an electric train. My dad screwed the train tracks to a Masonite board which could be leaned up against the wall when not in use.

From time to time, additions were made to this train set: more tracks, more cars, switches, a train station. I played with this train and learned quite a bit about electricity and mechanics. Sometimes dad would take me to see train layouts that some of the men around town had built. Since I didn't get my hands on them, they were not as interesting to me as to my dad.

When my mother would decorate the Christmas tree, I liked to help with the lights and see how they worked. Back in those days, each string of lights (at our house) was wired in series, with just one wire from one light to the next. Therefore, if one light didn't work, the whole string went out. It was a big job to fix enough lights for a big tree. I had enough vision to see one light at a time. I liked to help test the lights and put them on the tree. Each time a string would go out during the Christmas season, we had to test all the bulbs on that string until we found the bad one. We only kept a very few spares on hand and felt we could not afford to replace more than the one that burned out. I was very interested in how these strings of lights worked and why. We had a few bubble lights which had a tube of liquid sticking out of the top of the bulb. When the bulb heated up, the liquid at the bottom would boil, causing a bubble to rise to the top of the tube. I wanted to know how these worked and drove my mother crazy asking about them. When one burned out, I would take it apart.

When I was in junior high, one of the teachers at the School for the Blind became interested in ham radio, and the local ham radio club often met at the School for the Blind. Some other students and I also began to study to take the exams for licenses. The school established a ham radio station. I

THE POWER OF LOVE | 115

also talked my dad into buying me a ham radio station and putting up antennae at home. I got to do the design work on the antennae and help put them up. These antennae were supported from the top of the shop, the house, and a tree. One of them was 65 feet long, and one was 125 feet long.

I learned about a magazine called the *Braille Technical Press,* published by a blind ham in New York. Uncharacteristically for me, I read this magazine extensively and learned a great deal from it about electronics. I was also drawn to radio and TV shops in Griswold, and I hung out with an older student at school who repaired radios.

As a very young child in public school, I had tried hard to read print, both large and small. I could not see it well enough to read it. My mother tried darkening it and enlarging it, but I still couldn't see it well enough to read. I knew the letters and could print them. I could read the largest newspaper headlines one letter at a time, but this was frustrating. My mother read to me and to my sisters (who are also blind) from the time we were toddlers, and we all enjoyed it.

When I started attending the Iowa School for the Blind in second grade, they started teaching me Braille immediately, but I had already come to regard reading as a struggle. I worked at reading Braille, but never got fast. There weren't more than a few books in Braille in the school library that I really wanted to read, and there were a great many print books everywhere that I wanted to read if I could get someone to read aloud to me. I found a few recorded books about radio and other technical things I enjoyed, but it didn't help my

Braille skills or my attitude toward Braille. When I found Braille materials that were interesting, such as a booklet about atomic power, the American Brotherhood for the Blind's book of basic American documents, and the *Braille Technical Press,* I read them. I was still slow. While I have always used Braille daily for notes, etc. and read Braille articles occasionally, the *Braille Technical Press* was the only Braille magazine I have ever read extensively.

As I grew older, whenever I could get my mother to read to me, I took full advantage of it. Her time for this was limited, and she would fall asleep before I was ready to quit reading. I guess she was not as interested in electronics as I was.

Through my junior year of high school, I hoped to attend trade school and then open a TV repair shop as a career. In the fall of my senior year, one of the school staff encouraged me to go to college and study electrical engineering. I'm not sure how serious he was. He joked about getting a degree from Stanford University. It took me a while to make up my mind, but I decided to go for it.

A week or so after I graduated from high school, I enrolled as a student in the Orientation and Adjustment Center of the Iowa Commission for the Blind in Des Moines, Iowa. Dr. Kenneth Jernigan was director of the agency at that time. In addition to standard classes of cane travel, shop, etc., I was scheduled along with several other students for grammar with Dr. Jernigan. The class met weekly in the evening. That's when I really began to get to know Dr. Jernigan. He taught a way to analyze grammar that was new to me, and I took more interest in grammar than I ever had. Some Saturday mornings Dr. Jernigan invited students for breakfast and spent the morning with us.

One of the people I met when I arrived in Des Moines was Don Nading, chief of maintenance at the Commission's building. I began to visit with him in his office when he worked in the evenings. One of his projects was to install an intercom system in the building. Another was to install a telephone system to allow people inside to admit others at the front door without going down several floors to let them in. I took a strong interest in both of these projects. Don found my interest and suggestions helpful. When Dr. Jernigan became aware of my interest, he encouraged my involvement, too. By August, I was spending my shop class working with Don Nading.

Late in August I enrolled as a freshman in electrical engineering at Iowa State University, which is located in Ames just thirty miles north of Des Moines. Frequently on weekends, I took the bus to Des Moines to work on the intercom system and the phone system at the Commission for the Blind. These systems required both maintenance and expansion as the program grew. I continued to work on this equipment during college and afterward, long after Don Nading had left the Commission staff.

I was planning to study electrical engineering in college, and Dr. Jernigan encouraged me. I was accepted at Iowa State University and first went there in July for freshman orientation. I knew that Dr. Jernigan had some conversation with people at ISU. Clearly, they had some concerns about blindness. Part of what I learned at the training center at the Commission for the Blind was to present myself to professors and department heads to put them at ease about the way I dealt with blindness. I wanted them to know that I was motivated to succeed and had the skills to deal with blindness so they didn't have to worry about it. I knew I needed to do good enough work in college that my professors and department heads would want to recommend me to employers who trusted them. We had discussed at the training center the need for recommendations from our professors when we were seeking employment. There were a limited number of employers in Iowa who hired electrical engineers, and they worked closely with university staff.

During college I learned discipline, especially as math became tougher, but techniques to do the engineering work were not really a problem. By the time I graduated, the department people believed in me enough to recommend me to the in-state employers that believed in them. I applied for and was recommended for jobs at Collins Radio and at the phone company. Many contacts were made in my behalf, and I was offered a job at Collins Radio about a week after I was interviewed. I was expected to design some pieces of radio equipment under the leadership of a project engineer. Within a couple of months, we established that a known weakness in the existing design was more serious than anticipated, and I proposed a design approach that would overcome the weakness. With the support of my colleagues, I set to work to redesign the equipment, using my new approach. Because of time pressure, we tested the new design using the old circuit boards with major extra wiring. While still in the testing phase, we had customers visit from Canada. I was out of town, but the design worked. Since my design was an improvement on something many others had contributed to, this visit from Canada helped eliminate any doubt that may have remained about my ability to do the work. Both my colleagues and our managers became aware of what I was doing.

I got the same pay raises as others, until the company got into financial trouble. After about four years, Collins Radio hired another blind electrical engineer who had just graduated from Iowa State. That was about the time of the beginning of company financial trouble, so the second blind engineer took an early layoff. Eventually, I was also laid off.

Through the years I had worked on a variety of equipment at the Commission for the Blind. I was hired by Dr. Jernigan to do several short-term projects there. I designed a radio studio and a Braille adapter for a telephone operator using a new telephone console. All that time I was sending out résumés looking for work anywhere in the country. I was not aware of how much Dr. Jernigan was working with phone company people to get them to give me a chance to compete, but I now know he did quite a bit. I received an offer and started a new job there.

A few years after I started working at the phone company, I received a letter from Bell Laboratories thanking me and complimenting me for "helping us to solve a problem." I gave a copy of this letter to my supervisor at Northwestern Bell. I also gave a copy to Dr. Jernigan, thinking he might be interested. A few days later he called me up and asked what I had done. I told him that the phone company had a serious service-affecting problem causing communication lines to some large industrial customers to quit working during the heat of the summer when electrical power consumption was at its maximum. After studying the problem, I determined that signals were being passed between two locations using a method highly susceptible to interference from power lines. I realized that all of the necessary components for a less susceptible signaling method were present. All that was necessary to eliminate the problem was to make some wiring changes and remove a piece of equipment. The hardest part of the solution was to convince the equipment designers at Bell Laboratories that it was a good solution. Because I had carefully and clearly documented the problem and the proposed solution, the Bell Labs engineers understood. This was a long-standing problem, so others had tried to solve it previously. It was my work that made the solution happen. Dr. Jernigan thanked me for the explanation and hung up.

Later I heard him say in speeches that this letter caused him to do some soul searching about blindness and electrical engineers. Dr. Jernigan said he asked himself if he had truly believed that I (as well as other blind electrical engineers who had been educated and hired by that time) was truly competitive. He said he could not be sure. Even though he had helped several of us and said we were competitive; even though Collins Radio might have liked to have one blind engineer just for show, but they certainly didn't need two of us for show, still two were hired; and even though his contacts at the phone company seemed happy with my work; Dr. Jernigan said he was not totally sure until he read that letter and heard my explanation that he had absolutely no doubt about whether blindness might diminish the ability of an engineer. Since Dr. Jernigan had less knowledge and experience with electronics than an engineer has, he would not be expected to understand all of the specifics of what we do and how we do it. That must make some difference. Nevertheless, he said he never again had any doubt about my ability or how blindness might inconvenience an engineer.

Of course, blind engineers have to find a way to show the people around us what we want them to understand. Each blind engineer, like blind people in many professions, has to work out his or her preferred methods for this. The subject needs to be given considerable attention by blind people preparing to attend college in a wide variety of fields. Blind people need to acquire several techniques for making raised-line drawings; a facility for explaining complex diagrams and for getting others who think they can't to explain them to the blind person; and a facility for visualizing two-dimensional and three-dimensional objects and how they are represented on paper. Blind people with some residual vision need to learn what visual techniques they can use effectively. It is possible for a totally blind person to accomplish these things, but there is nothing wrong with using visual techniques if they really work. Blind people need to have the opportunity through their entire education to touch and examine tactilely the widest possible variety of objects. They need to learn to ask to touch, if possible, things that most other people do not touch. If a blind engineer has mastered these things, then communicating concepts to and from colleagues will not become an issue.

In 1977 I got an opportunity to work for a year as a consultant to Bell Laboratories in New Jersey. While there I became acquainted with a computer operating system called "Unix," which was not widely known outside Bell Labs at the time. Most of its programs were written in a language called "C," which was developed along with and for Unix. I had the opportunity to be a student in a course on C, in which the printed textbook was not available until part way through the course. I attended a seminar in which a brand new system command language or "shell" was introduced by a young Ph.D. named Stephen Bourne. Those who are familiar with Unix, Linux, or any of several other Unix-like systems will recognize the Bourne shell. At that time, Unix was entirely a text-based system and therefore accessibility was not an issue.

A few years after I returned to Iowa, I met a blind high school librarian who wanted access to her card catalog in order to help her students use the library. (This was before libraries commonly had computerized catalogs.) I proposed that a Unix-based computer, with a speech synthesizer to make it talk, would solve her problem. The Iowa Commission for the Blind agreed. I formed a company called Willoughby Enterprises to develop the system and sell it to the Commission for their client.

A year or two later, Willoughby Enterprises developed a system to allow a blind court reporter to record steno notes and read them back from a direct Braille representation of her key entries. This was before court reporting was computerized generally, so this young woman functioned much the same way sighted court reporters did. Dr. Jernigan encouraged me in all the Willoughby Enterprise projects.

In 1992-93 the office where I worked in Des Moines at the telephone company was closed. When I wrote résumés to seek other jobs, I had two basic skill sets which I thought would be valuable to employers. One was the circuit design work I had been doing, and the other was my knowledge of Unix. I circulated résumés highlighting both skill sets. Inside the phone company at that time, résumés had to be customized for each job opening. In July 1993 I had a telephone interview with a hiring manager and two of his assistants for a Unix job in Denver. I had enough Unix knowledge for them to make me an offer. I accepted the job and moved to Denver, beginning work September 1. The work was technical support of Unix computers located throughout fourteen states. Members of my group installed these computers, supported the network that interconnected them, provided telephone technical support for them, and supported the applications that ran on them. In a couple of years, there were several hundred of these computers in operation. Not many years after that, these computers began to be replaced by Windows computers. Of the four people who started when I did in September 1993, one left within a year to work for a development group, two were laid off, and I was the only one who continued through even more changes until I retired in 2001.

In addition to continuing my NFB work, since retiring from the phone company I have been volunteering with the

"Tuesday Crew," which does a variety of building maintenance and improvement projects at my church. I have also been doing substantial work at Colorado's reading service for the blind, where I support computer and audio systems.

I attended state conventions of the NFB while I was in college, and a few Des Moines chapter meetings. When I graduated from college and moved to Cedar Rapids, I joined the chapter there. I served in several positions on the chapter board. I served on boards of statewide chapters, as well as on the board of NFB of Iowa. Later I was elected for several terms as treasurer of the NFB of Iowa. My first NFB convention was in 1966, and I haven't missed one since. After moving to Colorado, I have held office in two different chapters.

I married Doris Koerner in 1967, and she has been a partner with me in the Federation ever since. She was a school teacher when I met her, and very early volunteered to be the supervising teacher for a blind student teacher who was enrolled in the State University of Iowa. Then Doris decided to become certified as a teacher of blind children. She went on to teach blind children and/or blind adults until she recently retired. She has been the primary author of four books about the education of the blind, all of which have been published by the NFB and have become important parts of Federation literature. The books are definitely hers, but I played a significant role in writing some of the chapters. I am pleased and proud that Doris has been interested and active in the work of the Federation and has made such major contributions.

From my first knowledge of the Federation, I have believed that its work is important and that concerted action is the only way that conditions affecting the blind can be improved. I was a member of the NFB Research and Development Committee for about thirty years. I was president of the NFB Amateur Radio Operators Group for about twenty years. In this capacity, I was in charge of a project to provide special receivers so that conventioneers who are hard of hearing or need Spanish translation of the convention program can listen to it.

For almost fifty years, I have been active in the Federation in a wide variety of ways. Those that I am best known for are mostly technical, which is not surprising since that is my profession. I have also supported the Federation with my presence, my leadership, and my financial contributions.

If my experience has been helpful to others, I am glad. I have also had a rewarding career. I will continue to do what I can as long as I can. It is hard for me now to sort out Dr. Jernigan's influence from all the other influences on my life and my work. However, his influence started immediately after high school graduation and continued as long as he lived. In fact, it continues today. I am not the only person who received unexpected phone calls from Dr. Jernigan from time to time, and I enjoyed talking with him whenever they came. When I had the opportunity to share a meal with him, it was always a special occasion. There is no question that both Doris's life and mine have been richer for having known and worked with Dr. Jernigan.

CHAPTER 10

THE SPARK THAT BECAME A FLAME

by Tony Cobb

Note: Kenneth Jernigan and Tony Cobb discovered each other while Dr. Jernigan was leading an effort to change accreditation for agencies serving the blind. During the 1960s and 70s, agencies serving the blind were often told their services were good by a group purporting to be a national accreditation council, while they treated blind people with condescension and their staff members behaved unethically. Below, Tony Cobb describes how he brought an example of this and himself to Dr. Jernigan's attention, and he describes how this began an important relationship between the two.

PERHAPS IT WAS CHANCE, PERHAPS NOT, THAT WE MET at that landing on Chicago's Palmer House stairs in 1975, but it certainly began a momentous change in my life, as encounters with Dr. Kenneth Jernigan have done for so many. Very few people who are described as "larger than life" really are, but I was to discover in the next few decades that Dr. Jernigan was one of them.

Anthony Cobb, 1987.

I had come to this, my first national convention of the National Federation of the Blind, at his invitation, fascinated by the little I already knew about the Federation and Dr. Jernigan, but I was definitely a very green newbie. So in this meeting on the stairs, he asked if after the two days I had been there I had any idea about what made the Federation work. To answer, therefore, I reached into my bag of jargon and pulled out, "Well, I guess it's the power of collective action, Sir."

Dr. Jernigan smiled slightly, signaling it was a nice try but not a bull's-eye and that I should listen up to what would come next. I listened up. "Mr. Cobb," he said, "the thing that makes the Federation work is love, and we are not afraid to say that." He then smiled again and went on his way, leaving me to ponder for a long time what he said.

I knew next to nothing about blindness in 1972, when I left teaching high school and college English to pursue school administration at the Tennessee School for the Blind (TSB) as assistant superintendent in charge of a variety of administrative operations. The only blind person I knew about at the time was an old man in an army overcoat with a cup full of pencils who played his ukulele and sang in front of Woolworth's on Fifth Avenue in Nashville. In this phase of my learning the truth about blindness, ignorance was the bliss of being taught first about blindness by members of the National Federation of the Blind and not the careerists at the School for the Blind. Each month Mr. J. M. Warren, a veteran Federationist who had latched on to me as someone to educate before I could do any real damage, brought me a copy of the latest *Braille Monitor* and urged me to read it, and read it I did avidly because it was very well written, and the topics it treated were engaging. There was always something in it by Dr. Jernigan or about his activities, and I began to feel I knew at least a little about him. The approach he took to blindness made more and more sense as I watched the custodial treatment of blind children in the protective environment of TSB.

The school was accredited by the National Accreditation Council for Agencies Serving the Blind and Visually

Handicapped (NAC), and as I learned from Dr. Jernigan's articles and speeches that was surely not a good thing for the students and staff of the school. At length I had tangible proof when NAC ignored violation of its own standards, causing me to write the chairman of its board a very critical letter taking NAC to task for its negligence, and I copied Dr. Jernigan almost as an afterthought simply because I thought he'd be interested as an alumnus of and former teacher at the school in addition to being a national leader.

About two weeks later my office telephone rang, and in a voice of authority Dr. Jernigan introduced himself. He wanted to know if I really wrote that letter or whether I had someone else write it and then merely signed it. I assured him at least twice that indeed I was the writer, not fully knowing whether he appreciated being copied on a letter written by this unknown administrator or considered it an act of wanton presumption.

Dr. Jernigan was, however, among other things a talent scout. Apparently he suspected, after reading the letter and ascertaining I was its author, that I was able to contribute something of value to the Federation and the Iowa Commission for the Blind that he and the NFB had led to such great accomplishments that he had received a formal commendation from President Johnson in 1968. He went to work on the telephone: Would I come to the NFB national convention in Chicago? Would I then ride back to Des Moines with him and look over the Iowa Commission while he looked me over with no commitment whatsoever? I was fascinated that he seemed just as impressive as I had imagined, and I took about two seconds to agree to the trip, a small step to decades of adventure and lifelong learning.

One thing a person learned about Dr. Jernigan rather quickly was that he did not waste time or words and that he was very thorough. If I thought the week at the convention would be an interesting but ordinary and leisurely garden-variety conference, I quickly discovered otherwise. It was most exciting. If I thought he'd pay little attention to me while I was there, I soon figured out that he had an amazing attention span focused on any number of things and people at once. Assigned to be monitored and mentored at the convention by Mrs. tenBroek, I passed inspection for the trip to Des Moines.

He showed me for two days around the magnificent Iowa Commission building, quizzed me about philosophy, literature, and history, and in general tried to determine my interests, my specific abilities, and value as an investment of his time and energy. At one point he asked me, for example, if I knew the name of Alexander the Great's horse. The really funny thing was that I did, having actually named one of the family horses after Bucephalus, but for the life of me I could not come up with the name under those unfamiliar circumstances. We had a debate about Platonic and Aristotelian philosophy which he clearly and quickly won hands down but from which he apparently concluded that we shared some interests. I read things he gave me and answered his penetrating questions about them. There was no bluffing my way through the answers, and he tried his best to rattle me a little to see of what I was made.

I later learned that he wanted to see how I handled all that. If I had taken umbrage and felt I could hardly wait to get out of there, he would have known, and I would have self-selected out of his process. If, on the other hand, I found the place and him fascinating and wanted to know more, he'd let me prove it by word and deed. It was one of many experiences in this story that remain vivid memories, and there would be many more. I apparently made the cut in his rigorous process, however, because the following month found me working at the Iowa Commission for the Blind, sharing an office complex with no less a Federation leader than Jim Omvig.

Fairly quickly followed the seminar for new staff, in which Jim and Dr. Jernigan set about making real Federationists out of me, Lorraine Rovig, and another new staff member who unfortunately washed out and left the corps after a short while. Lorraine and I—both possessing 20/20 vision—were charged with not only learning to travel with a long white cane and without vision under special blindfolds called sleep shades, but we also were required to learn the skills well enough to teach travel to others. We did a great deal of travel for several weeks, things like riding the bus into work and back home completely without using vision, negotiating what is called a "drop-off" by our instructor, who took us blindfolded into separate unfamiliar areas of the city and let us out of the car with instructions to find the way back to the Commission using only our nonvisual travel ability. In general we mastered the skills well enough to be confident. We educated the public who tried to take us across intersections to places we had not intended to go. We dealt with the unexpected sidewalk hazards and survived. We emerged at last with a passing grade from teacher Dick Davis and from Dr. Jernigan, and that was better than a diploma.

Those who have seen our video "We Know Who We Are" will remember a great deal about students at the Iowa Commission and their learning to travel, especially the episode in which Dr. Jernigan arrives at a student's room one morning and tells her that he and she are going out on travel and are actually going to run while they are out. She gulps and says she does not know if she's ready, but responds, "If you say we're going to run, we'll run." Many of us had our counterparts with Dr. Jernigan. Likely one of my first was being summoned one morning to Dr. Jernigan's office and told my assignment was to go alone to get a twenty-eight-foot rental truck, drive it to the Hoover State Office Building on the East Side, pick up two vending machines, and deliver them to the Army Ammunition Vending Facility in Burlington, Iowa, nearly 200 miles away. The conversation went something like this:

"By myself?" I protested, "But I have never driven a twenty-eight-foot truck."

"You have a driver's license, don't you?"

"Well, … yes Sir."

"You told me you learned to drive a straight shift, didn't you?"

"Well, yes Sir."

"Well, the truck has a straight shift, and there will be an appliance dolly in the truck. You'll do fine."

Now when one of us heard the "You'll do fine," the conversation was at an end, and you were to just go do whatever was under discussion. I did. And indeed I did fine.

This episode revealed to me something I saw Dr. Jernigan demonstrate time after time: an almost uncanny ability to judge where you as a newly-blinded adult orientation student or as a new staff member were with respect to your comfort zone and to push just enough to get you out of it without pushing so hard that you'd break. The objective was to grow you through successive experiences into a self-confident individual with the ability to confront new challenges, use your head, and come out on top. That was how he worked, and he wanted to develop you into someone who would likewise be one of the best marchers in the movement on behalf of the blind individuals we serve. He did not want whiners or people petrified to try the difficult or even what some might think is impossible.

He also wanted us to understand that blind persons are frequently denied opportunities for many of the experiences we take for granted. Sometimes overprotective families fear to allow them to do the things their sighted peers do all the time. Employers may pass them up because they believe blind people in the workplace will be a liability or even an insurance risk. We think nothing, for example, of jumping on commercial flights to any number of places, but Dr. Jernigan discovered that there in the mid-seventies three students at the Iowa

Commission for the Blind's Orientation and Adjustment Center for training blind adults had never flown on an airplane, and he thought they should have that experience, so common even then in business and pleasure. He was going to be in Chicago at a meeting to which he had driven the relatively short distance from Des Moines, and he seized the opportunity to have the three young women fly to Chicago, meet him there, and drive back to Des Moines with him later in the day. When he paged me over the Commission intercom the day before, little did I know he would put me in charge of the expedition to Chicago. He would take over for the return drive, but it was up to me to guide the mission and its not-yet-intrepid explorers to that point.

The three women were new students, and it was clear as we planned the trip they were apprehensive, but we took a cab to the airport, checked in, and boarded the jet. As it taxied to the runway, there was quietly agitated conversation between them over the unfamiliar sensations and the unknown ones ahead. As we taxied to the top of the runway and were cleared for takeoff, they were glued to their seats with white knuckles. The airplane tore down the runway and lifted off with the trio stone silent for most of the one-hour flight to Chicago. Finally, we landed with a rush of the jet engines suddenly reversing noisily to slow the plane down. At that point I thought the three were all going to come out of their seatbelts, experiencing for the very first time one of the common sensations of air travel most of us take for granted.

On the drive home Dr. Jernigan was the teacher and mentor supreme, drawing from them at some length their mixed reactions to the experience and questioning them about whether they thought they would fly without fear from that point on. As I reflected on the day, I was aware of the honor he gave me in making me part of his providing that growth experience for them, and I felt genuinely grateful for his confidence and trust that I'd help pull it off.

He taught us to be perceptive observers of this world in which we seek to change what it means to be blind, assessing people and situations realistically. He studied the people with whom he worked carefully, learning about both their strengths and weaknesses, as well as their preferences and pet causes. Once as we walked to a meeting down Grand Avenue on the East Side of Des Moines, I complained to him bitterly about an elected official who was not being helpful to the state's blind people and whom I considered, therefore, uninformed and downright bereft of understanding. My implication was clearly that the man was just plain ignorant and obstinate. "Mr. Cobb," Dr. Jernigan said patiently, "he's been reelected six times, and hostile though he may be, you need to give him some credit for the ability to do that." The degree of respectful humility that comment reflected was a facet of Dr. Jernigan that some of us were to observe more often than others even in the thick of our battles for equitable treatment, but I believe he always was sincere about it.

He expected you to think and to be resourceful. He wanted you, he said, to be the kind who, if dropped by parachute onto a Pacific Island, would in two or three days find out if there were others on the island, organize the place, and be running it. If there were no other humans on the island, he'd expect you to make yourself very comfortable. He made you think that doing the uniquely difficult would be fun the way he thought it was.

He also made clear he expected you to analyze and react appropriately in each new situation. He admonished, "If I give you a set of directions, and on the way to carry them out you get new data that suggest you should act in a different manner, you are just as accountable for disregarding my instructions and acting appropriately on the new data as you would be for disregarding the original instructions in the absence of the new data." In other words, you were not to come back and lamely take refuge in insisting that you just did what he told you. He did not suffer such foolishness gladly.

It is too trite to say merely that he taught me about life in this period, but I think he really did take me where he found me and stretched me into living fully. He termed it learning to "get on in the world." To this day I recall frequently words of counsel here and there, many moments of playfulness and fun, and occasionally the smarting of tough love when he pointed out an obvious mistake on my part. But he always let me know I was loved and that while I sometimes failed to apply my abilities, he nevertheless found me capable under the high standard by which he measured performance. And the side of him many of us discovered over the years was that he loved faithfully and passionately, and he gave to those he loved all he had, even when one on occasion disappointed him. I became one who simply had to love him back and want more than anything not to let him down. Rarely does a leader succeed at fostering that spirit to the degree he did.

The story continued as Dr. Jernigan left Iowa in 1978 to come east to Baltimore and establish the permanent national headquarters of the National Federation of the Blind, now known as the National Federation of the Blind Jernigan Institute. In early 1986 I received the second momentous telephone call from him, asking if I would consider coming to look over the headquarters and explore with him becoming a part of the staff of the national office. Once again I answered his call, came to Baltimore, and worked for a short tryout with the young blind attorney on the staff named Marc Maurer who was soon to be elected our leader. I was offered a job, returned to Iowa to pack up my earthly goods in a rental truck, and came back to Baltimore for good to join the staff on May 19, 1986. Yes, as I loaded a rental truck in Des Moines for the second and probably last time, I did remember that other encounter about driving a truck that by then seemed so long ago.

It was a mere ten years after that fateful encounter on the Palmer House stairs that set the tone for my Federation career and much of my adult life, that he would say to us all as he said so often over the years at other times and in other places:

> "We know what we must do, and we have counted the cost. We fight not only for ourselves but also for those who went before us, for Dr. tenBroek and the other founders of our movement—and for those who come after, the blind of the next generation, the children and the children to be. And we will not fail. The stakes are too high and the alternative too terrible. Tomorrow is bright with promise. We go to meet it with gladness: And we

take with us all that we have—our hopes and our dreams, our will to work and our knowledge of deprivation, our faith and our purpose, and our heritage of slavery. And this also we take—our trust in ourselves, our love for each other, and our belief in the ultimate goodness of people. My brothers and my sisters, the future is ours! Come, join me!—and we will march together to freedom!" (*Blindness: The Pattern of Freedom*, 1985 National Convention Banquet Speech in Louisville)

He was to spend the next twelve years before his death helping Dr. Maurer take the helm after him as our President, and in that time he worked very hard even through the acute illness that took him from us, challenging us to keep the faith and press on with the struggle for equality for the blind of the nation. Every experience I had with Dr. Jernigan and every step of the way in my now nearly thirty-seven years as a marcher in this movement have reinforced that notion planted so long ago by my teacher and friend, Dr. Jernigan, that love is what makes us who we are and makes us also a tight family and an unstoppable movement. Love and devotion to his duty to us were certainly the hallmarks of his life, and his spirit of love and commitment abides with us as we continue the journey.

CHAPTER 11

ON PLANNING AND DETAILS

by Duane Gerstenberger

Note: Duane Gerstenberger worked with Dr. Jernigan for nearly twenty-five years. Then he moved with his family across the country to Washington State. In this short chapter, he shares some of his observations about Kenneth Jernigan's work style, and he notes that the influence has continued to the present time.

During the 1970s, Duane Gerstenberger was the assistant director of the Iowa Commission for the Blind (now the Iowa Department for the Blind) in charge of Library Services. During the 1980s and 1990s, he supervised much of the work at the national office of the Federation in Baltimore. The position he held at the time he resigned was executive director. In Washington State, he has been employed in private business in financial planning.

Duane Gerstenberger, 1996.

DR. KENNETH JERNIGAN STEPPED INTO MY LIFE WHEN I was twenty-seven years old; he was forty-six. We spent the next twenty-five years as associates, colleagues, and friends. Here is how he kindly reflected on our years together when I left employment with the National Federation of the Blind (NFB) in early 1997: "I first met Mr. Gerstenberger in 1973 when I employed him as a librarian at the Iowa Commission for the Blind. Shortly after the National Center for the Blind was established in Baltimore, he left Iowa [December 1979] to take employment with the Federation. During the last few years he has served as our Executive Director ... he is resigning to move to the state of Washington ... Though sighted, he understands, believes, and lives our philosophy on a daily basis ... On a personal note, I trust and rely on Mr. Gerstenberger to the ultimate. That will not change as he leaves formal employment with the Federation. He will be in New Orleans this summer, supervising the exhibit hall as usual." [*Braille Monitor*, February 1997]

I did attend the NFB national convention that summer in New Orleans. The next time we were together was September 1998 at his home in Baltimore a few weeks before his death.

When a fellow works twenty-five years for one man who is twenty years his senior, it's inevitable that the older will influence the younger. And when the senior in the relationship is a man with Dr. Jernigan's knowledge, talents, experience, wisdom, and energy, that influence is profound and lasting. In the following paragraphs, I write about just two of the valuable concepts I learned from Dr. Jernigan. Like most concepts that I learned at his side, they have these two factors in common: they can help generate ordinary, private achievement as well as historic, public achievement; and they pass the one test that Dr. Jernigan used to measure any concept's effectiveness— they work.

Dr. Jernigan believed in the power of incremental effort. He knew that growth, change, accomplishment, and success most often occur incrementally—bit by bit, piece by piece, step by step. Success rarely comes immediately. Federation history is replete with struggles won that stretch across years and, more often, decades. Just heft a copy of *Walking Alone and Marching Together: A History of the Organized Blind Movement in the United States, 1940-1990* by Dr. Floyd

Matson, and you're holding a story that chronicles fifty years of success driven by incremental effort.

When he spoke of this concept—and he often did—he introduced it with this familiar riddle: "How do you eat an elephant? One bite at a time." He used this riddle in formal presentations to large audiences; he used it in casual, one-on-one conversations; he used it inside and outside the Federation; he used it with new acquaintances; and he used it as a reminder to those whom he knew had heard it many times before.

While it reminds one of "The Tortoise and the Hare" fable ("Don't brag about your lightning pace, for Slow and Steady won the race!"), it's important to note that the power of incremental effort always requires steady application but not necessarily slow application. Likewise, it may be applied singularly or collectively. Certainly if a diner sits down to eat his elephant alone it will be a lengthy meal. However, he may invite friends to join him, and if enough do, it may be a brief, light lunch. But either way, the beast is devoured "One bite at a time."

Let me leave the elephant, the tortoise, and the hare to tell of the first major project that Dr. Jernigan and I worked on together, which used the power of incremental effort.

When the National Center for the Blind was established in Baltimore in mid-1978, the NFB National Headquarters had been housed in the Randolph Hotel building in downtown Des Moines—just a few blocks from the Iowa Commission for the

Blind building—for a decade. As a hostelry, the Randolph's best days were behind it. The public spaces had not been updated for years. The tenants were primarily weekly or monthly renters and travelers who wanted a low-budget room downtown. Guest services were minimal.

The NFB offices, work area, and storage spaces provided a marked contrast to the rest of the building: they were clean, comfortable, and convenient. While the Randolph had served our purposes well, it was now moving time for the national office. Every lock, stock, and barrel—including miles of shelved literature and materials—had to be packed and loaded for the trip to Baltimore. I was part of the force Dr. Jernigan marshaled to get the job done as quickly and efficiently as possible.

Here, thirty-two years later, is my compressed recollection of the Randolph Hotel exit:

The drum beat was pack, load, and ship. National office staff worked exclusively on the move. Volunteers from the local NFB chapter pitched in. Several Commission employees volunteered evenings and weekends. Temporary laborers were hired. Food and drink were supplied on the premises. Work began early and ran late into the night. Crews worked through the weekends.

Literature flew off the shelves into boxes. Boxes leapt onto carts. Carts moved telepathically down aisles and around corners to the elevator. The elevator stood ready at the floor needed; the elevator walls flexed to accommodate any load. An empty semi-trailer appeared in the alley; it vacuumed boxes aboard; it moved when full; another empty trailer immediately took its place. Then one Saturday we put the last lock (it might have been a stock or a barrel) in the NFB van. We closed the offices. The Randolph had been vacated.

But here is, as Paul Harvey used to say, the rest of the story.

The national office staff was just two people. The National Headquarters were spread across several floors of the Randolph. There was only one small, attendant-operated passenger elevator and no freight elevator. Since the Randolph had no conventional loading dock, we loaded the trailers from a side door in the alley. No more than two workers could stand on a narrow ledge outside the door and hand boxes and other materials to workers inside the trailer. The temporary laborers (recruited two at a time) were given one four-hour shift to demonstrate their capacity. If the person in charge of the operation of that shift thought they were keeping pace, we asked them to come back after lunch. Most didn't make the cut, and a few decided that it was more than they wanted; only one fellow stuck with us from the day he started to the last day. My recollection of the total semi-tractor trailers loaded is uncertain, but I believe it was in the twenty-five to twenty-seven range.

If ever a project demanded the power of incremental effort, it was moving the national office out of the Randolph Hotel building. Yes, we threw all the workers that we could muster at the task; we developed workflow patterns to maximize operations in a limited space; and we worked at a rapid pace.

But it was the incremental box-by-box, cart-by-cart, hour-by-hour, day-by-day, and trailer-by-trailer approach that carried us to success.

Dr. Jernigan believed in the power of incidental events. Life sometimes provides an obvious opportunity that we grab because it means almost certain success; and life sometimes provides a profound—nearly miraculous—opportunity that virtually chooses us and grants us nearly instant success. (Something like *Little Dorrit*'s fortune in the Dickens novel of the same name.) Yet most of life's opportunities are small and come to us in brief, seemingly ordinary circumstances—maybe so ordinary that they can be missed if we've not learned to anticipate them. Perhaps we fail to see an opportunity that seems ordinary but actually is a bit extraordinary; or we fail to see an opportunity that accrues from the concurrence of several ordinary opportunities because we consider them individually and not collectively.

The power of incidental events depends both on opportunity and awareness. Opportunity can be accidental, but it also can be planned if we put ourselves in the position to maximize our exposure to incidental events. Awareness is not accidental; it's a talent that must be learned and applied. Dr. Jernigan knew how to plan, and he was aware.

He was a master at what I call solicited serendipity. Serendipity is generally defined as an aptitude for making desirable discoveries by accident; solicited serendipity I define as an aptitude for making desirable discoveries by consciously putting yourself in a position to make those discoveries.

While director of the Iowa Commission for the Blind, Dr. Jernigan would occasionally step into the office of the deputy director and say, "We're going over to the capitol this morning." The Commission building was only a few minutes by car from the state capitol building, so it was an easy trip. The first time he announced one of these unscheduled visits to a particular deputy director she asked, "Why are we going?" He responded, "I don't know. We'll leave here at ten." On the way over to the capitol the deputy director inquired, "Whom are you going to see?" "Nobody particular," he replied. "Is there a problem?" she asked. "No," he replied. "Then why are we going?" she asked. He replied again, "I don't know."

Over the years Dr. Jernigan made a number of such visits to the Iowa Capitol Building. He, of course, also made a number of scheduled visits: to speak with the governor, to testify before a legislative budget committee, to seek a particular senator's or representative's assistance, or to consult with the attorney general—the type of trip many state agency department heads made from time to time. But why these impromptu visits? He went to engage the power of incidental events.

Dr. Jernigan literally did not know specifically why he was going, but he did know that by being in and around the capitol building for no particular purpose—where the governor, the other constitutionally elected officials, legislators, and all their staff worked and congregated—he usually learned something that accrued to the benefit of the Commission and those it served. He didn't need to slink around in the back hallways or listen at any keyholes or doors left ajar. He would simply pass through the public spaces and be stopped by a legislator or state official who wanted to chat.

One time a visit might do nothing more than continue or enhance a friendship—and plenty of friends under the Golden Dome in Des Moines was a good thing for the director of a state agency to have. Another time what Dr. Jernigan learned might offer an immediate and critical opportunity for the Commission; another time it might be an opportunity that would lay dormant for months or even years but eventually prove valuable; and another time what he learned might have value only when matched with one or more additional opportunities—perhaps one gathered during an earlier visit or a subsequent incidental visit to the state capitol.

For the last five years I've commuted to work in Bellevue from our home in north Seattle via bus across Lake Washington. Once across the lake I can transfer to another bus and consistently be home around 4:25 p.m. If I walk home (twenty-five blocks) from the transfer point, I can consistently be home around 4:30 p.m. Most days I walk. That's one of my incremental efforts for maintaining good health. However, the walk is also a source of valuable incidental events.

My usual route takes me through the eclectic University District next to the University of Washington, through Cowen Park, past the Roosevelt High School athletic field, and into three distinct residential neighborhoods. During every trip I am exposed to a variety of interesting people and activities. If I stay alert and aware, I often spot something that causes me to stop and watch briefly; sometimes I stop to pick up something of value.

In the U-District I pass a private, co-operative elementary school. One afternoon last summer I noticed out front a wood table with removable legs that had a sign attached saying "FREE TABLE." On inspection I found it to be in very good condition. While we didn't need a table, and I didn't know precisely what we would do with this one, it seemed too good at the price to pass up. The obvious problem was how to get it home. I had twenty more blocks to walk.

The table itself was not heavy, but it measured 32 inches by 60 inches; the four legs were metal but hollow, so not heavy either. I stuffed the legs in the main compartment of my backpack, snuggled them together between two zippers, hoisted the table on my back and set off. About halfway home I shifted the table to my head and balanced it there with both hands. While a bit stiff in my neck and back when I got home, it was a successful trip. Seeing no immediate use for it, we stashed the table in the basement.

Recently our younger daughter, Jennifer, moved into a new apartment. She had moved back to Seattle five months ago after three years in New York City. In order to return here by plane, she sold all of her furnishings back in New York. With the move, she needed furniture at her new place; specifically, she needed a table much like the one in our basement. Thanks to the power of incidental events, she has one—delivered to her in the car.

Dr. Jernigan was a master at using the power of incremental effort and the power of incidental events. Much of his historic, public success was achieved using these two concepts. Fueled by his unrelenting focus and discipline, they were powerful twin engines that delivered remarkable and critical achievements across five decades for the National Federation of the Blind. I learned the value of these concepts during my early years under his direction and influence. They are still at work in my life every day providing many private, ordinary achievements.

CHAPTER 12

GROWTH AND INNOVATION IN LOUISIANA AND BEYOND

by Joanne Wilson

Note: Joanne Wilson retired from the position of executive director in charge of Affiliate Action for the National Federation of the Blind. She founded and directed the Louisiana Center for the Blind for sixteen years, and then was appointed by President George W. Bush to serve as the Rehabilitation Services Administration Commissioner in the U.S. Department of Education. This chapter shows how her work was modeled after the example she saw in Iowa and in the National Federation of the Blind when Dr. Jernigan was leading each of those organizations.

THE YEAR WAS 1966; I WAS A YOUNG COLLEGE STUDENT struggling with the problems of how to function as a blind person. I was dragged to my first encounter with blind people, which was a student seminar held at the Iowa Commission for the Blind.

Joanne Wilson, 2001.

After the day's events the students were invited to a fancy restaurant to relax and enjoy each other. I was seated next to Dr. Jernigan. I sat in awe and listened and knew that something important was about to happen. As I was leaning over the candle in the middle of the table trying to read my bill so I could pay for my meal, Dr. Jernigan suddenly asked me, "Joanne, are you blind?" I said, "No, no, I'm not blind—I just can't see very well." He held up his hand and said, "How many fingers do I have up?" I said, "Well, I can sort of see your hand there, but I can't exactly tell how many fingers you have up." He said, "Joanne, you're blind." The talk that followed was like nothing I had ever heard. That night and in the months and years to follow, a voice was put to all the confusion and funny notions about blindness that I had in my mind. I was taught to define philosophy. I was given knowledge, belief, and most of all hope.

I was a student at the Iowa Commission for the Blind, and I learned many things, including skills and a philosophy about blindness. I learned how to get political influence and how to build an organization, how to be a leader, how to get elected and stay elected, how to give a speech, how to be an advocate, how to have discipline and work really hard. I also learned how to play and how to love ... and I learned how to give.

Dr. Jernigan was always teaching. Everything that he did— from the ordinary to the spectacular, from ordering a meal to giving a banquet speech—always seemed to have a purpose and to be a part of something bigger. It was a part of building a great movement. All of Dr. Jernigan's actions and his works were directed toward large accomplishments.

He taught me how to make my day-to-day activities count. I remember one day when we students were sitting in our discussion group, Dr. Jernigan came into the room and started telling us about a legislative banquet that we were going to have in a couple of weeks. He started assigning jobs to us— explaining how we were going to help set up the tables and get things organized and mix and mingle with the legislators. Then he told us we needed to buy our tickets and pay for another person's ticket. We said, "What? We don't have any money—why, we ought to get our meal for free. We're going to do all this other work." Well, a discussion ensued. It was the first time I heard the words, "There ain't no such thing as a free lunch." At that legislative banquet we all stood with pride and dignity when Dr. Jernigan got up and said to the legislators, "Your meal has been bought by a blind person."

I remember another time. It was about 5:30 in the morning. I was sound asleep in my dorm room at the Iowa Commission for the Blind, and suddenly there was a rap at the door. My heart pounded, and I heard Dr. Jernigan out there saying, "Hurry, hurry Joanne, come to my apartment immediately. It's urgent." I heard him go up and down the hall, knocking on other students' doors saying, "Hurry, hurry, come immediately to my apartment." We all rushed down there. We had our robes on, and I had big rollers in my hair and my flip flops on, and my night cream was dripping from my face. We ran in there with our hearts pounding. We gathered in his living room, and he said, "Surprise, come-as-you-are party."

We learned, and we began to live what we learned. Where were you when you heard of the death of Dr. Jernigan? On that October 12th, I was in a fancy restaurant in Little Rock, Arkansas, relaxing after a hard day of rock climbing with the students at the Louisiana Center for the Blind. My cell phone rang; I took the phone and went to a quiet part of the restaurant and heard the news. On my way back to my table in the restaurant, I felt confused and sad. I felt empty and uncomfortable. What should I do next?

I sat down at my table and looked around. There at my table were young college students and others struggling with the problems of how to function as competent blind people. I thought, "Dr. Jernigan, even at this moment you are teaching me a lesson." I had a flashback to my first dinner with Dr. Jernigan, and I knew he was telling me to pass it on. We had made the full circle. I was there to give the knowledge, the belief, and the dreams to these blind students. I was there to be their guide and to give them a defined philosophy about blindness. As Dr. Jernigan did for me, I did my best to help my students set their sights high and learn the skills and confidence to reach their goals.

The NFB had come a long way in Louisiana since I first arrived there in 1978. I was proud of what we had accomplished, and I think Dr. Jernigan was proud too. I couldn't have done what I did without the foundation he gave me in Iowa. I was thrilled to be able to carry it across the country to yet another generation of blind people, both young and old.

When I was in Iowa, working in the NFB was safe and comfortable because there were so many people involved. Dr. Jernigan had been building there for eight years before I ever met him. He had found and trained a great many people— those who worked in the blindness field and blind people who lived and worked all over the state. I was president of a new chapter and for a time vice president of the NFB of Iowa, but my activities and actions did not seem critical to me.

My husband got a job in Ruston, Louisiana. I had three children, including a brand new baby. I knew I had been fortunate to be in Iowa because things were better for the blind there. But I had no way of really knowing how fortunate until later. When we moved to Louisiana, there was a dramatic dose of reality because there was so much difference.

The NFB in Louisiana was both weak and fragmented internally. I did not find a national focus; no one was really dedicated to the organization; there was no depth of commitment, nor even the understanding of blindness that I had learned in Iowa from Dr. Jernigan. In Louisiana, blind people were not using white canes or traveling independently, and most were not employed. I realized that the blind in Louisiana were years behind and lacked positive leadership.

At my first state convention, Dr. Jernigan was there and asked the hotel manager to donate to the national organization. In order to motivate the members of the affiliate, Dr. Jernigan told them that he had asked for and received this contribution. The majority of the members were embarrassed that he had done this. They actually voted to return the donation to the hotel manager.

The NFB of Louisiana was receiving some gambling money from the state, and most of its time was spent arguing about how to spend this money. I started going to state board meetings which lasted an entire weekend. Most of the time was spent fighting. I decided to try to bring new members into the organization, so I volunteered to recruit new people in Ruston. The old timers thought I couldn't do it, but we had forty people at an organizing meeting. The leaders of the NFB of Louisiana came to the meeting, and they were shocked!

Before long Dr. Jernigan asked me if I had considered running for office. I had learned in Iowa that you have to count the votes before you run. I got the old leadership to permit me to organize new chapters. They thought they knew all the blind people, but I was able to find new members and organize chapters in other parts of the state, just as I had in Ruston. I made phone calls during my kids' nap time. WHEN I went to meetings, I took the kids with me, even to the first meetings of new chapters. I had no one to leave them with. I brought toys and books for them, and many of the blind people seemed glad to meet them. I mentored the new members in these new chapters, mostly by telephone. Of course, my manner was different from Dr. Jernigan's, but I didn't even think about it. The blind people I met understood that I cared and that I understood something about blindness they needed to know.

I also worked on making friends with some of the long-time members. At the next convention, we were able to make some changes in the constitution of the NFB of Louisiana, changes that required a two-thirds majority vote. And I was elected president. The people I wanted on the state Board were also elected. Not everybody was happy about all this change. One of the large old chapters from Lafayette walked out shouting and cursing, and they never came back.

After I was elected, there were still too many fights. I had to lead a series of expulsions of people who were stealing money. Those people took this problem to court, and it was hard on both old and new members. Unfortunately, some racial prejudice was involved, but that was not the primary issue. I was proud of many who made sacrifices to help the blind move forward. It took about two years for us to have peace, unity, and loyalty to the NFB in the Louisiana affiliate, and it has been peaceful ever since.

We also experienced phenomenal growth. The members were ready to focus on progress for the blind. We kept organizing new groups—a Student Division and a Parents of Blind Children Division were two of the first groups we organized. We also kept organizing new chapters in new cities and working to strengthen the existing chapters.

There was an effort in the state to build a huge building to house all programs for blind children and adults. The NFB knew that the people in charge of this project would not provide the kinds of services that blind people needed. I got people all over the state to help write letters and talk to their legislators about what was really needed, which was a high-quality rehabilitation center modeled after the one in Iowa where I had received training. Our members also traveled to Baton Rouge to meet with legislators in the Capitol. We made friends with state senators and representatives such as Mary Landrieu, who later served as a United States senator from Louisiana. When Senator Landrieu was new in the Louisiana legislature, she went with a bunch of Federationists to Governor Edwin Edwards's office to tell him what we needed. When we left, she stayed with the governor a little longer. When she came out, she told me that we needed to write an amendment to the governor's budget, which we did immediately.

At the NFB convention in Louisville, Kentucky, in 1985 I received the message that Governor Edwards was recommending more than a quarter million dollars for the establishment of a training center for the blind in Louisiana.

Then I looked for a center director, but no one wanted to do it. There were reasons: We only had funding for one year, and we would not be able to pay large salaries. I was not going to let this opportunity fail. I had taught elementary school, but I didn't think I had the administrative experience needed. Still, I decided to start the center myself until somebody else could be found. We had learned about the money in July, and less than three months later on October 1, we opened the center. By the end of October we had five students. I hired teachers from South Carolina, California, Iowa, and Louisiana. The staff saw the opportunity, and the students soon understood too. We knew we were breaking ground and doing something important, both for the blind of Louisiana and for the whole country. The support of the National Federation of the Blind gave us the strength and determination to do what we had to do.

We really believed that we were making a difference and expanding the dream of making rehabilitation better in Louisiana and far beyond. Our mission was to carry forward the dream first articulated by Dr. tenBroek and Dr. Jernigan, the dream of putting Federation philosophy and ideas into a training center that would ultimately improve all rehabilitation for the blind everywhere. And I think what we did in Louisiana and what continues there today has made a difference to blind individuals. It has helped to set a higher standard for other programs in other states.

We all made sacrifices. There were times when I had to ask the Center staff to do what nobody should have to do. Salaries were not large, and our teachers often worked day and night. Sometimes I had to ask for volunteers to take a delay in getting their paychecks because state officials were dragging their feet in getting money to us—money that was already authorized for us. Students also had to make sacrifices. We had to drive 200 miles to hearings in Baton Rouge numerous times in the process of securing second-year funding. That meant leaving Ruston at 4:00 a.m. to be at hearings by 8:00 a.m. We called ourselves the pioneers because we knew that our sacrifices would be a part of changing rehabilitation. For us it was a cause, a mission of the National Federation of the Blind. We felt we were a part of the nationwide effort. Louisiana just happened to be where our work was needed at that particular time.

Directing the Center was one kind of activity that had its own crises and accomplishments. It is extremely rewarding to help blind students become more competent by learning to believe in themselves, learning new skills, and learning to think differently about blindness and sell themselves to employers. Dealing with the budget and legislators was another kind of activity—important and intense. There were criticisms and threats from people who did not understand the value of what we were doing and who did not want us to succeed.

On Mother's Day 1986, I remember NFB members from all over Louisiana sitting at an appropriations hearing where they were discussing our second-year budget. One of the representatives asked where our critics were. They were not there because it was Mother's Day. But we were there, and they voted eleven to one to give us the funding. This kind of thing happened over and over again. With just a few hours' notice, we would manage to let people know, and we would gather NFB members in large numbers at appropriations hearings.

By the third year, the reputation of the Louisiana Center was good enough with many of the rehabilitation counselors that payment for the training would be authorized by that agency. Payment by rehab then covered our costs.

We took our students to the various rehab offices where they told their stories of how the Center helped them. I was following what Dr. Jernigan did when I was a student. I knew that people would be impressed by hearing what the students had to say instead of hearing stories from me or other staff members—and they were.

After we rented facilities for the first two years, the governor helped us get funds to buy an office and classroom building that is currently the headquarters of the Louisiana Center for the Blind. The city of Ruston loved to have us there. The more they learned about what we were doing, the more they were proud to have us. They saw the students learning to travel independently with their white canes, and they came to visit when we had open houses. The community became very valuable to the Louisiana Center for the Blind.

I had learned from Dr. Jernigan to sell the program to the community and the state. Dr. Jernigan gave tours of the Iowa Commission for the Blind, invited groups to have banquets in the commission building, and sent students and staff out to make presentations for all kinds of groups. We did the same thing in Louisiana, and the community helped us with the governor and the legislature. Local senators and representatives in the Ruston area wanted to help us also. Dr. Jernigan was a master at building this kind of support.

At the Ruston Civic Center, we had the largest banquet ever held in the city. Governor Edwards was there. Before he spoke, I had all of the students talk about their experiences. The governor threw out his prepared talk and wrote a new one on a napkin. He said the things we wanted him to say. This helped us get funds for the classroom and office building. Then we got money to buy apartments where students could live during training so we did not have to rent living space for them. We asked the community of Ruston for help to build an activity center for meetings and social get-togethers. People from the community volunteered and donated their expertise and materials to build an entire building. When I left Louisiana, the Center included a large classroom and office building, another classroom building that housed a shop, a career center, the activity center, and two apartment complexes.

One day one of our students, Barry Adkins, came in with a big old school bell and a cross-stitched plaque that read, "When the bell sounds, all of us have gained new ground." Starting that day, whenever a student achieved something he or she didn't believe a blind person could do, we rang the "Freedom Bell." We rang the bell when someone crossed the street, finished his/her first Braille book, cooked a meal for forty, graduated from college, or got married. We did this for current students. Past students would call us and ask us to ring the bell, and announce their accomplishments. Not only was this a great way to share information, it also gave hope to the new students who heard about the achievements of their predecessors. We heard when our graduates traveled across Europe, had babies, got new jobs, bought their first homes, and more. Ringing the Freedom Bell became an important way to congratulate individuals who made progress. Dr. Jernigan named one of the Kernel Books *The Freedom Bell* and included an article about the Louisiana Center for the Blind.

Then we started giving to each of our graduates a smaller version of this bell engraved with their names and dates of graduation, followed by the words "Louisiana Center for the Blind, Together we are changing what it means to be blind." All of these small accomplishments together are opening doors and changing what blindness is like for this generation. Other NFB training centers like this practice and inaugurated it as well. Now these bells sound across the country and symbolize what we are doing whenever there is a new accomplishment for the blind. Governor Buddy Rohmer came to one of our banquets. When he got up to talk, he said that he had diabetes and expected to be blind one day. He was very supportive of our Center. We gave him a Freedom Bell, which he displayed in his office. I believe it remained there as long as he was governor of Louisiana.

The Louisiana Center for the Blind expanded into summer programs for blind elementary school children and another program for blind teenagers. We sought and received a grant for the early intervention programs for blind infants and toddlers throughout the state. Every blind infant and toddler in Louisiana is supposed to be referred to the Louisiana Center. Half a dozen staff members contact parents and work with blind and visually impaired children throughout the state. That work also continues today.

Then we did the same thing for blind seniors. We got a grant and hired people to go to the homes of seniors who are losing vision. And there are a great many more seniors than children. These newly blind people receive instruction in the techniques and attitudes that will make it so they can live more productively and independently.

Louisiana was the first state to setup newspaper accessibility by telephone called NFB NEWSLINE®, which the NFB created. Now 373 newspapers and forty-eight magazines are accessible to the blind by touchtone telephone in most parts of the country. Dr. Jernigan worked hard to build this program in the 1990s. All we had to do was to find a little money to provide this service.

We started the Professional Development and Research Institute on Blindness at Louisiana Tech University in Ruston. It began with two Master's degree programs, one degree in O and M (Orientation and Mobility), and the other degree is in teaching blind students. The Center was well enough established in Ruston that I called Dr. Dan Reno, president of the Louisiana Tech University, and I got an appointment. I proposed starting a degree program there, and he liked the idea. We agreed to seek funding to get it started, which we did. We both liked building new programs and reaching out to people who needed them. Dr. Reno's background was in medical programs, but he was glad to help and to offer these new degrees. He understood that this was an important way to change rehabilitation for the blind. Every year between five and fifteen people, both blind and sighted, receive degrees in Orientation and Mobility. The graduates are employed at many different training centers around the country. Some of them work for programs that were already doing work the way the NFB does it. Other graduates are employed where the NFB approach has not been popular. The graduates of Louisiana Tech are effective teachers. Their travel students become more independent than those who are taught by teachers with degrees from other programs. This is another very exciting way to help blind people become independent and employed.

After George W. Bush was elected President in 2000, I received a phone call from NFB President Marc Maurer asking me if I would be interested in applying for the Rehabilitation Services Administration (RSA) Commissioner position in the federal Department of Education. This is a political position appointed by the President of the United States. It had been formerly held by Federationist Fred Schroeder. The thought of such a thing had never entered my mind. I was shocked at the very idea! I told Dr. Maurer that I would think about it. Then I received phone calls from other Federationists, including Mary Ellen Jernigan, who also urged me to apply. I talked to my family and thought about what would be necessary to get appointed and how it would benefit the Federation and the blind, and I decided to apply. All of this took a week or two.

I began to gather support from other organizations of people with disabilities, congressmen and senators that I knew, the governor of Louisiana, state legislators, and prominent contributors to President Bush's campaign. Federationists around the country were helping in their own states to gather support for my nomination. I learned in April that President Bush intended to nominate me, but I could not say anything about it. Bush actually announced publicly that he would send my name to the US Senate for confirmation in July. The Senate confirmation occurred early in August. I had been looking at houses in Virginia, and after the confirmation I had to finalize the arrangements and move as quickly as possible. My youngest daughter Jennica had one more year of high school to complete, so she needed to be enrolled in Arlington, Virginia. My husband Harold found employment in Virginia as well.

On August 27, 2000, we had a swearing-in ceremony attended by Federationists, Senator Mary Landrieu, and Representative from Louisiana John Cooksey. I would be working under the Secretary of Education, Rod Page, who conducted the swearing-in. That was the first time I met a lot of the RSA staff and other top officials of the Department of Education. It took a little time for me to learn to know the people I would be working with and the processes I would need to follow in this position. Lots of different organizations and state rehabilitation agency directors who report to the

Department of Education came to meet and share with me their priorities and agendas.

My philosophy was that my most important opportunity was to offer to the rehabilitation field a strong message. That was the one that was taught to me by Dr. Jernigan. He stressed that if you want a strong agency, you need to have strong consumer organizations. Many of the rehab agency directors were worried about the continued existence of rehabilitation. I insisted to them that if they gave service to their consumers, then in turn those consumers would support and protect the agencies when that was necessary. Most of the directors had not really understood the value of strong organizations of consumers. I wanted to put in place a pattern that rehabilitation personnel would work closely with consumers and consumer organizations of people with disabilities. I started talking about this with everyone I met from the very beginning of my work in Washington.

There was pressure to submerge all of rehabilitation in the Department of Labor. That would be a great disadvantage for the blind. In the Rehab Act, there are provisions for assisting blind seniors and blind businessmen and women. It calls for specialized training for the blind in Braille, independent travel, and adapted computers. It is possible to have two rehab agencies in each state, one for the blind and another for general rehabilitation. It is difficult enough under the current system for the blind to receive the assistance that makes it possible to have the kind of life I have had, the kind of life I have worked so hard to help my students achieve. Putting the federal vocational rehab program under the Department of Labor would definitely make it more difficult for the state programs to offer what is needed. In the long run, it would cost a lot of money if blind people were not self-supporting—a huge step backwards. Now I was a federal official. I could not lobby publicly, but I knew consumers could and would support the program.

I had learned long ago from Dr. Jernigan that good quality training included mentoring and being exposed to positive role models. This was a missing element I found in most rehabilitation agencies. I was successful in getting grant funding to setup mentoring programs where individuals with disabilities would be mentored by successful and competent role models who had the same disability. Organizations of the disabled and rehab agencies all over the country could apply for grants to establish this program. During my tenure as RSA commissioner, there were two different requests for proposals for these grants. I know that the agencies that received these grants were strengthened by them, and so were the services they provided.

Another project I created was a national conference called "Cutting Edge Practices—Expectations, Empowerment, and Employment: National Conference for Residential Training Centers for the Blind" for administrators and staff who ran residential training programs for blind adults. The first three-day conference was in Albuquerque in November 2002 and was well attended. Immediately after it, I began receiving requests for another one which occurred in Nashville a year and a half later. There are about ninety residential training programs for the blind in the country, and all were invited.

About 200 people participated in each conference. Many of the participants were members of the NFB who led quite a few of the discussions. This was another chance for us to pass on Dr. Jernigan's concepts about good rehabilitation training and high expectations for the blind. Our speakers talked about independent travel with a long cane which we have come to call the "Structured Discovery Method." There were discussions about the need for philosophy class to explore students' needs and expectations about blindness. The tone of the conferences was that expectations of blind people should be higher than they have been thought traditionally. Use of blindfolds for people with partial vision was a major topic. Techniques to use for adults who are new Braille readers to become effective in Braille reading and writing were another popular topic. Dr. Jernigan proved the value of this approach in Iowa; I proved it in Louisiana, and it is now believed and practiced more widely than ever before. A controversial issue was training staff under sleep shades or blindfolds in order to help them to be more effective teachers. We discussed the role of confidence-building activities outside the classroom, such as rock climbing, white water rafting, water skiing, and cutting wood with chain saws. Each day at the conferences there were multiple workshops and general sessions to explore all the components of training centers for the blind. I welcomed participants to the conferences and gave a presentation at the beginning. Former RSA Commissioner Fred Schroeder made the final presentation for both. The feedback I got was very positive.

In 2005 at the NFB headquarters, Dr. Maurer decided to establish a department for affiliate action, and he offered me the opportunity to direct it. It sounded very exciting to me because I would have the freedom to help the Federation grow throughout the national arena. I felt good about what I did for the federal government, but I was tired of the processes I had to follow.

My husband and I moved to Baltimore in 2005, where I had the opportunity to continue to develop and find new ways to help blind people grow and become integrated more completely into society.

I appreciate what I learned from Dr. Jernigan, and I have done my best to pass it on to the next generation. If I have added to it, I am glad. My outlook for the blind in the future is very bright. We still need time to reach more people and to train more staff to work in more places—but we are making progress. And I am fortunate to know well many younger people who are ready and eager to continue the work. Dr. Maurer is a wonderful leader, and so is our new President, Mark Riccobono, but they cannot do it by themselves, just as Dr. Jernigan could not. The National Federation of the Blind is bigger and stronger now than ever before, and I believe that our momentum will continue to increase as it has for the last half century or more.

CHAPTER 13

THE POWER OF THE MAN AND THE MOVEMENT IN MY LIFE

by James Gashel

Note: Jim Gashel first met Dr. Jernigan in 1964 when he was a new high school graduate and became a student at the Orientation and Adjustment Center at the Iowa Commission for the Blind. After graduating from college, Jim Gashel worked closely with Dr. Jernigan in several different capacities, but he is best known for his work in Washington, DC, representing the blind to congressmen and senators and federal agency officials, which he did from 1974 until 2007, and for his work as vice president of Business Development at K-NFB Reading Technology from 2007 to 2015.

Administrators of the Social Security Administration said that Jim Gashel knew their rules and policies better than anyone who worked at SSA. Similar statements could be made with regard to his knowledge of the Americans with Disabilities Act, the Randolph-Sheppard Act, the Rehabilitation Act, the Individuals with Disabilities Education Act, and other legislation affecting the blind. Throughout this time, he helped to create new services

for the blind, such as job opportunities for the blind, and to connect individuals and programs whose work could complement each other.

In addition to his work on Capitol Hill, Jim Gashel was the first staff member at the National Center for the Blind when the facility was inaugurated in 1978, and one of the key leaders there until his retirement in 2007. Further, he has been a leader in developing new technology for the blind, including Jobline, NFB NEWSLINE®, the K-NFB reader, and more. It is easy to understand why the relationship between Kenneth Jernigan and Jim Gashel was close and productive for so long.

Jim Gashel, 1970.

IT IS NOT AN EXAGGERATION TO SAY THAT KENNETH Jernigan became absolutely the most important force to guide me in positive directions toward success. Dr. Jernigan's life on earth ended in October 1998, but his presence is still very much a part of who I am, what I do, and what I have become. As I reflect on my association with Dr. Jernigan, first as his student, then as his employee and a soldier in the movement, the power of his personality and leadership are still with me every day.

While presenting to Dr. Jernigan a special citation from US President Lyndon B. Johnson, Harold Russell (then Chairman of the President's Committee on Employment of the Handicapped) said in 1968: "If a person must be blind, it is better to be blind in Iowa than anywhere else in the nation or the world." I was born in Mason City, Iowa, and was a senior at the University of Northern Iowa at the time, and I knew firsthand the truth of Harold Russell's words. What I could not thoroughly comprehend at that time was the transformative effect Dr. Jernigan's leadership of programs for the blind in Iowa would have on opportunities for the blind throughout the rest of the United States and around the world. The chance for me to serve the movement as one of Dr. Jernigan's principal lieutenants was yet to come.

I first met Kenneth Jernigan on June 11, 1964, at approximately 3:00 p.m. central daylight time. It was a Friday afternoon, exactly two weeks after my high school graduation. Dr. Jernigan was director of the Iowa Commission for the Blind, and we met in his office in Des Moines. I remember that meeting as though it was taking place all over again right now.

The meeting had been arranged by Jim Glaza, my rehabilitation counselor. Mr. Glaza was insisting that I begin a nine-month course of training at the Commission's adult Orientation and Adjustment Center, but I was hoping to get in and get out so I could start as an incoming freshman that fall at the State College of Iowa (SCI) in Cedar Falls, now the University of Northern Iowa. My plan was to become a teacher, and SCI was the state's school for training teachers.

Not very far into the meeting with Dr. Jernigan, I figured out that he agreed with Jim Glaza and not with Jim Gashel. Although I tried hard not to admit it, both Jernigan and Glaza were absolutely right; I did need serious adjustment to blindness training in spite of the fact (or perhaps because of the fact) that I had attended the Iowa Braille and Sight Saving School (the state school for blind children) for thirteen years. Having lived under the school's influence and control for nine months every year from age four to seventeen, I thought that I should know everything there was to know about blindness. That's what I wanted to think in my heart, but my mind knew better.

I remember standing in the director's outer office as Dr. Jernigan stepped briskly through the doorway with his hand outstretched to greet me. No blind person had ever before approached me with such confidence. I was both impressed and terrified as Dr. Jernigan invited me into the office, closed the door, and stepped behind his desk. There I was in a room alone with the most decisive and fully in-charge individual I had ever met, not to mention the fact that he was also blind.

He had everything I wanted but didn't have and wasn't sure I could ever get.

Dr. Jernigan had planned ahead. Knowing that I had hopes of completing training in something like ninety days, he announced that the date for me to begin would be August 10. This made my plan to start at SCI in the fall a practical impossibility, and Dr. Jernigan was fully aware of it. I either had to ditch the training altogether or put off my enrollment at SCI. During the meeting my inadequate responses to Dr. Jernigan's probing questions proved to both of us that blindness would continue to be a serious obstacle throughout my adult life unless I decided to do something about it. So, on August 10, 1964, I reported for my first day of classes as one of Dr. Jernigan's students. I turned the page to begin a new chapter of my life.

I soon learned to fear him and to love him. The love came from knowing how much Dr. Jernigan cared about each of us, taking as much time as we needed from his demanding schedule. His role was to encourage, guide, and challenge us. More than once did I lose a bet with Dr. Jernigan as he tried to pound important points of grammar into my head. He pointed out with great glee that there is more than one way to pay for education, and I did.

The fear of Dr. Jernigan came from knowing that he would always find out whenever we were selling ourselves short. The challenges he put before us were always right around the corner, and you never knew exactly when they would come. It might be 5:30 in the morning when Dr. Jernigan would show up for gym class and see who could jump rope without missing longer than he could. It might be while cutting wood. Dr. Jernigan would grab a two-man cross-cut saw and insist that you join him on the other end. This created a sufficient supply of fireplace wood to get through the coldest months of a normal Iowa winter. Feeling inadequate or inferior due to blindness is the last thing on your mind after spending a day sawing wood with Dr. Jernigan. Try as we all did to avoid facing up to our fears of competing in a world where everyone else can see, Dr. Jernigan made us know we could do it, and he always seemed to know exactly when we were most vulnerable to our deepest doubts.

Grammar class, gym class, and wood cutting are among my most memorable experiences while I was a student with Dr. Jernigan in charge. However, nothing can top his challenge to three of us to build a new kitchen for the home economics department at the Center. The discussion about needing a new kitchen came up more or less out of the blue one day when Dr. Jernigan dropped in for a visit with our 12:30 p.m. men's home ec class taught by Ruth Schroeder. The students were sitting around the dining room table having a normal conversation with Ruth and Dr. Jernigan when one of us suggested that our cooking activities would be far more efficient if a new kitchen could be built in an area then only partially developed and poorly arranged. We were pleasantly surprised when Dr. Jernigan readily agreed; not so pleasantly surprised with the plan he offered. As I recall, his exact words were: "Fine. You build it."

Imagine our response when faced with this proposition which amounted to throwing down the gauntlet. We were like deer in the headlights, and Dr. Jernigan was driving the fast-approaching car. How could we get out of this situation? The best excuse we could think of was that we all had regular classes. We did not want to delay our training. The answer which I will never forget was, "Building the kitchen is your class. You have no other class until the kitchen is finished."

So on a crisp clear Iowa Monday morning in late October 1964, rather than attending our previously scheduled classes, our kitchen-building class started with three students—Merve Flander, Monte Rathbun, and me—and no shop instructor. We were strictly on our own to sink or swim. And swim we did, quite literally. That happened at one point near the end of the project when I was holding a board in place, and one of my kitchen crew colleagues was pounding a nail which made an unplanned penetration into a water pipe. There followed several anxious minutes while we wondered where a valve might be to shut off the water, which had started to spray like a geyser from the punctured line.

Although I am not certain to this day just how we got the water to stop pouring from the punctured pipe, the point is that we did, and the kitchen project was completed in less than three months. That was just in time to show it off to members of the Iowa state legislature who toured the Commission building in January. The kitchen project resulted in two kitchens in one room complete with stoves, ovens, sinks, counters, and cupboards, but only one refrigerator. We showed off the physical facilities with pride. And even more important, the thing we actually built was the foundation for a whole new perspective on blindness and ourselves. Although the kitchen project is several decades in the past, I still use the lessons learned from that experience in responding to other new challenges in my life. Of course, this is exactly what Dr. Jernigan had in mind when he told us that no other class would be more important than building the kitchen. You could say that rising to Dr. Jernigan's challenge to build the kitchen has actually become an important metaphor for many activities in my life.

In the fall of 1965, only a few weeks into my first semester at SCI on my way to the teaching career I had planned, my public speaking professor strongly advised me to sign up for the inter-collegiate competitive debating team. This was another new challenge. Keeping up with my classes and all the homework reading required seemed to me enough. Was this just an excuse? How could I as a blind person expect to compete on the same level with sighted students when documents used to build and support a winning case are only in print? I reasoned that my professor had obviously not considered my circumstances. Then I thought about the kitchen. How could I be true to the lessons learned there and not sign up for debate? The answer was simple. The nature of this challenge was exactly the same.

I would be selling myself short if I accepted the rationalization that my classes and homework were enough. With fear and determination, I decided not to let blindness get in the way. I signed up and earned a spot on the SCI debate team for the next four years. I found that thinking about blindness as an obstacle was only an excuse. I found ways of reading the print. My research was often more thorough than that of my opponents who could see. More than that, my ability to read my notes in Braille turned into an advantage. I could maintain eye contact with the judges better than print readers. This is what Dr. Jernigan would have called turning lemons into lemonade.

After college graduation, I worked successfully in Pipestone, Minnesota, as a junior high and high school teacher and coached the high school debate team. Then I returned to Des Moines and worked under Dr. Jernigan as a teacher in the Orientation and Adjustment Center where I had earlier been a student. In December of 1973, I moved to Washington, DC, to become chief of the Washington Office of the National Federation of the Blind, and a new chapter of my life began. What on earth was I thinking? I was barely twenty-seven years old, but the challenge was to go to Washington and get laws passed on behalf of the blind. I had experience writing and speaking, but would anyone in Congress pay attention? Never in my life, not once, had I worked to get a law passed, but Dr. Jernigan seemed to think I could do it.

With little else but that vote of confidence, I packed my bags and flew east. The position at the NFB evolved from chief of the Washington Office to director of Governmental Affairs to executive director for Strategic Initiatives in the twenty-first century. Over a period of more than thirty years, I helped to get laws passed and to improve opportunities and services for the blind, and I interacted with government agencies and Washington officials. There is not as much difference as some might think between getting laws passed and building a kitchen. Both are a challenge, and meeting the challenge begins with what you believe you can do.

Changing the Social Security law that penalized blind people for working was one of my first assignments. The earnings limit for the blind was $140 a month. Any amount above that a blind person earned would cause a complete loss of benefits, not only for the blind person but also for any dependents on the wage earner's record. Getting almost any job would cause the complete loss of benefits, forcing most blind people to choose between the security of a monthly check or to work for less money. Our goal: remove the limit on earnings altogether. My responsibility working under Dr. Jernigan as our leader was to make it happen.

Blind people were literally penalized for going to work. Although the goal itself seemed simple, the prevailing view in Congress seemed to be that continued payment of cash benefits should be conditioned on little or no work allowed. Never mind that there would be tax benefits resulting from blind Social Security beneficiaries becoming wage earners. So the battle lines were drawn, and Dr. Jernigan was counting on me to make a difference. It was just like building the kitchen all over again.

It is one thing to get a bill introduced in Congress, but something else altogether to get the Congress to consider the bill itself. Most of the five thousand or six thousand bills introduced during the course of a two-year Congress fail to move, and fewer than five hundred actually become law. Of those that do become law, a surprisingly high percentage are passed to recognize or commemorate persons or events of particular significance to those backing the commemoration. Changing the limits on earnings allowed by the blind who receive Social Security disability benefits may be important to the blind, but something of this magnitude is just not at the top of the Congressional agenda. A strategy was required to force the issue. One thing I knew about Dr. Jernigan (win or lose) was that allowing Congress to ignore our issue was not an option.

In 1977, three years after I arrived in Washington and started to learn how things got done in Congress, we got our opportunity to do something about the earnings limit problem. I say "opportunity," but at the beginning it was hard to know whether we would be facing an opportunity or a curse. The issue was a funding crisis looming over the entire Social Security system, threatening that the system would become insolvent and unable to meet current benefit obligations. To say that this was understood as a crisis forcing Congress to act is an understatement.

Raising or removing the limit on earnings by the blind was not viewed as a cost-saving approach, even though more blind people would have the opportunity to work and pay taxes. Congress was in a cost-cutting mood and loath to add any new obligations to the system. Who aside from Dr. Jernigan would think that Congress would relax the limit and allow blind people to earn more while trying to keep Social Security afloat?

Anyone who followed the 1977 debate in Congress to shore up Social Security might have thought that I was nuts for seeking more benefits to allow the blind to work. And if it hadn't been for Dr. Jernigan who continued to insist that our cause was right and the time was now, I might also have had reason to question my sanity. But when the dust settled, President Jimmy Carter signed the Social Security Financing Amendments of 1977 into law. The limit on earnings allowed for blind people was immediately raised to $334 a month, combined with mandated increases for each of the next five years, and automatic adjustments based on annual wage growth for every year in the future. This result was far less than we wanted, but it was progress nonetheless. The limit has increased from $140 in 1977 to $1,640 in 2011, and it is still climbing with the cost of living year after year.

Although Dr. Jernigan had never spent a single day working the halls of Congress, he had a keen understanding of both politics and human nature. He was in fact a master politician, as well as a master teacher of how to use the political process to get things done. More than once I found myself questioning an approach he insisted we should take only to find that his way worked just right when mine would almost certainly have failed.

Another example of this occurred during President Reagan's second term. The General Services Administration was preparing to disregard opportunities for blind businessmen and women under the Randolph-Sheppard Act. The commissioner of the Public Building Services decided to raise revenue for the federal treasury by leasing space to fast food chains, such as

McDonalds, Burger King, Pizza Hut, and the like. Contrary to the federal Randolph-Sheppard Act, the commissioner's so-called "out-leasing" program did not include a priority for blind people to operate food service or vending facility businesses in the areas set aside for commercial enterprises. There was also no provision to protect blind vendors already operating food service and other businesses in federal buildings from unwarranted and quite likely illegal competition from the fast food giants and their branded product lines.

When Dr. Jernigan first got wind that this plan was in the works, he did not hesitate for a moment. His remedy: mount a major public protest in the Congress and in the streets of Washington, DC, to embarrass the Reagan Administration for running rough-shod over business opportunities for the blind provided by law. But the approach I favored was far less grandiose. Rather than taking to the streets, I reasoned that the appeal rights already set forth in the Randolph-Sheppard Act should be used to challenge the commissioner's "out-leasing" plan, and there would be no need for a public brouhaha. I was concerned that mounting a public protest might just fuel a confrontation and end up with nothing more than an acrimonious public battle we couldn't win. Worse than that, I feared that the public protest might harm our chances to overturn the "out-leasing" plan through the more quiet legal means if that should be necessary.

Looking back, it is possible that recourse to the law might have worked, but it certainly would have taken time—perhaps several years—during which the fast food giants would have made a killing at the expense of blind businessmen and women. Dr. Jernigan obviously understood this, and I didn't. Rather than spending money on lawyers and losing out on opportunities for the blind in the meantime, all it took was the threat of a public protest, and the commissioner decided that proceeding with his "out-leasing" program was not worth a public confrontation with the blind. Imagine the pride we all felt that February as Dr. Jernigan read the commissioner's letter of concession to more than five hundred members and leaders of the NFB assembled for our annual Washington Seminar! Dr. Jernigan knew better than I when a demonstration could shortcut a long, difficult legal appeal, and I learned again how keen was his judgment.

From the time I became his student in August 1964 until his death more than thirty-four years later, Dr. Jernigan taught me how to live and succeed in the world, as he did many others. In the last year of his life, and particularly in the last few months, he also taught me how to die. Knowing that he would not live to see the completion of our new building at the National Center for the Blind, he led the initial planning and talked about its importance for decades to come. I remember with particular clarity how Dr. Jernigan placed his hands on the tactile model of the new building to be erected on Wells Street and joined to the existing structure on Johnson Street in South Baltimore. But building for the future aside, Dr. Jernigan knew he could help us most even after death by offering us a challenge. For me it was much like the challenge of building the kitchen, but this time it was our new President Dr. Marc Maurer who continued to lead the project and urge us on to success.

Five years and $20 million later, we celebrated the grand opening of our brand new Jernigan Institute, the world's first institute of its kind where cutting-edge research and pioneering training programs relating to blindness are planned and directed by the blind themselves. Since that time our accomplishments have been many, but it is only the beginning. Dr. Jernigan taught us to dream and never to be satisfied with anything less than the best. I shared with my wife Betsy, the first director of the new Institute, the thrills of innovation as she dared to undertake the kinds of projects Dr. Jernigan would have loved. Then we met the blind driver challenge. Mark Riccobono, the second director of the Jernigan Institute (and now the new President of the National Federation), drove the first car designed for the blind. Dr. Jernigan would have loved to have been behind the wheel, and in every way that really counts, he was.

In July of 2007, I decided that a new career challenge would be good for me and equally good for the NFB. At age 61, I considered that it was time to make room for the next generation at a time when I would still be around to share my experience. Dr. Jernigan showed us the value of selecting his successor and making a good transition in the Presidency of the NFB. I recognized a similar opportunity, although somewhat less critical. It gives me pleasure to report that the process has worked equally well, and I commend my successor John Paré and other staff and NFB members on their excellent performance.

As for me, my position as vice president of Business Development at K-NFB Reading Technology has been a rewarding new opportunity to fulfill our needs as blind people with the functionality and promise of innovative technology in the digital age. Our company was formed in December 2005 as a joint venture by the National Federation of the Blind and world famous inventor and futurist, Dr. Raymond Kurzweil. I first met Ray Kurzweil in 1975 and introduced him to Dr. Jernigan at our national convention that summer in Chicago. I knew then that cutting edge technology would begin to play an increasingly important role in changing what it means to be blind. Both Dr. Kurzweil and Dr. Jernigan understood that too. It has been a pleasure for me to watch this evolution of technology for the blind ever since that time. My role is exciting and challenging.

In November 2007, just as my wife, Dr. Betsy Zaborowski, was dying from the recurrence of Retinal Blastoma she had suffered as a child in the 1950s, we moved across the country from Baltimore to Denver, Colorado. Thus I began a new chapter in my life without Betsy, with a new job, and living in a community that was entirely new to me. I was proud to know that Betsy had been the founding director of our NFB Jernigan Institute for research and training, and it was time for me to meet a new challenge. It is a huge understatement to say that my continued work in the National Federation of the Blind and the many friends I have in our movement have been an invaluable source of support.

I have a new passion for downhill skiing which has also helped, a fact which Betsy knew in planning our move during the last few weeks of her life. I don't know how fast I go when skiing down steep black diamond runs, which I now do as often as I can, but I do know that Dr. Jernigan is with me when I do it. We used to run together on the streets of Des Moines, when Dr. Jernigan was director of the Iowa Commission for the Blind and I was one of his students, so I know he liked to go fast. If he were still alive and had ever learned the joy of downhill skiing, Dr. Jernigan would be skiing down black diamond runs too. In fact, by teaching me I could build a kitchen he also taught me I could ski. Dr. Jernigan would be proud of many of his students and the progress of the Federation. I have remarried, and my wife Susan is an attorney and a partner in the Federation. The reading technology developed by K-NFB Reading Technologies is now the property of the NFB and has helped to make reading materials far more accessible to the blind than ever before. Since reading was a passion of Dr. Jernigan, this would matter to him a great deal.

In September 1998 when it was clear that Dr. Jernigan had only a few weeks to live, I sent him a personal letter in Braille to express my thoughts and say good-bye. I suppose this was also a form of closure to a part of my life that will never be closed. Here is what I said at that time and say again now:

"Baltimore, Maryland
September 14, 1998

Dear Dr. Jernigan:
I'm not sure when it was that I last wrote a letter to you, but I think it may have been as long as thirty years ago back in Iowa. I guess this is so because I have had the honor to work by

your side each and every day for the better part of this time. Now I must write to say good-bye.

It is an understatement to say that this is not easy. You have spent your entire life giving to us, and now we have only a few weeks left and very little that we can give to you in return. In the short term, I guess that just giving you time finally to be at peace is best.

Beyond that you should be comforted in knowing that the purpose to which you devoted your life is now shared among tens of thousands of us. It is true that your voice will be silent and your hand will not be on the tiller, but the course will be as steady as it has ever been.

You gave this assurance to Dr. tenBroek thirty years ago, and now we give it to you. One thing you know for sure is that the National Federation of the Blind is as strong as it has ever been. The trust that we now have is to keep it that way and to build on the progress you helped to make. Please know that this will happen. You have done everything you could possibly have hoped to do to make it that way.

You have said that there is no force on earth that can stop our progress. When you first said those words many years ago, it may have been a matter of faith, but now it has become a matter of fact. Through the patience of your teaching and the example of your life, the fire of your commitment to blind people has ignited an eternal flame which we will fuel and in our turn pass along.

So, Dr. Jernigan, as it has been during the journey of your life so far, it will continue to be during the journey you are now making. In ways that really count, you are not alone. I will miss your strength and your wisdom, but I promise you that my commitment to the mission of your life will always remain true.

Yours with thanks for all that you have meant and mean.

James Gashel"

CHAPTER 14

FROM TOLEDO TO KELOWNA

by Mary Ellen Gabias

Note: Mary Ellen Gabias married a Canadian and moved to Canada almost twenty-five years ago. She and her husband Paul have four children, mostly grown up now, and work to bring change for the blind in Canada. Here she discusses her activities in that country attempting to improve the lives of the blind. She is only one of Dr. Jernigan's students who has ended up in a foreign country and realized how great the need is among the blind there. Kenneth Jernigan taught his colleagues and students that each must work in the climates and circumstances in which she finds herself. We will never know of all the examples around the world where this has happened.

WHEN I WAS A YOUNG WOMAN OF TWENTY-ONE, I thought of myself as a college kid. I knew I was good at schoolwork, but I had trouble imagining myself shouldering adult responsibilities. As a result of the work I had done organizing students for the NFB in my home state of Ohio, I had been elected secretary of the national student division in 1973. But in my mind this was all practice; responsibility for the Federation belonged to the national President, Board members, and state leaders—to the real adults. So, when Dr. Jernigan called to invite me to a leadership seminar in Des Moines over the 1973 Labor Day weekend, I was expecting a course for students. I read the literature I was sent as if I were preparing for an exam.

Mary Ellen Gabias stands with Kenneth Jernigan
during her wedding reception, 1989.

When I arrived at the seminar, it didn't take me long to realize that this was no academic exercise; nor was it a practice session for some future date when I might grow up and do some leading. Dr. Jernigan thought of me as both an adult and a responsible colleague. He made it absolutely clear that every person at the seminar was expected to carry part of the load—even scared, college-kid me.

Dr. Jernigan knew I was feeling overwhelmed. He did everything he could to reassure me at the same time he was presenting me with the toughest challenge I had ever faced. He went out of his way to make me feel I belonged.

On the first night in Des Moines we went to a restaurant where customers chose and prepared their own steaks. Another seminarian—a woman with more courage and honesty than I possessed—told him before we went that she didn't want to grill her own steak. She said she had never learned to grill them properly. She knew that other blind people could do it, but not she. "Don't worry," Dr. Jernigan replied. "You'll do just fine. I'll show you what you need to know. Grilling steaks is fun. How do you feel about grilling a steak, Mary Ellen?"

I had probably eaten fewer than ten steaks in my life! Not only had I never grilled one, I was not even sure whether I would know how a good steak should taste. I was embarrassed to admit my ignorance, but I knew it would be readily apparent as soon as we got to the restaurant. So I answered Dr. Jernigan's question in what seemed to me to be the safest way possible. "Well, sir," I replied, "I've never grilled a steak, but there's no harm in trying."

"There's no virtue in it, either," was his astonishing reply. "There's nothing more obnoxious than a blind person who's so touchy about his independence that he won't accept help when doing so would be more efficient and graceful. That sort of behavior says more about insecurity than independence." Someone showed me how to grill my steak, but that evening is memorable because of what it gave me to chew over in my mind. Dr. Jernigan was not a person who could be satisfied with a glib, safe, and self-serving answer.

The next day we started before eight in the morning and finished at ten in the evening. There was more to do than we could possibly get done. That's the way it always is in the Federation. We worked hard, laughed a lot, and cried sometimes.

The experience changed the way I thought about myself. I began to understand that Dr. Jernigan could not carry the load alone. He could write and speak about blindness better than anyone else; his thinking was innovative; his courage was beyond question; but he also needed my help. He had shown me what the Federation meant to blind people. He had given the deepest and best part of himself to the movement. He had ceased to be an intimidating stranger and had become a trusted friend. For the rest of my life I will never forget that the responsibility for the work that needs doing belongs as much to me as to anyone else. The most successful projects the Federation does begin because someone in the organization sees a need and starts thinking of ways to meet it.

Dr. Jernigan hired me to work at NFB headquarters, now known as the NFB Jernigan Institute, in October 1982. He knew how to make hard work fun. The staff called themselves "citizens" and met from time to time to celebrate birthdays and to decide on crucial matters, such as what brand of peanut butter we would buy for the lunchroom. Citizens of the National Center, like citizens the world over, paid "taxes" to cover the cost of coffee and some food staples. There was a great deal of politicking to get the commodities various people wanted. Dr. Jernigan made alliances and brokered deals. Sometimes his side won, but not always.

Citizens who left items on the lunchroom counters or tables were subject to small fines that went into the treasury with the taxes. This boosted revenues and kept the lunchroom tidy. More than once a gleeful voice came over the public address system: "Dr. Jernigan, please retrieve your possession from the lunchroom and pay your fine." He paid without a murmur of protest, but he also never missed an opportunity to collect fines from his colleagues. He modeled disciplined behavior and proved that discipline can be taught without sacrificing playfulness and fun. I've since discovered that my own family runs more smoothly when I remember that.

Dr. Jernigan loved to entertain. Every year he invited the staff to his home for a picnic. We also had a potluck Christmas dinner. One year I made ratatouille. "Ratatouille," he said the word several times. Then he asked, "If you have just a little ratatouille, would you have mouse-atouille?"

He teased me a lot about my love of baseball, particularly my fondness for the Toledo Mudhens. "A coot can't mate with a mallard, but a mudhen can mate with either a coot or a mallard."

I wondered where in the world he had gotten that information about water fowl. "That shows that mudhens are very flexible," I responded.

"No," he answered. "That shows that mudhens are very promiscuous."

One day, when I was still very new on the staff, I told him I was afraid of making a mistake that would cause harm to a blind person. "You will. You can count on it. The only people who never get it wrong are the ones who do nothing. Those people who always play it safe avoid mistakes at the expense of making the worst mistake of all, failing to do what they can."

When he was working, he worked very hard. When he wasn't working, he resisted working at all. One evening I was a guest at his home. The conversation around the dinner table was about politics, wine, the weather. I was thinking about something I was doing at work and asked him a question about it. He answered politely in one sentence and went back to discussing politics, wine, and the weather. Two more times I brought up questions about work with the same result. I finally got the message. As the Bible says, "To everything there is a season."

Chapters and state affiliates frequently came to NFB Headquarters to tour their property, talk to Dr. Jernigan and Dr. Maurer, buy aids and appliances, and enjoy good food and the excitement that comes from being at the nerve center of the National Federation of the Blind. Dr. Jernigan would often work late into the evening discussing the Federation with the members of the affiliates. At the end of a very long weekend he told a departing state affiliate that he was going to go and clean the bedroom and bathroom he had used while staying at the Center. One person said in an astonished tone, "He's the leader of the Federation, and he still cleans toilets!" Dr. Jernigan replied that it would be an irresponsible waste of the Federation's resources if he spent very much time cleaning toilets, but that if he was unwilling to spend some time cleaning, he didn't deserve to lead.

Our opponents were often unnerved by his ability to change his approach when the situation warranted change. He could be unflinchingly confrontational when the rights of blind people were being trampled. He could also accept the need to work with people who disliked the Federation if doing so would safeguard the rights of blind people. I once asked him how he could keep from hating such snakes. "If a snake is going to bite you, you have to kill it. But you should always love the snake, even while you're killing it. A fat lot of good it does the snake, I suppose, but it does you a lot of good." Bitterness and hatred were not part of his character.

Dr. Jernigan was the first person outside of our immediate families to learn of my engagement to Paul Gabias. Paul grew up in Quebec province and came to the United States to get his PhD from New York University. Then he worked in this country for several years.

The year 1989 was a truly eventful one! Paul and I were married in January; I discovered I was pregnant on the Fourth of July; I quit my job at the NFB in mid-August; and we arrived in Fredericton, New Brunswick in Canada in time for Paul to begin teaching there in early September. Packing up and moving to a new country added to my sense of adventure, especially since I believed we would be there only one year, just enough time to feel as though we were more than tourists, but not enough time to put down roots.

Moving into our rented house and adjusting to the prospect of becoming parents occupied all our attention for the first month or so. We had little energy for the organized blind movement—until a municipal issue reminded us that Federationism cannot be separated from daily living.

Downtown Fredericton had several intersections with a traffic pattern that was new to us. First the north-south traffic would move. Then the east-west traffic took its turn. The "don't walk" sign remained on during both cycles. Finally, the walk signal lit up for pedestrians in all directions. You could walk straight across the street or cross diagonally; all cars stopped, and people had full possession of the intersection. I'd never encountered such a "scatter crossing" traffic pattern before; it was just one more fascinating and unique aspect of my new community.

Then we heard that the chief administrator of the New Brunswick Division of the Canadian National Institute for the Blind (CNIB) was attempting to get rid of the "scatter" cycle and have it replaced with a standard "walk/don't walk" pattern. Her reasoning? The "scatter" system was just too dangerous for blind people.

We went to the city council meeting where the issue was debated and spoke up in favor of Fredericton's unique downtown and against the notion that blind people couldn't manage something as simple as a variation in traffic flow. It was a new experience for me to hear the mayor of the city called "Your Worship," but other than that, the city council reminded me of others I had visited.

Unfortunately, CNIB had its way, although Paul was interviewed by a local radio station and took the opportunity to talk about blind people as normal, competent individuals.

After that episode, we decided we'd better become active if we didn't want to live with the restricted image being promoted by the service agency. We joined the local organization of blind people, a social club. In the midst of attending Christmas parties and discussing plans for next spring's lawn bowling league, we began talking with blind people about their aspirations and sharing what the Federation meant to us. It was a time for learning a lot and teaching a little. Our new friends taught us that, when it comes to adopting a philosophy of blindness, the border doesn't really matter. We're all seeking to make our lives full of opportunity and to put the concept of blindness as tragedy to rest. The Federation has articulated the dream better than any other organization I know, but the dream of full and equal participation is universal.

Our efforts in Fredericton were tentative because our focus was on our expected baby, and we believed we would be in Canada only one year. Even so, we made friends for ourselves and for Federationism.

Dr. Jernigan was one of the people we called the following February when our daughter Joanne was born with an infection that collapsed her lung and almost killed her. He rejoiced with us at her recovery and later at the births of our sons Jeffrey and Philip.

Our fourth child, Elliott, was born on September 3, 1998— exactly twenty-five years after the First Seminar in Des Moines. Though he was weak and short of breath and knew his death was not far off, Dr. Jernigan rejoiced with us again. Without Dr. Jernigan's work, how many Federation families would never have come to be? The children of those families are truly his Federation grandchildren.

We've always thought of ourselves as particularly fortunate because we have two families, our biological family and our Federation family that now encompasses two countries. We didn't realize in February 1990 how much the Canadian Federation family would come to mean to us.

Summer 1990 brought another move, but not back to the United States as we had expected. Instead, Paul took a position at Okanagan College in Kelowna, British Columbia.

So we packed up our belongings and headed for the opposite side of the continent, with a stop at the NFB convention in Dallas en route. That was the year we began a pattern of bringing Canadians to the convention with us. One of our New Brunswick friends returned from that trip to Dallas with a long white cane. Before that convention, he'd resisted using anything but a short folding cane—and that only at night or for identification.

In the overall scheme of things, one man deciding that a white cane is a useful tool and nothing to be ashamed of is a small matter. For us at that time, it was confirmation of what we already deeply believed. Attending a national convention of the NFB can be a life-changing experience. Paul and I would have liked to offer more support to this gentleman than we could from across the country. Nevertheless, he never went back to being ashamed of his blindness and hiding it.

Since Paul grew up in Canada, he was very eager to bring the kind of change to the blind of that country that he had found in the United States. I was happy to assist, but my priority was my new baby. Further, I had to learn more about Canada before I could lead the way toward change.

We continued meeting blind people and inviting them to explore Federationism. As we talked with more and more activists, it became clear to us that no existing organization of the blind operated with a Federation philosophy. So we explored the possibility of starting a new one.

Throughout this time we had been in touch with Dr. Jernigan from time to time. He told us how in the 1950s he had helped transform a group that was a Federation chapter in name only into a thriving integral part of the organization. He urged us to join the local social club, graciously plan picnics and parties, and make friends. Then he said the sentence that came to define the work we did together for the rest of his life. "I can tell you what I think I would do, but you're there, and I'm not."

With Dr. Jernigan urging us to help transform an existing social group, and activists in Canada telling us to stay away from all social groups, we were in a quandary. So we did a little of both. We made friends with anyone we could, whether elderly members of social clubs or young activists, and formed two chapters of an organization we thought of as the Federation in Canada.

Not surprisingly, we met with resistance, some of it vicious. A man visited our fledgling group in Vancouver and attacked our character and competence, even though he had never met us. Our president there, a young woman with enthusiasm but little experience, became discouraged and the group fell apart.

Yet persistence was also one of the lessons we learned from Dr. Jernigan. Though progress was painfully slow, we continued talking to blind Canadians. Each year we brought new people to the NFB convention. Each year we talked about creating a more positive future with blind Canadians.

In 1995 our fledgling organization received its charitable status from the federal government, and for the first time we were able to raise a significant amount of money. By 1997 Canada had a delegation of ninety people at the NFB convention in New Orleans.

We grew rapidly, perhaps too rapidly. There was a hunger for change in the country, but change meant something different to almost every person. Some in our fledgling group did not fully believe in the possibility that blindness could ever become just one of thousands of characteristics; to them it would always be a serious disability that could be ameliorated but never conceived of as a normal characteristic. By the end of the decade those of us who wanted to be the Federation in Canada founded the Canadian Federation of the Blind. Now there are two organizations in Canada seeking change that can trace their beginnings to Dr. Jernigan's influence.

The Canadian Federation of the Blind faces a daunting task that would be overwhelming without our ties to Federationism and the legacy of Dr. Jernigan. The Canadian people are warm and courteous, quite prepared to treat blind people with dignity and respect. Not surprisingly, those with little or no experience don't know very much about blindness. They've been led to believe that CNIB, the giant service agency in the country, meets all of our blindness needs. Because the public believes it's the best way to help us, they happily contribute money to CNIB, which is a private charity. Most Canadians believe CNIB is a part of government; few realize that neither the federal government nor the provinces provide rehabilitation or library services to adult blind people.

Governments at all levels within Canada also accept the service agency as speaking for blind people. Because government officials know little about blindness and feel ill equipped to make decisions about services, they are happy to think of CNIB as expert and refer any questions or critiques to that agency. The result is that governments are not used to blind people having an independent voice, and blind people aren't accustomed to dealing with government directly. The CNIB depends on private contributions and is not able to do what government agencies do in the United States. Further, there has never been an organization like the Federation in Canada to advocate for the kind of change we are seeking. As everyone knows, the population of Canada is relatively small and spread out, approximately 34 million. From Toronto to Calgary (perhaps 2000 miles), there is not a single city as large as a million people. Therefore most of our work has been with the blind of western Canada, and we would love to coordinate more with blind people in Quebec and Ontario provinces as well as in the middle of the country.

Dr. Jernigan used to say that the only way to eat an elephant is one bite at a time. Our elephant in Canada is working to make decent training available for the blind and getting governments and the public to recognize that blind people need to have an independent voice. We cannot be represented by a monolithic service agency. There are now at least twelve blind Canadians who have developed skills similar to those Paul and I learned in the United States and understand the needs. We have helped some of them find funding to go to the United States and take training in one of the NFB centers there. Of course, most people cannot do this and do not wish to be that far away from home for several months. Maybe we will be eating two or three elephants, but we've begun the huge task of creating decent government-funded rehabilitation by asking the province of British Columbia to support blind people to go to one of the three NFB centers.

Now Paul's attention is focused primarily on earning a living and raising three teenage boys. He still helps in the NFB, and I'm still mom in a very active family, but it has fallen to me to take the lead for seeking change for the blind in Canada. I never dreamed I could do such a thing. I know Dr. Jernigan would be less surprised about it than I am.

Our ultimate responsibility is to raise the expectations blind people have of themselves and their potential for living as fully equal members of Canadian society. We do that by mentoring one another and reaching out to blind people who are seeking what Federationism has to offer. The only way to build an organization of the blind is to find one member at a time.

I first began to understand Dr. Jernigan's commitment to building individuals, not just membership rosters, at my first meeting with him during that long ago 1973 leadership seminar. Because of his influence, the Canadian Federation of the Blind is thoroughly grounded in commitment to and respect for blind people and the belief that each of us is responsible for the organization's future. Working together, we are capable of creating a positive future for ourselves and for those who will follow.

CHAPTER 15

WHAT ARE YOU DOING ABOUT IT?

by Barbara Loos

Note: Barbara Loos is a mature and conscientious blind woman. After the death of her first husband, Jim Walker, she raised their children, seven and five at the time, alone. Now she is remarried and helping to raise her step-children. She has been employed as supervisor of the training center for the blind in Nebraska and as a teacher of adaptive technology for the blind. She has served as both president and treasurer of the National Federation of the Blind of Nebraska and has been its Lincoln Chapter president as well. She was appointed by the Nebraska governor as a member of the Nebraska Commission for the Blind and Visually Impaired Board of Commissioners and was elected to be its first chairperson. She has mentored blind youth, both formally and informally. For two years she served as a member of AmeriCorps. She now serves as president of the American Action Fund for Blind Children and Adults, is active in both the NFB and her church, and continues to teach and mentor.

She has selected portions of several of her speeches delivered over a period of more than twenty-five years. Using this material, she tells of the influence of Dr. Jernigan on her life and work.

Barbara Loos, 2005.

IN HIS BOOK, *HOW GOOD DO WE HAVE TO BE*, RABBI Harold Kushner tells a story he read in a book which he calls a fairy tale for adults. It is called "The Missing Piece," and it goes like this:

"Once there was a circle that was missing a piece. A large triangular wedge had been cut out of it. The circle wanted to be whole, with nothing missing, so it went around looking for its missing piece. But because it was incomplete, it could only roll very slowly as it rolled through the world.

"And as it rolled slowly, it admired the flowers along the way. It chatted with butterflies and enjoyed the sunshine. It found lots of pieces, but none of them fit, so it left them all by the side of the road and kept on searching.

"Then, one day, it found a piece that fit perfectly. It was so happy. Now it could be whole, with nothing missing. It incorporated the missing piece into itself and began to roll.

"Now it was a perfect circle, and it could roll very fast—too fast to notice the flowers, too fast to talk to the butterflies.

"When it realized how different the world seemed when it rolled through it so quickly, it stopped, left its missing piece by the side of the road, and rolled slowly away, looking for its missing piece."

When I first read that story, I felt uneasy. Even as a child I didn't like fairy tales that seemed either far-fetched or unfinished. Life is teaching me that reality itself is often far-fetched; and the journey can be worthwhile, regardless of the outcome. Still I felt disturbed. After all, why couldn't this one have ended with the words, "satisfied with its new-found wisdom" rather than "looking for its missing piece"—especially since it had already found the piece? Had it so soon forgotten? What was going on?

As I read and thought about what Rabbi Kushner said that the lesson of the story was for him, I found myself thinking about the first time I met Dr. Kenneth Jernigan. He was then both President of the National Federation of the Blind and Director of the Iowa Commission for the Blind.

Rabbi Kushner says, in part, "The lesson of the story was that, in some strange sense, we are more whole when we're incomplete—when we're missing something. There is a wholeness about the person who can give himself away—who can give his time, his money, his strength to others—and not feel diminished when he does so. There is a wholeness about the person who has come to terms with his limitations, who knows who he is and what he can and cannot do; the person who has been brave enough to let go of his unrealistic dreams and not feel like a failure for doing so … To be whole means to rise beyond the need to pretend that we're perfect; to rise above the fear that we'll be rejected for not being perfect. It means having the integrity not to let the inevitable moments of weakness and selfishness become permanent parts of our character."

As I mentioned before, this description of wholeness took me back to my first meeting with Dr. Jernigan. It was December 4, 1974. I sat in Dr. Jernigan's office at the Iowa Commission for the Blind. I had spent the two previous days observing the commission's program for the purpose of broadening my professional education and getting some direction as a rehabilitation teacher of the blind. By that time, I had been working at the agency for the blind in Nebraska for over a year. A lot of things that we did seemed absolutely ridiculous to me.

I remember the time in early 1974 when we had an open house. One of the things that we were to do to prove to the world that blind people were using whatever abilities they had was to Braille everything. And I do mean everything! I went through six rolls of dymo tape labeling drawers, counters, bottles of catsup, even a hammer. I was very naïve when I started working at the agency. I knew I was being paid less than other people but thought the reason was that there were specific positions open for specific pay, and because there wasn't an opening for a teacher, I was getting less money. When a sighted person was hired to do exactly what I was doing and received a full-time salary, and when I subsequently overheard one administrator say about me to another something like, "She seems happy to be working, whatever the pay," I felt both duped and trapped.

The day the director called me into his office and asked me to Braille some material and then read it back to him, ultimately exclaiming in a tone of amazed surprise, "That's exactly what I told you to write," I bristled at the sting of belittlement but felt powerless to counteract it.

I had personal reasons for going to Iowa, too. I had heard much about the Iowa Commission for the Blind and the National Federation of the Blind. I wanted to know if the Commission really was all that it was cracked up to be and wanted to know why Federationists from Iowa kept coming to Nebraska to deal with legislative and other matters which I presumed were none of their business. I had also wondered why Nebraska Federationists seemed to welcome what I saw as interference from the Iowans.

Dr. Jernigan listened to my questions. I now know it may have been the millionth time he had heard such things. Then he calmly asked me without judgment or malice, "And what are you doing about it?"

I sat for a moment reflecting on what I had just done. I had just told the national president of an organization to which I didn't belong what was wrong with a local component of that organization, where I could be (but hadn't been) doing something about it. Having already discovered during that visit that I had many misconceptions about the Federation and its workings, I decided that the very least I could do was to go back to my job and the Lincoln chapter of the Federation and look upon both with the love and respect I had been shown, and with the new understanding of the Federation's approach to issues which I was gaining. It is no exaggeration to say that the few days I spent in an environment where the underlying assumption was that it is respectable to be blind changed my life. And my meeting with Dr. Jernigan was the climax of that visit.

I left that meeting personally exhilarated by the growing conviction that I had found the key to improving my life and the lives of other blind people. I was also keenly aware that what I was about to do was not going to be easy.

I joined the Federation in January 1975, and within a month I was elected president of the Lincoln chapter. In July, I experienced the magic of my first national convention. That was where I became inextricably a part of the Federation family. It was there that I committed myself to involvement in improvements in Nebraska's school, agency, and library for the blind, as well as other issues facing us as blind people— no matter how controversial things might become—because I believe in the rightness of doing so.

From the beginning, Dr. Jernigan showed me that it is not what we do that makes us so strong, important as that is. Our real strength lies in our love, respect, and commitment to one another. I continue to dedicate much of my time and energy to the Federation because of the real lives of the real people which those issues affect. It is, I believe, a worthwhile struggle.

Dr. Jernigan's message was both clear and compelling: with the proper training and opportunity the characteristic of blindness can be reduced to the level of a nuisance, making it possible for the average blind person to do the average job in the average place of business, and do it as well as his or her sighted neighbor. This was, he said, the core of the philosophy of the National Federation of the Blind. Dr. Jernigan both lived this philosophy and helped it to reach fruition in the lives of his students, staff, and colleagues in the movement.

When I met Dr. Jernigan, I was in my mid-twenties, having lived almost twenty-four years searching for, or trying to compensate for, my missing piece. I believed then that I knew what that missing piece was. It was the fact of my physical blindness. But for the first time I wasn't hearing about being incomplete or unwhole because I was blind. I wasn't hearing that the only viable answer for earning full inclusion in the world was to find a way physically to see. I went home both exhilarated and unnerved. It buoyed me up to know that, to this experienced, highly-respected blind person, I had neither to pretend nor to prove anything. But at the same time it was sobering to accept the responsibilities inherent in the kind of wholeness Dr. Jernigan both embodied and offered to me.

He helped me to understand that my missing piece—the thing that kept me from feeling and being perceived as whole—was not the physical fact of blindness. At least part of it consisted of the misconceptions which I and all of society around me had about blindness and blind people.

His words and his presence awakened something in me that gave me courage to try harder to find ways to participate more fully in life. But along with that came the realization if I were to be honest with myself and others, I must be willing to question behavior in others and myself which, unchecked, could stifle growth. For me, accepting the gift of that knowledge of wholeness was very hard. I really don't like making waves.

But Dr. Jernigan that day gave me something every bit as precious as the recognition of my wholeness just as I was. He gave me, as he has to so many before and after me, the key to the National Federation of the Blind—the vehicle through which we, the blind, are finding for ourselves the missing pieces of security, equality, and opportunity for all blind people in our society and putting them into place.

It is hard to articulate the difference that knowing this wholeness and being part of the Federation have made in my life. Perhaps a recounting of something tangible may help to express it.

During my first meeting with Dr. Jernigan he offered me some banana chips and other snacks I had never tasted. The banana chips were my favorite. Over the years thoughts of that meeting have often brought those chips to mind.

In the spring of 1997 I saw an infomercial on television about a food dehydrator. My first thought (after considering the cost, of course) was, "I could make banana chips!" It was wonderful to have that instantaneous response. I did not feel, as I once would have, anxious about cutting myself while slicing, hung up about making uniform slices, troubled about the possibility of burning myself on whatever generated heat for drying things, or convinced that I would need sight in order to use the machine effectively. I made room in my budget and placed an order, thanking God and the National Federation of the Blind for the changes in my attitude which made this possible.

Later that same year, as both an expression of gratitude and a symbol of my progress as a blind person, I gave Dr. Jernigan some banana chips and other fruit I had dried myself. It was a small gesture, but his gracious and understanding acceptance of my gift made it a poignantly unforgettable moment for me. It is, I believe, mostly through such simple, day-to-day actions and statements that each of us comes closer to finding the missing pieces in our lives.

It is neither necessary nor possible for everyone to make the tremendous and far-reaching impact in the world that Dr. Jernigan and other Presidents of the National Federation of the Blind have made. It is necessary and possible for each of us to do and be what we can to reach out to give the gifts of knowledge of wholeness and the National Federation of the Blind to all blind people so that we can search on an equal footing with our sighted peers for that ever-present, still-elusive missing piece—whatever and wherever it might be.

[In 1998 at the memorial service after Dr. Jernigan's death, I made the following remarks:] Somewhere in our National Center for the Blind, I once helped to secure a nail. I don't know exactly where it is or even if, in the course of remodeling, it's still there. But the lessons of that nail will always be a part of the building of my life. My instructor was Dr. Kenneth Jernigan.

I believe the year was 1979. The occasion was a meeting of the American Brotherhood for the Blind, now the American Action Fund for Blind Children and Adults. The place was an old run-down building at 1800 Johnson Street in Baltimore.

We gathered in an enormous, echoey room where we were given the opportunity to nail down a section of floor covering. Some on the Board eagerly accepted the hammer and nails Dr. Jernigan offered and went immediately to work.

As he handed me a nail (the biggest one I had ever seen), Dr. Jernigan quietly asked me if I had ever driven one. Embarrassed and a bit apprehensive, I said "No."

With irresistible enthusiasm he drew me into the process of building. Neither the nail itself nor the driving of it was insignificant to him. He showed me how to choose where to place it, taking into consideration its function and its proximity to other nails. He then invited me to observe the placement of his hands as he held the nail firmly upright while tapping it gently, saying that it was important not only to get it started straight but also to hold it steady until its direction was established and it was solidly grounded. After that, it was a matter of rhythm, coordination, and confirmation of the nail's position and progress. This he accomplished by touching the head of the nail between hammer strokes.

When he handed me the hammer, there was still room for the nail to bend if I hit it wrong, but it had a good straight start. My first taps were tentative. The nail didn't bend, but neither did it progress. Dr. Jernigan pointed out that, even if you're doing the right thing, if you do it without conviction, it's all for naught. "Make it count!" he urged. "Make it count!"

My next swing of the hammer was both true and convincing. The nail went deeper. When I hesitated between swings, Dr. Jernigan said the job would be done more quickly and with less chance of error if I just got into the rhythm and drove the nail home.

He was right. As I concentrated on the goal, bringing my whole self into synchronizing the components, most of my swings were productive, and the nail went down, resting at last flush with the flooring. When, upon completion, Dr. Jernigan voiced his approval, I felt at once proud of having made a small contribution to our building and awed by the impact of the wise counsel I had just received from this master builder.

As if reading my thoughts, Dr. Jernigan proclaimed, intermittently slapping a nearby pillar for emphasis, that each of us had now contributed to the structure of the National Center for the Blind. He hoped we felt proud of our investment and personally responsible for maintaining and improving upon it. I did and still do.

As I reflect on that moment with Dr. Jernigan, I recall many similar lessons in building within the context of Action Fund business. Mostly they have to do, not with nails, but with people's lives. For just as he took, more than once in his lifetime, shabby and dilapidated structures and dreamed them into grand and functional facilities, so too did he take broken and dispirited human beings and love them into independent and fulfilled people.

Dr. Jernigan taught us, in all we do, to be builders. Sometimes we build with intangibles—hope, encouragement, or truth about blindness. Sometimes we build with things—grants, equipment, or books in Braille. But whatever the setting, whatever the tools, our job is, as it was for me the day I learned to drive a nail, to answer Dr. Jernigan's challenge and "make it count!"

[From November 2005 through November 2007 I participated in a formal mentoring program through the Jernigan Institute's National Center on Mentoring Excellence, which I enjoyed very much.] I first met Hannah Lindner, a blind teenager, in Aurora, Nebraska, at the kickoff event of the NFB's mentoring program. One activity that weekend took us to a mall with specific assignments. We efficiently completed our mission, learning in the process that we both take expectations seriously while finding humor in much of what happens along the way.

Everything we have done since that time has continued to help us to get to know each other. We are regularly in touch by phone and via email. We spent one afternoon at Hannah's grandparents' place sharing snacks and conversation with them as well as with her mother and one of her sisters. At Brad's and my home, we have baked rhubarb bread, worked on the computer, downloaded and Brailled lyrics to a song we want to learn, and met over supper with another mentor/mentee team to discuss techniques of blindness they have used in anatomy classes, something Hannah anticipates needing in order to pursue her current post-high school goals. We have also attended events of the National Federation of the Blind of Nebraska's Lincoln chapter, giving us both food for thought and opportunities to network with other blind people. When the latest *Harry Potter* movie came to our Mopix Theater, we donned wireless earphones and availed ourselves of audio descriptions of the visual happenings taking place on the screen.

And overarching all we do are five essential elements of success for blind people. Those elements are: coming to believe both emotionally and intellectually that it is respectable to be blind; learning the skills and mastering the alternative techniques of blindness; knowing how to cope with people's misconceptions about blindness; possessing the discipline, the flexibility, and the work ethic, grooming, and appearance to blend in; giving back both to other blind people and to society.

I agreed to do this because I love young people and enjoy the opportunity to interact with blind youth, whom I see, among other things, as the future of the blind, for better or worse. I still remember Dr. Kenneth Jernigan's question: "And what are you doing about it?" some thirty years ago, after I had complained to him about what I saw as a lack of effort on the part of blind Nebraskans. Then and there, I determined to become part of the solution rather than the problem. Through a commitment to this mentoring program, I hope to continue to do something about improving life for at least two blind people—Hannah and me.

We both agreed that a mentor-mentee relationship does not have to be a commitment that you wonder how you are going to fulfill. It can provide help, security, fun, friendship, and satisfaction for both people. In our case, we found that by growing in our acceptance of the respectability of being blind, improving upon our blindness skills, coping with both public and private attitudes about blindness, exploring ways of blending in and taking advantage of opportunities to give back, together we were able truly to change what it means to be blind in positive ways.

I will share two brief stories I first related in an article I wrote about employment of the blind, which may serve to sum up my continued response to Dr. Jernigan's question concerning what we can do to keep moving forward as blind people.

The minister in my church recently told a story about a boy and his mother walking in their flower garden. The child, gazing at the splendor all around and leaning to drink in the fragrance of the flower nearest him, asked "Mommy, how does God make flowers?"

Before she could decide what to answer, he exclaimed, tearing open a bud, "Oh, I know! God makes them from the inside out!"

The lad had discovered not only the truth about flowers, but also the key to all creation and creativity—that it comes from within …

There are those who have said that, since we can't make everyone understand what blindness is really all about, our task is hopeless. I'm reminded of the child walking along the beach and throwing starfish back into the water. Someone tells him he's wasting his time. He can't ever save all those starfish stranded on the sand. Undaunted, tossing another in, he replies "But I made a difference to that one."

The bud-holding boy shows us that we must create change from within. And the starfishsaving boy reminds us that it will happen one person at a time. Dr. Jernigan modeled this in his life and work. I will do my best as long as I live to do likewise. When times are tough and I am tempted to quit or complain, I still hear that quiet yet compelling voice asking: "And what are you doing about it?"

I seek to find answers which will preserve our foundation of love and respect.

CHAPTER 16

THE BELLY LAUGH

by Richard Davis

Note: Dick Davis was hired by Dr. Jernigan as a 22-year-old sighted college graduate. He became a close friend and colleague. Others had somewhat similar experiences. His story shows an important part of why Kenneth Jernigan accomplished so much and drew so many people into his activities. This account is as entertaining as Dr. Jernigan himself.

WHEN I STARTED WORKING AT THE ORIENTATION Center of the Iowa Commission for the Blind, Kenneth Jernigan, the Commission's director, told me that an orientation center was like an atom bomb. To function properly, it always had to be ready to explode. Seventeen years later the New Mexico Commission for the Blind Orientation Center, which I then ran, had gone beyond critical mass and was ready to blow.

New Mexico is a big state and Alamogordo, where the Center is located, is 225 miles south of the Commission's headquarters in Santa Fe. Oversight of its operations under the Department of Vocational Rehabilitation had been largely nonexistent, and the people who ran it had been permitted for years to do anything they pleased without fear of repercussions. Its reputation was so bad that it had become a dumping ground for some of the agency's most difficult clients. But in 1986, Fred Schroeder, a blind NFB leader, was hired to direct the newly-created New Mexico Commission for the Blind, and Fred was working hard to make it a modern agency. He wanted somebody who could turn the Center around, restore its reputation, and do so with minimal supervision.

Richard Davis, 2013

In my first year on the job, I had to deal with break-ins, drug dealers, and violent alcoholics with suicidal tendencies. Some of the dormitory staff took every opportunity to undercut what I was doing with the students. The teaching staff also had their problems, and it took a lot of time working with all the staff to get them moving in the right direction. I brought in some new people, and it took time to get them and the old-timers working together. For the first couple of years, I avoided trips away from the Center because of the crises that erupted in my absence.

In the popular game show, "Who Wants to Be a Millionaire," contestants are given a lifeline, a friend or relative they can call for advice on how to answer the question. Sometimes I needed Dr. Jernigan for my lifeline. When a problem seemed to be beyond my abilities to solve, I'd give him a call. He always had my best interests and those of the blind people I served in mind, and I trusted him completely. In fact, he'd recommended me to Fred Schroeder. Some people had questioned whether a sighted person could run an orientation center, but Dr. Jernigan had no doubts about my ability.

When I called him one night, I was facing a whopper of a problem that I had no idea how to solve. It was evening in Alamogordo and two hours later in Baltimore, but Dr. Jernigan picked up the phone, as he always did when I called. I described the problem in gory detail and asked for his help solving it. To my surprise, he started laughing—not just a chuckle—but a real belly laugh that went on and on. Finally, he got enough control over himself to say, "You know, until you called I had forgotten how glad I am not to be running an orientation center anymore! Thank you for reminding me." After laughing a while longer, he said, "Well, I'm sure you'll figure it out," and hung up.

Dr. Jernigan had his personal idiosyncrasies–once he had spent a day pretending to be a computer and answering all of his phone calls like one–but even so, I was stunned. I thought of calling him back but decided not to. His laughter had diminished the stress, and instead of being overwhelmed, I fixed the problem so completely that today I can't even remember what it was. Dr. Jernigan could have given me the advice I sought, but he chose to let me figure it out on my own. That was one of the training methods he used. By his reaction, he showed me he had faith in my ability to solve the problem, and once again he was right. If his response seems cavalier and his training methods tough, you might not have liked working for him. But I did. The seven years I spent working for him at the Iowa Commission for the Blind were some of the best of my life.

When Dr. Jernigan hired me he said, "I want someone I can set down naked in a jungle, and when I return a year later, he'll be flourishing, if not actually running the place." He had no tolerance for people, blind or sighted, who thought of themselves as victims and believed the world owed them a living. When an Iowa student told Dr. Jernigan that it was the staff's responsibility to find him a job, Dr. Jernigan responded: "No, it isn't. Go find your own job!" When I was teaching at the Iowa Orientation Center, I complained to Dr. Jernigan about my frustration with the behavior of some of the students. After listening for a while, he asked me, "Do you think of yourself as an innocent victim?" After some thinking and a little prodding by him, I admitted that I did. "Well, you aren't an innocent victim," he said, "you're a mover and shaker, so go fix the problem!"

The first time I met Dr. Jernigan was when I interviewed for the position of deputy director of the Iowa Commission for the Blind, which was located in Des Moines. My future father-in-law, Bill Paquette, who ran the Career Planning and Placement Office at Drake University, suggested I apply for the job. When I reminded him that I was 22 years old and had no administrative experience, he suggested I apply anyway; if they didn't hire me for that job, maybe they'd hire me for a different one.

When I called to ask about the job, I was referred to Jim Valliant, the deputy director who was leaving. He asked me a series of trivia questions that seemed completely unrelated to the job, and I answered them to the best of my ability. Satisfied with my responses, Mr. Valliant invited me to come in for an interview with Dr. Jernigan. When I got there, Dr. Jernigan's secretary helped me with my coat, then led me into his office. I found myself face-to-face with an impeccably dressed, physically solid, good-looking man who was standing there holding out his hand. I suddenly realized he was blind. Why that possibility had never occurred to me, I don't know. Fortunately I had the presence of mind to take his hand and shake it.

After the icebreaker questions common to job interviews, he resumed the trivia questions I had experienced with Mr. Valliant. Dr. Jernigan asked me to tell him the circumference of the earth and identify a long list of historic and present-day individuals, most of whose names I fortunately knew. When I didn't know an answer, he asked me to guess. If I guessed wrong, he told me the correct answer. He asked me to name the parts of a sentence, describe the periodic table of elements, and answer some mathematical questions. Since I always had an aptitude for trivia, I found the interview interesting, if a bit strange. It wasn't the kind of interview I was used to.

After the trivia questions, he gave me some judgment problems to solve. Some had to do with what I would do in different situations, but others were more cerebral. When he asked me to define "a desk," I told him it was "a flat surface used for paperwork." He nodded, opened the door to his conference room, pointed to the large u-shaped table inside, and said, "That's a flat surface used for paperwork. Is it a desk?" "We call it a conference table," I responded. He told me I was ducking the question. After thinking a while I said, "Yes, it is a desk, a desk used by a large number of people!" He agreed and closed the door.

He then did something that I saw him do many times; he explained the reasons behind his thoughts and actions, even though he had no obligation to do so. In life, he said, it was necessary for a person to be able to come up with a working definition, as I did for the desk, and be willing to stick with it, even if it wasn't perfect. He said the trivia questions were his way of determining how broad an education I had. He told me he hired people with many different kinds of training and experience so they'd avoid bias and be collectively able to solve whatever problems they encountered. For those reasons, he chose not to staff the agency with people who had degrees in rehabilitation, although he said he didn't discriminate and had hired at least one of them, too. That diversity of training and experience produced the most intelligent and creative group of people with whom I have ever worked.

Dr. Jernigan finished the interview by offering me a chance to work for him for a week on an unpaid basis so he could get to know me, and more accurately assess my qualifications for the job. For the next week, the Commission's assistant directors and professional staff asked me questions, answered mine, and gave me challenging work assignments. They explained what they did and the reasons why, and allowed me to shadow them as they did their jobs. I was given some of Dr. Jernigan's speeches to read, and I was asked what I thought about them. I said that they were the best I had ever read. I had no idea at the time how important the ideas in these speeches would become in my life.

On Thursday of that week, I was assigned by Florence Grannis, assistant director in charge of the Iowa Library for the Blind, to create a catalog of recorded and Braille books about foreign countries. It was a real job assignment, not a "make work" exercise. I had to figure out how to do it myself, although I could ask questions of anyone who worked there. By the end of the day I had to find ten books that needed to be in it, make a list of them, and translate its title, "Reading International," into French, German, and Spanish.

Getting the translation done proved to be the most difficult part of the assignment. I went to the public library and looked in language dictionaries. While I found the word "international," "reading" eluded me. Since I was running out of time, I asked the reference librarian if there was someone who could translate the phrase into the three languages. She referred me to a multilingual interpreter who did it for free, even though I offered to pay her out of my own pocket.

I returned to the Commission and worked on the rest of my assignment until 9:00 p.m., stopping only briefly for dinner. It was at that point that Mrs. Grannis found me. She reviewed my work and pronounced it competently done, but she was curious to know how I had translated the title. When I told her, she said she was pleased with my approach because it showed that I knew how to use the resources of a public library. She then told me that if I wanted to buy a house, she could help me find one because she was a licensed real estate agent. That made me optimistic about the next day's outcome.

The next morning, I met with Dr. Jernigan and learned that I had come in second out of the three applicants for deputy director. But Bill Paquette's prediction came true when Dr. Jernigan offered me a job as a cane travel teacher. I was delighted because I thought the job was very interesting. Then Dr. Jernigan asked me how much I thought he should pay me for that job. Since I knew how much public school jobs usually paid, I said around $7,000. He asked me if I thought $8,000 would be fair. I said it would. How about $9,000? That was even better. $10,000? By that point, I was amazed because salary negotiations never went that way. He finally decided on $9,900 because he said it would keep me humble. That was more money than I'd ever seen in my life.

I began work at the Iowa Commission for the Blind on February 8, 1971, and spent the next four months in training, wearing blindfolds so I could learn the techniques of a totally blind person and come to believe in them. After a short amount of time in all of the classes, I began a routine in the morning of four hours training to use the long white cane for independent travel while wearing a blindfold and four hours in the afternoon of reading the *Braille Monitor*, the monthly publication of the National Federation of the Blind. I started at its first issue and read to the present time. It taught me the history of blind people and gave me the perspective I needed to understand it. Periodically, Dr. Jernigan or another member of his staff conducted seminars for the staff trainees. He continued to monitor my progress, even following me on cane travel assignments, and when he decided I was ready to teach, he divided up the cane travel students and gave me half of them.

While I was still in training I was assigned to drive a group of college students to a meeting in Ames about forty miles north of Des Moines. I would be driving Moby Dick, the Commission's white school bus. The shop instructor, Paul Hahle, would go with me Saturday morning before the trip to instruct me on driving the bus. I practiced driving the bus on ice-encrusted roads at state fairgrounds, then drove the bus back to the Commission building, picked up the students, and headed off to Ames. I did pretty well driving Moby on the interstate where there was very little ice and was even able to parallel park it at the university. The trip back to Des Moines was uneventful.

When Monday rolled around, I told a number of people how difficult the assignment had been in order to build myself up in their estimation. Soon Dr. Jernigan called me to his office. He recited my words back to me with great accuracy and then asked why I thought the trip was such a big ordeal. I said it was because I had gotten only two hours of training. He asked me if I hadn't driven the bus competently, without any problems. I agreed that I had. "Then," he said, "two hours of training were exactly what you needed!" End of discussion.

One of Dr. Jernigan's gifts was his ability to "chew you out" and have you leave his office glad that he did. Whenever he corrected me, he took time afterward to share something interesting that he was doing, and sometimes ask for my advice. That told me that even though I'd made a mistake, he still regarded me as a valuable member of his team. Part of his mythology was that he was a rough tough guy who would "beat on" people to get them to do things. That may have been the case with his adversaries, but I never found that to be the case with his staff. Instead, I found him to be a gentle man who took the time to explain the reasons why he wanted you to do something, and usually you would come to agree with him.

The best example of this was when he wanted me to move from the orientation center to field operations and become a rehabilitation counselor. He said that the assistant director in charge of the orientation center was a liberal who had surrounded himself with others of that persuasion. That had affected center discipline and had resulted in a number of student problems. His plan was to restore balance by moving some liberals out and replacing them with older people who had a more conservative outlook. But instead of telling me I would be changing jobs, which he had every right to do, he took a lot of time to explain the job to me and tell me all the ways I would benefit from the change.

After we discussed his plan for a while, he asked me to go away and think about it, and then come back in a couple of days and tell him what I wanted to do. He said he'd be willing to reconsider his plan if I gave him some good reasons why I should stay in my current job. I considered his offer for a couple of days, and then told him I was willing to give it a try. After that, he called the assistant director in charge of field operations and told him what he wanted to do. Since there were no counselor vacancies, I agreed to work as a rehabilitation teacher. Dr. Jernigan thought I would like that job better, and he was right. Before long, I became field trainer for all the new rehabilitation teachers.

One of the things I liked about the jobs in field operations was the degree of autonomy each of us was given. By and large, we were expected to make our own decisions, create our own schedules, and work with agency clients in whatever way we thought best. It wasn't that we weren't supervised; Joe Balderston read all our contact reports and reviewed the rehabilitation plans and funding authorizations that we wrote. He, too, had a gentle touch. Whenever he saw something he didn't like, he would call me on the phone and say half humorously, "Come to my office—I've got a bone to pick with you!" Then he would patiently explain my error and suggest an alternative course of action.

I was used to working in factories where your supervisor yelled at you whenever you did anything wrong. In those positions, if I got any supervision at all, it was a brief orientation to the job, after which I was handed off to an experienced coworker who taught me what to do. But in the Iowa Commission for the Blind, even the managers showed a real interest in you. I was never treated like a kid, and nobody yelled at me. We all made mistakes, but as long as they were honest ones we were given an opportunity to correct them and guided to a better course. I had no fear at all about admitting my mistakes to Mr. Balderston and asking him for guidance.

Being expected to make my own decisions and take full responsibility for them turned me into a self-reliant person who knew how to think on his feet and make choices effectively. As a 27-year-old rehabilitation teacher, I had the authority to work with area special education directors to set up programs for blind children, help hire the staff, and train and mentor them. I was also given the responsibility of orienting the new field staff to their jobs.

When I became a rehabilitation counselor, Mr. Balderston told me that I was the equal of anyone. If I needed to, I could walk into a company and speak to the president. I was expected to set people up in business, buy equipment and supplies, help with legal arrangements if necessary—all as a representative of the Commission for the Blind assisting blind people who were seeking competitive employment. With this experience, I acquired the knowledge and skill base I needed to later become an orientation center administrator, a rehabilitation supervisor, and ultimately, director of a state agency for the blind.

As director of the Iowa Commission for the Blind, Dr. Jernigan, along with the staff he hired and supervised, had proved that the Federation's belief in blind people was justified. He both defined and articulated the Federation's philosophy: "With proper training and opportunity, the average blind person can do the average job in the average place of business, and do it as well as his sighted neighbor." "It is respectable to be blind." "Blindness can be reduced to the level of a physical nuisance." Everyone at the Iowa Commission for the Blind learned to live this philosophy day in and day out.

However, the success of the modern, consumer-focused programs at the Iowa agency caused resentment and bitterness among agencies that preferred the old methods of custodialism and control over the lives of their blind clients. In 1968 Dr. Jernigan became president of the National Federation of the Blind (NFB) and became the leader of the blind civil rights movement in this country. For several years the NFB challenged the practices of many custodial agencies and the corrupt body that accredited them. Eventually some of these agencies decided to fight back by attacking Dr. Jernigan and the Iowa program.

In order to draw fire away from the Iowa agency, Dr. Jernigan initially considered leaving the Federation presidency, but he finally came to the conclusion that he needed to resign as director of the Iowa Commission for the Blind, which he did in the spring of 1978. It was a very hard thing for him to leave the job he had held for twenty years and all the friends he had made, move to Baltimore, and start all over again. As a rehab counselor, I continued to work at the Commission another eight years.

In 1980 I made a number of weekend trips to Baltimore to meet with Dr. Jernigan. He had me read key documents about the Commission for the Blind, and taught me the intricacies of its policies and finances. This gave me enough information and training to do detailed program and financial analysis. A side effect of those trips to Baltimore was that Dr. Jernigan and I became very close friends.

One Sunday we were sitting in his office working on some financial calculations. He'd grown up on a farm in Tennessee and liked to wear bib overalls and a flannel shirt on the weekends. After working for a while, Dr. Jernigan (using a talking calculator and I using a print one) leaned back, sighed, and said, "You know, doing math can make you crazy." At that point, all the authority with which he had cloaked himself at the Commission fell away, and I was able to see him as just a human being—one I liked, and one who liked me.

Because I'm sighted, I'd become used to a support role and felt uncomfortable being suddenly thrust into the leadership in the NFB of Iowa. Dr. Jernigan assured me that sighted people could be Federation leaders too. Even though I held no elective office, I functioned as one of the key leaders in the state.

As I said earlier, Dr. Jernigan recommended me to Fred Schroeder for the job of administrator of the New Mexico

Commission for the Blind Orientation Center, and Fred hired me. Running an orientation center is like nothing else in the world. The only way to deal successfully with blindness is to confront the idea that blind people are less capable than sighted people. That kind of confrontation causes stress, but it also brings about the changes necessary to lead blind students to self-confidence, which enables them to be fully functioning citizens on the job, at home, and in their communities. If things get too relaxed, change ceases to occur; but if they get too stressful, too much change occurs, and that destabilizes the whole program. Hence, the "atom bomb," or as I refer to it, the "nuclear reactor" effect.

The work, while challenging and occasionally unnerving, is always energizing and exciting. There is always a "rush" when a student breaks through self-imposed and society-imposed limitations and goes off and gets a job. Because of what Dr. Jernigan had taught me, I was able to make a successful transition to the new job and the new state. In addition to running the Center, I was the southern area rehabilitation supervisor for four years and was responsible for training new agency staff, much of which occurred at the Center. While I held this position, we turned the New Mexico Training Center completely around and made it a source of pride to the state, restored its reputation with the local politicians, and it came to be regarded as an asset to the state and the community. I still have many friends in the NFB of New Mexico today.

I stayed in touch with Dr. Jernigan, and when six years later he suggested I move on to direct a state agency and recommended me for the directorship of Minnesota State

Services for the Blind, I took his advice once again. That turned out to be my least favorite job, because I worked for people who continually preyed on State Services for the Blind and tried to use its resources for generic programs that would mostly benefit sighted people. Twice they tried to merge State Services for the Blind with other parts of the department, but because of the things Dr. Jernigan taught me and my subsequent experience, I knew that would be a disaster for blind people of the state. Twice I was able successfully to resist those merger attempts, always knowing I was supported by the NFB of Minnesota. I lost my job because of that resistance, but State Services for the Blind in Minnesota remains an independent agency to this day.

Dr. Jernigan taught me many principles and techniques that helped me become a better administrator and a better, stronger human being. When I close my eyes today, I can still hear his words: "You've got to be able to turn your anger on and off like a water faucet;" "You've got to make people love you before you can get them to do anything else;" "As director, you've got to set the tone of your agency;" and "Never use up all your margins." Once he told me, "I've spent all of my working life lying to people." That was a shocking statement, but what he really meant was that he expressed a level of confidence in people that was often unjustified, hoping that they would rise to meet his expectations. Most of the time, it worked. I used that technique and the others that he taught me for years, and I continue to use them today in my job as assistant director of BLIND, Inc., one of the three NFB training centers. All of them were based on the Iowa model but have expanded beyond it as Dr. Jernigan intended.

One thing Dr. Jernigan told me at the end of my job interview has lasted longer than anything else. When he had asked if I had any questions, I blurted out, "But—I have no experience with blind people and don't know what to do!" He smiled and told me, "We'll see that you come to know many interesting blind people and develop meaningful lifelong friendships with them." Over the past forty years, I have met and worked with literally thousands of blind people from all walks of life and have come to know many of them as friends. Dr. Jernigan completely transformed my life. I cannot imagine what it would have been like without him. He continues to live on in my heart and in the hearts of the thousands of other people, blind and sighted, whose lives he influenced.

CHAPTER 17

WHAT HE GAVE TO ME

by Ramona Walhof

Note: What can I add to all of these accounts? I am another person whose life was changed totally by the lessons I learned from Kenneth Jernigan. For me it didn't happen suddenly, but gradually. Partly because of the need to get things done, partly because of his confidence in blind people, and partly because of his imaginative approach to work and living; he repeatedly offered me new opportunities and ideas. More than once he said what he gave could be repaid by passing it on to someone else in the future. I have and will forever try to do this, but I fear I can never pass on anything near what I received from Kenneth Jernigan. The foundation was and is love. The result is miraculous change in thousands of lives.

Dr. Jernigan used so many techniques with so many people that they cannot all be included in a single volume. But perhaps my personal experience can fill in some of the gaps. And it is one more example of how one student found ways of furthering the work of the National Federation of

the Blind, at first only with firm pushing from Dr. Jernigan, and later with my own creativity and confidence.

Ramona Walhof speaks from the podium during the banquet of the 2010 NFB National Convention.

I FIRST MET DR. JERNIGAN THE SUMMER AFTER I graduated from high school. I enrolled as a student in the Orientation and Adjustment Center at the Iowa Commission for the Blind in Des Moines. I was afraid to travel with a long white cane alone but determined to learn. This was my primary reason for attending the center. Soon after I arrived for training I was informed that my name had been sent in as a potential student in a course in Washington, DC, offering foreign language study to young blind adults. The first question posed to me was: Would I like to go to Kansas City to take the test to qualify? There was no reason not to take the test, so I did.

Dr. Jernigan was intimidating to me, but his conversation was always fascinating. When he came to the discussion class, there was often something unexpected he wanted the students to do. For example, he asked the students to determine the length and dates of their summer break. When he taught grammar class, there were very sensible rules to follow to understand and use the English language. When he invited us to his apartment or up to the roof for a cookout, there was good food and new ideas. I tried to keep quiet, thinking I did not know much, but Dr. Jernigan always got around to me. During one discussion class we talked about the girls who had just graduated from the school for the blind and why we did not shave our legs. We had never before been expected to do so, but we were not flattered to have this pointed out to the entire student body. We all went out and bought raisers immediately.

One afternoon Dr. Jernigan asked me to shape raw hamburger meat into patties and place them in racks for grilling. When I took the racks to him, he pronounced the hamburgers too small and sent me back to "lick my calf over." He used lots of folksy expressions. This one, he said, was something his mother used to say.

I did not have time that summer to read many of the books on Dr. Jernigan's recommended reading list. During the next ten years, I read most of them. Many of the books I discovered this way became an important part of my education. He never tried to describe to me what he looked for in a good book, but I soon understood that success and power were parts of it. And the subject matter was diverse: politics, westerns, history, motivational and inspirational material, science fiction, and more. Dr. Jernigan also read some stories aloud in classes or to individuals on weekends. He used his voice like a musical instrument, causing anything he read aloud to be even more memorable than the average story or book. Eventually I found a few books and stories to recommend to him, and we both found delight in sharing them. President Marc Maurer also shared with leaders of the NFB a few of Dr. Jernigan's favorite stories read and recorded by the master, and Maurer has also discovered some to add to the collection.

While I was a student in Des Moines, one evening somebody told me Dr. Jernigan wanted to see me in his apartment. That seemed odd, because I knew he had not been in his office that day. He had had his wisdom teeth removed. However, I timidly knocked on the door. Dr. Jernigan first told me about the removal of his wisdom teeth. I would learn that he was always willing to share medical details with those around him. His curiosity reached out for new experiences, whatever they were, and he was always happy to share this information. I listened to his description politely, knowing that it was not the primary reason I had been invited to his home.

Then I was informed that the test results from Kansas City had arrived that day. He told me that two of the other students from Iowa had ranked high enough to be accepted into the course. "And you," he said, his voice dripping with delight and pride, "Ranked in the top ten!" He paused and then asked, "Would you like to go to Washington, DC, to college?" It was clear that he thought this was, indeed, a good opportunity! I said, "I guess I would." Then he asked, "What will your mother think?" I said I thought she'd be all right. Dr. Jernigan told me I should let him talk to my mother. This seemed very strange, but I had no objections. Later, I realized precisely what his reasoning was. It was clear that I was not as sure as he that this was a good opportunity or that I wanted it. He had no questions at all, and he wanted my mother to be excited. She didn't say much, but she did help me gather things I would need and get ready to go. Dr. Jernigan told both of us that he would have a student from Iowa who had already been studying in Washington meet me and help me get settled, which he did. The rest was up to me, and I felt obligated to make the most of it, if for no other reason than to meet expectations and prove his confidence in me was not misplaced. Not to do well would have been like refusing to accept a gift, which was offered by the giver with joy.

I know that Dr. Jernigan never worried about how I would travel around Washington, DC, although I had just begun cane travel lessons. He paid blind people the compliment of giving them the opportunity to succeed and providing what training he could, then turning them loose. If I qualified for the course, he would see that I had the financial help necessary, and the rest was up to me. As director of a state rehabilitation agency for the blind, he believed it was his responsibility to do what he could to create opportunities. He had enough confidence in blind people to know that most of us would find a way, which we did. In order to be equal, we also must have the opportunity to fail, and some did. Although he often said he did not expect things to go well, he behaved as though he expected blind people to succeed. That gave me and many hundreds of others a huge boost toward success.

Academically I was unprepared for college, and socially I was definitely not ready for Georgetown University. I had been introduced to the philosophy that blind people can succeed, and I felt obligated to do so. It never occurred to me that I could not find a way, mostly because Dr. Jernigan seemed so sure I would.

After I completed the two-year course in the Russian language, I decided to finish my bachelor's degree at Georgetown University. I had no idea how unusual it was for a rehabilitation agency to pay tuition at a school such as Georgetown. I knew it was expensive and that I was expected to get good grades, and I did my best. One summer I went to Vermont and enrolled in an intensive course of Russian, where we were expected to speak only Russian for six weeks, and it was paid for by the Iowa Commission for the Blind. Another summer I traveled to Europe and spent two months in Russia, (the Soviet Union at the time), again with the help of the Iowa agency.

While I was in college, Dr. Jernigan kept in touch. I was young and made mistakes, but he never complained or criticized. When he came to DC on business, he sometimes would phone me or invite me to join his party for dinner. These dinners were always in a fancy restaurant, such as Trader Vic's, or at a hotel where the food would often be something I had never eaten before.

In the spring of 1965, Dr. Jernigan was planning the NFB convention which would occur that summer at the Mayflower hotel in Washington. He invited me and others to join him there for dinner and a yard of beer. Then he invited me to a meeting of the DC affiliate of the NFB to learn about the convention. I avoided the planning, but I attended most of the convention and discovered that this Federation had more to it than I had ever dreamed.

After the convention another Iowa student and a friend of mine, Tom Bickford, asked me to join the DC chapter. Tom was running for NFB of DC president and said he needed my vote. That was something I could do, and I knew that Tom would be a good president.

The summer after I graduated from Georgetown in 1967, I went to the NFB convention in Los Angeles. That was the year the NFB Student Division was organized. I got involved in planning and was elected secretary. Dr. Jernigan did not tell us what to do. Soon we were invited to go to Montreal to help organize students in Canada. Dr. Jernigan saw to it that we had the money to go. The newly-elected student Division president, Jim Gashel, and I took the Greyhound bus from Des Moines to Chicago and the train on to Montreal, and we did, indeed, help the Canadian students get organized.

After we returned to Des Moines, Dr. Jernigan got Dr. tenBroek on the phone so we could tell him what had occurred. Although he never said he was pleased with our work, we understood from this telephone call that he wanted to share with the NFB President something that mattered. Dr. tenBroek told us that whenever we wanted to organize blind people in another foreign country, that he would do what he could to help. We all had a good laugh when we said that we would soon be organizing in Illinois, and Dr. tenBroek said that would be considered a foreign country. There was no NFB affiliate in Illinois at the time.

The Board of the Student Division decided to write a *Handbook for Blind College Students*. When we had the text written, we had no idea how to get it printed or how to design a cover. Dr. Jernigan helped us find the money to print 500 copies, but he offered no input about anything else. However, the day we received delivery of the first 500 Handbooks, we also received an order from the Library of Congress for 500 Student Handbooks. How did the Library of Congress know about it in the first place? And what would they do with so many little booklets? I never knew. But Dr. Jernigan knew people at the Library of Congress, and so did the librarian at the Iowa Commission for the Blind, Florence Grannis. We had surprised ourselves with the success of this project. We ordered a second printing and continued to sell them for one dollar each. That publication has been re-written several times since, and I think each group of students who worked on it has learned.

Some events that Dr. Jernigan put in motion could not have been planned in detail, but he seemed prepared for anything. The second vice president of the NFB Student Division, Chuck Walhof, came to Iowa to study the programs during his winter break. The new director of the Idaho Commission for the Blind, another student of Dr. Jernigan, was planning to hire this young man as soon as he completed his college degree in the spring. Chuck took Braille, cane travel, and some other classes. Dr. Jernigan called me to his office one afternoon and asked me how I was getting along with the fellow from Idaho. I said I thought he was doing okay. Dr. Jernigan never underestimated the dynamics when young people got together. He said, "I have not been able to get this fellow to warm up to me. Why don't you take him on as a project?" I am sure I succeeded at that project. Chuck was already more committed to the Federation than I was, and his influence on me was considerable. The next summer I received a diamond ring at convention, a little matter that actually was announced in *The Des Moines Register.*

At the 1968 NFB convention in Des Moines, we held a seminar for blind college students. There were certainly a lot more students at that convention than the one before, many times more students! Federationists around the country had been inviting blind students to meetings and organizing groups. The Student Division didn't have much trouble planning an exciting agenda and conducting the program. Dr. Jernigan had kept an eye on us, but he turned us loose to learn as we progressed. One of his assistants made a few suggestions. We got advice from whomever we wanted; I don't remember all of the details. I just know it worked, and the number of students in the NFB began to increase in many parts of the country. I only served one year on that Board; my husband served two, and I think Jim Gashel served four years. The Student Division has changed many times since the 1960s, sometimes for better and sometimes not. The NFB has become stronger for recruiting blind students when they are young.

Dr. tenBroek died of cancer in the spring of 1968, and Dr. Jernigan moved from first vice president to become President of the NFB. Although he had helped plan conventions before, this one was his sole responsibility, and it was in Des Moines. He passed out jobs to all kinds of people. I was teaching in the training center at the time, and he asked me and the leader of a women's group to co-chair a committee to organize a tour of the Iowa Commission for the Blind building. All conventioneers would be invited to take this tour one afternoon. After the tour we would serve hamburgers to be grilled on the roof, Iowa sweet corn, and ice cream. It was my job to find people to be drivers, tour guides, and to be present at every stop along the tour. Commission staff, former students, and current students were well-trained, so I can't be sure whether I deserve much of the credit, but the activity that afternoon was very popular and seemed to work well. I only talked to Dr. Jernigan once or twice, but there were a lot of people involved in this tour, and he would have known if plans were not progressing well.

After a struggle because of my blindness, I was accepted in a Master of Arts in Teaching Russian program at the University of Chicago. Dr. Jernigan told me that he thought I should get that degree but take a year first and teach in the orientation center in Des Moines. I am sure he correctly understood that I had not yet attained as much confidence as would be desirable. That was a hard decision for me because I knew I would lose skill with the Russian language if I did not use it for a year. Nevertheless, I decided to take the job. I did learn a lot that year, but I never did go back for the Master's degree.

I was part of the organizing team that went to Illinois in August 1968 and immediately afterward I moved to Idaho. Chuck and I were married October 26, and then we spent a few days in Portland, Oregon. The morning after we returned to our new apartment in Boise, literally, before we had got out of bed, the telephone rang. Chuck answered it and passed it to me. Dr. Jernigan was putting an organizing team together to go to Kansas and wanted me to lead it. I was enrolled in some courses to get a teaching credential in Idaho, but my real concern about spending two weeks in Kansas was being away from my brand new husband. So I said I would think about it. However, Chuck was very practical about the matter. He said, "Right now the NFB values what you can do. If you don't do it, they may not ask again. I think you should go." It meant being away for almost two weeks after we had been married about that long. But I spent ten days in Kansas, and we organized a new affiliate there before Thanksgiving. Of course, I learned more than I gave.

When an organizing team went into a state where the NFB had no affiliate, it worked like this. We took with us a list of names of blind people. First we had to find each person, then go to visit him/her at home. The NFB representative would find out something about the blind person, and then tell him or her something about the Federation and what it meant to each of us personally. We would also ask for names of other blind people in the area. We came across very needy blind individuals and some with good leadership potential. Sometimes that blind person would get excited, but often he or she would not want to join. There were many reasons for this, from simple lack of motivation to fear of reprisals from local agencies or friends. Dr. Jernigan almost always came to the organizing meeting at the end of the work in that state. If organizers could get a person to that meeting, very often the new people would be excited by Dr. Jernigan and what he had to say. As an organizer, I always was fascinated to watch this process as Dr. Jernigan would read and discuss a constitution, answer questions, and then hold an election for officers. By 1975 we had NFB affiliates in every state and the District of Columbia, and later we organized in Puerto Rico.

During the last forty years, I have used the same process for organizing chapters in various cities with considerable success, but Dr. Jernigan's charm and presence were always an extra bonus. Kansas was organized in 1968. The next summer I helped to organize in Tennessee, North Carolina, Michigan, and Washington State. Later on I organized in Oregon and North Dakota. Many young Federationists became better leaders by participating on these organizing teams.

When we were married, Chuck was first vice president of the NFB of Idaho, and he had helped convince the Idaho legislature to create the Idaho Commission for the Blind. The new director of the Idaho agency had been a student of Dr. Jernigan's, and Chuck was hired as a rehab counselor immediately after he graduated from Boise State College (now Boise State University). We were both active in the NFB of Idaho, and I looked for and found jobs I could help with. We also had two babies. I worked for Head Start, taught a little Russian at Boise State College, and ran a food service business. By the time our son was born just before Christmas 1971, it was clear that my husband had serious diabetic kidney disease, and he lived only another four months.

When I left Iowa, Dr. Jernigan had said to me: If you ever need a job, you should contact me. I did not expect I would need to do that, but I did not forget. So after my husband died, I called Dr. Jernigan. He had a job for me if I could get there by the end of June. I was able to sell my house, pack up all our belongings, move to Des Moines with my two-year old daughter and five-month old son, find a babysitter and an apartment, and start work early in June. All this activity was in some ways the best therapy for a young widow.

Dr. Jernigan always had projects for the people around him. One day in 1973 he called me to his office and informed me that the NFB was going to make a film at the next convention. He said the theme would be "The Blind: An Emerging Minority." Then he said, "We have hired a film crew, and it will be your job to see that they film and record the right things." I was appalled! I was sure I could not do such a thing, and I said so. I explained that there were other people who could do it much better! Dr. Jernigan wanted to know who they were. I began to list some people, all of whom had more experience in the Federation than I. Dr. Jernigan patiently told me that each was either too busy at the convention or that I would do a better job than some I named. I had no difficulty with the idea that some people were too busy. However, it had never occurred to me that anybody might think I could do something better than those on the other list. I was so astonished that I had very little to say. I just told him I would do my best and left his office as fast as I could.

The convention was in Chicago, and Sharon Grosteven was assigned to work with the film crew as well. I realized that I did know who the right people were to be filmed, and they were very cooperative about scheduling appointments. We tried to get interesting pictures, but we ended up with too many "talking heads." After the convention we decided to shoot a little more film to add visual interest. Mary Ellen Anderson, now Mrs. Jernigan, was also assigned to work on the visual part of the film. When it was done, it did tell the story of the National Federation of the Blind. It was surprising how much we could squeeze into a half-hour. People were very complimentary about the film. They were not talking to me personally, but I always wondered if I really had done as good a job getting the material together as somebody else would have, especially if they knew more about film making. Then one of the commission staff members went to a meeting of rehabilitation personnel in Chicago. When he returned, he reported that some of the people who did not like the Federation (they said we were too radical) were talking about our film. They were complaining because it had been shown on TV—all twenty-seven minutes of it. The reason they were complaining was because the film was so good! It was so effective at presenting the story of the Federation! For the first time, I really believed I had accomplished what Dr. Jernigan had asked me to do. Although others did the technical work, I had done my part. If our detractors thought the film was good, what better compliment could be paid!

Dr. Jernigan always said that a measure of intelligence was that a person could be dropped naked in a strange city or country and come out well. I never hoped to put it to the test, but I did begin to think of changing things, and I began to want to try some new ideas.

I thought our students could learn Braille faster and be better readers and writers if we presented Braille lessons differently, and I started to work on some new lessons. There was another Braille teacher, Mabel Nading, at the Iowa Commission for the Blind who had far more experience teaching Braille than I did. After I persuaded her to help, we worked on *Beginning Braille for Adults* together. I wrote the lessons, and Mabel and I both tested them with our students. Mabel found errors and made valuable suggestions for changes. When I talked to Dr. Jernigan, he cautioned me not to let it interfere with the classes we were teaching. He agreed that the Braille production people in the library could help too.

The Braille lessons that had formerly been used were in three volumes, and many students did not complete them. Braille includes about two hundred abbreviations, and using these increases the speed of most readers and writers. But confronting the prospect of learning them seems daunting to most beginners, so I thought we could introduce these contractions earlier and faster. We could also give encouragement right in the book as the lessons progressed. All of this turned out to be true. One of our students completed our new lessons in three weeks and built her speed to 150 words per minute in six months. As far as I know, this had never happened before. However, it has been repeated! Just the other day, I met a young woman who told me she had learned Braille using our book. She said the best words she ever read were, "You can proudly tell your friends that you have learned the Braille alphabet!" That kind of feedback is the best possible reward for all the work invested in writing.

Ramona Walhof stands between her children, Chris Walhof and Laura Baumgartner, after receiving the Jacobus tenBroek Award in 2007.

When I had time, I wrote an article about raising my children as a single blind mother. When I showed it to Dr. Jernigan, he suggested a different title: "I am a Blind Mother Striving to Keep My Children from Corruption." He said this article would be useful, and it has been. Then I wrote a small book entitled *Questions Kids Ask about Blindness.* I was not a particularly good writer, but I thought there was a need for some materials about blindness not already available. *Questions Kids Ask About Blindness* has been circulating for more than thirty years, and *Beginning Braille for Adults* has been reprinted at least three times and revised once. Then Dr. Jernigan asked me to try to write something about compliance with Section 504 of the Rehabilitation Act. In order to do this I had to learn more about the Act. He took what I gave him, added to it, and printed it. I think it was useful as well. So I have been writing various things about blindness and programs for the blind for more than thirty years. I have never made any money as a writer, but I hope the materials I have written have provided guidance and support for those for whom they were intended. And I meet people who tell me that is so.

In 1979 Dr. Jernigan opened the new headquarters for the National Federation of the Blind in Baltimore. He took charge of remodeling old buildings at 1800 Johnson Street to change it into a modern and effective facility.

Unfortunately, his successor at the Iowa Commission for the Blind was a disappointment to many who thought the agency would continue to operate largely the way it had under Dr. Jernigan's leadership. Because this did not happen, several staff members from Iowa also moved to Maryland when positions at NFB headquarters became available. I moved in March of 1979. My first position was director of the National Blindness Information Center. I handled correspondence, gave tours of the new facility, called members for a variety of reasons, and continued to write new materials. My second position was assistant director of Job Opportunities for the Blind, a project in partnership with the US Department of Labor. This was an opportunity to develop new employment for the blind, educate employers about blindness, and help blind people search for jobs. It became an effective project. I liked the work, and I liked living in Baltimore.

However, one day Dr. Jernigan called me to his office to tell me that the Idaho Commission for the Blind needed a new director. Chairman Norm Gardner and Dr. Jernigan offered me the opportunity to travel to Boise for an interview. Since my husband had been part of the group who worked so hard to create the independent Idaho agency twelve years earlier, I wanted to help maintain that governmental structure. After an interview with the Commission Board in Idaho, I was offered the job and accepted it. My children and I moved to Idaho immediately to the dismay of my children who were then in middle school.

We all believed that the Idaho Commission for the Blind had been modeled after the Iowa Commission for the Blind, which Dr. Jernigan had directed for twenty years from 1958 to 1978. When I arrived in Idaho I discovered problems I had not expected, and before long, I was in trouble. Some of the staff resented my attempts to bring the agency in line with what it needed to be. Dr. Jernigan soon began to say, "You are on the scene. You know better than I what to do, and you must make the decisions." I had to lean on him less!

I made mistakes, but some things I did worked very well, and the Orientation Center thrived. I understood it the best because of six years of experience in a similar center in Iowa. Our students made wonderful progress, but I was not able to win the confidence of all of the staff. And the governor wanted to reorganize, placing the Commission for the Blind under another agency. I had been hired with the understanding that we must do everything possible to resist this, and I did. About sixteen months after I arrived in Idaho, I was fired. My dismissal was a blow to the NFB of Idaho and to many on the Commission staff. The chairman of the Commission Board was also the president of the NFB of Idaho, and he stood rock-solid. When his term was over, he was not reappointed by the governor. This was the first time since the creation of the agency that the NFB of Idaho president had not served on the Idaho Commission for the Blind Board. It was the beginning of some bad times in Idaho. We could rebuild the Idaho affiliate and the agency, but it would take time.

I felt I had to stay in Idaho in order to support those who had supported me. I needed a job and decided to go into business. Dr. Jernigan put me in touch with a fundraiser who had done very well for some of the NFB affiliates. I spent a week in Utah studying what they were doing. Because the population of the state was so small, I was concerned that it would not work in Idaho. Dr. Jernigan said, "You have to decide. I am not going to make this decision." Of course, I didn't really want him to make the decision, but he understood that I would have taken seriously any suggestion he made. The agreement I made with the fundraiser was such that I would not lose money for the first few months. If I could be successful in Idaho, the affiliate certainly needed the money. I decided to give it a try.

Before the end of three months, I knew that the process was wrong. I tried to discuss this with the man who was sponsoring the business, but he had no wish to talk about it. So I just kept going. As the figures grew worse, my sponsor said nothing to me, but he did tell Dr. Jernigan that he wanted out of Idaho. By then, I was pretty sure I knew how to correct the problems. So we reached a financial agreement, and I proceeded on my own.

The first year was in the black! In time, I was able to open three additional offices in other states, but the first one was the best. I managed the Boise office, and it did a lot of work for the Federation besides fundraising. It was a challenge to keep strong managers in the other offices. They all raised needed funds, and we did a lot of other things: found blind people who needed the Federation, wrote and printed brochures and flyers about blindness, and distributed a lot of information. I continued in this business for more than twenty years.

Before the end of the 1980s, I was elected president of the NFB of Idaho and re-elected every two years for more than a decade. I served on the national NFB Board for most of this time. Through the years, I had become tougher and more imaginative. Dr. Jernigan and I kept in touch until he died, but the relationship evolved and changed.

Dr. Jernigan asked for my input on many matters outside Idaho, as well, and often he used my suggestions. As long as he lived, I thoroughly enjoyed spending time with my mentor and friend. Whether it was a meeting, a dinner, or a phone call, he always had something interesting to say. Surprising to me, he was equally interested in what I had to say. He liked to know what his friends were doing and why, and he had lots of friends. Many of his students grew into friends. Many of his business associates evolved into friends. Many of his colleagues in the NFB became close friends. Even many of those who began by disagreeing with him wound up becoming friends. He was loved and admired both by those who worked with him on a daily basis and by those who heard his speeches and read what he wrote, but had relatively little immediate association with him. I counted my friendship with Dr. Jernigan as one of the most valuable in my life. No one outside my immediate family has had more influence on me and my thinking or brought me more satisfaction and joy. The fact that I am only one of many who feels this way is eloquent testimony to the wonder and scope of the man.

CHAPTER 18

THE TIES THAT BIND

by Barbara Pierce

Note: Barbara Pierce has worked tirelessly in the National Federation of the Blind for more than forty years. She is an articulate, thoughtful, and charming spokeswoman for the organization in Ohio and throughout the country. She is perhaps best known as the past editor of the largest and most influential magazine in work with the blind, the *Braille Monitor.* However, she has also worked actively for decades as a member of the NFB Scholarship and Resolutions Committees; assisted parents of blind children; served as president of the NFB of Ohio; and represented the NFB president at conferences inside and outside of the Federation. Barbara has handled press relations at national conventions, Washington seminars, NFB demonstrations, and numerous other events.

Barbara and her husband Bob raised three children, spent Bob's sabbaticals in England, held positions of leadership in their church, and are well known as contributing citizens in Oberlin, Ohio. In the following pages Barbara describes herself and her relationship with Dr. Jernigan. Her comments demonstrate how and

why she is one of the people who learned from him to continue to build and refine opportunities for the blind around the world.

Barbara Pierce mixes up some NFB tea with Dr. Jernigan at the National Center for the Blind, 1990.

I CONSIDER THAT I KNEW DR. JERNIGAN FROM January of 1974 until his death. That January was the first time I listened to recordings of his speeches, and doing so gave me the feeling that I had met the mind and spirit of this remarkable man. It was not until that June that I actually had direct contact with him. I had written him a letter. I am not sure how I expected him to respond, but it was certainly not the long, thoughtful, prompt letter I received. I could not have been more surprised or delighted if the letter had come from the president of the United States or the queen of England. That was always my experience of Dr. Jernigan—a man who gave and expected more of himself and me than I did.

Part of his genius was challenging the people around him to do more than they thought themselves capable of. For example, he told me fairly early in my life as a Federationist that he wanted me to begin representing the NFB in media interviews. This was unsettling news, but, since he had assigned me the job, I began reading the *Braille Monitor* even more carefully and listening to presidential releases with great attention. Then I went out and did my best. You always wanted to do your best for him because he always gave his best to all of us, and that best was very good indeed.

Living as he did on the public stage, every evolution in his thought, every change in a lifetime of behavior became public property. I remember his reflections in print when he concluded that he must walk a picket line. As one who came of age in the sixties, I found nothing perturbing about picketing, but I was powerfully impressed at Dr. Jernigan's willingness to rethink his long-held values and to reveal his conclusions with everyone who read the *Braille Monitor*. When I became the *Monitor* editor, I tried to draw on his example as I found myself telling thousands of readers my personal and professional struggle to grow. I have come to understand that such honesty and openness help to strengthen the ties that bind this movement together as a family whose members genuinely care for and respect each other.

His courage, humanity, integrity, and leadership notwithstanding, the most wide-reaching impact that Dr. Jernigan had on my life was his teaching me to use and appreciate language. I was an English major in college, so I already had a working knowledge of grammar and correct punctuation when I found the Federation. But I hated to write. I suspect that, even in my earliest days in the Federation, President Jernigan recognized that I could write a literate sentence, and he ensured that I would have plenty of opportunity to use that skill. He appointed me to the public relations committee and saw that I was invited to a PR seminar. I began helping to write press releases at national conventions and even coauthored a PR handbook. I was far from comfortable carrying out these assignments, but the NFB has always challenged its members to reach beyond their knowledge of themselves and their strengths to see what more they can accomplish.

By 1987 I had been chairing the PR committee for about seven years and had been president of the NFB of Ohio since 1984. I was working full time for Oberlin College—a job that I had found the courage to apply for, accept, and succeed in largely because of what the NFB had taught me about my ability to compete on terms of equality with my sighted colleagues. My husband and I had three growing children, a son at Yale and two daughters in high school. I was busy and happy and felt that I was doing my best to embody the Federation's philosophy.

I was sitting in a 1987 convention session when Dr. Jernigan called me to the platform to speak to him. To my astonishment and dismay he asked me to try my hand at writing that year's convention roundup. He told me to study what he had written the year before and then give it a try. I was dubious about my ability to produce anything that would save him time, but again I did my best, and with a bit of first-aid he was able to use it.

In 1988, when Dr. Jernigan asked me to write the convention roundup for the second time, I should have been suspicious. After all, he had been telling the world that he had to find a *Monitor* editor because after ten years he could not continue to do that job along with all the other responsibilities he was carrying. I can't remember exactly what I was thinking, but I had only a nebulous sinking feeling in my stomach when he asked me to come to Baltimore in August. His invitation in that visit to leave my job in order to become associate editor of the *Braille Monitor* made me a bit sick. I had never before done anything like editing. I did not think of myself as a writer, even though much of my Oberlin job was writing everything from letters to brochures. Deciding to accept his invitation was one of the braver decisions I have ever made. Looking back on it, it was also one of the best steps I have ever taken.

For almost ten years I had the privilege of working closely with Dr. Jernigan. Watching him write was fascinating. He usually began an article seated at his desk, his secretary in the chair across from him with a steno pad on her knee. After thinking a moment, he would dictate a title. He might throw out two or three suggestions before he got it right, but he never began writing without at least a working title. Then the sentences began coming, word by word, complete with correct punctuation. Soon the phone would ring. He would

262 | NATIONAL FEDERATION OF THE BLIND

stop and deal with whatever the call brought; then he would ask to hear the last paragraph or, more often, everything he had written so far. He might well make changes or even rewrite or insert an entire sentence or paragraph. Eventually he might get up to pace around his office as he dictated or corrected text. I often marveled that his secretaries could decipher the layers of correction. So it went, interruption after interruption, hour after hour. Some time late in that first day of observation he turned to me and said: "People think that those who write well throw long touchdown passes; they don't realize that we have to grind out our progress yard by yard on the ground, just like everybody else."

When he completed a draft or a day's work on a draft, he would ask for the text in Braille. That's what he took home to read over. The next day he was back, draft in hand, to read the text aloud and make the changes he had decided upon so his secretary could pencil them in on a print copy. He would listen carefully to his own voice as he read. His ear told him when a subtle alteration in the text would improve the work. "That will have a better ring," he would comment as he substituted a word, and, when you thought about it, he was right.

That was how he began teaching me to shape my own writing. Gradually I learned to avoid word repetition, the passive voice, and jargon words like "utilize" or "usage" instead of short, vigorous words like "use." Having seen the merciless rigor with which he edited his own writing, I found it exciting rather than depressing to watch him tinker with and rework my text. The process was always instructive.

Not until I began to train my successor did I fully appreciate how much faith, tact, and patience I had received at Dr. Jernigan's gentle hands. He never tried to alter my voice. In fact he warned me that I must find my own voice and outlook. I could not, he warned, make myself into an imitation of him. I could only succeed as *Monitor* editor if I made myself independent. Then he had the discipline to keep his hands off my writing enough to let me find my own way, and gradually I did. He was so subtle and sure-handed that I was hardly aware of the training that was going on. Only once did he insist on a prohibition. He told me that I was forbidden to use the word "desperately" for an entire year. I realized that I was overusing the word, thereby undermining its impact. Even today I hardly ever use that word in my writing.

Then there were the Braille lessons. I mastered the Braille code as a teenager, but I never bothered to work on reading speed. Decoding those little dots was slow and hard, and I never saw anyone read quickly. Not until I listened to those speeches in 1974 did I realize that it was possible to read Braille at speaking speed and faster. And not until I began working closely with Dr. Jernigan did anyone suggest that there was any point in my trying to make up the deficit in my education rather than complaining about it.

As usual, Dr. Jernigan didn't just suggest that I do something about it. When I hesitantly asked whether he thought I could increase my speed, he offered to help. That was the beginning of a remarkable period of investigation and discovery. Dr. Jernigan undertook to analyze how he used his hands when he read. He taught me to anchor my left hand and read the first few words of each line with that index finger while the rest of the hand marked the place and held on to the page—a handy skill when reading standing up. Meanwhile he explained that the right index finger reads the right two thirds of the line, and the middle and ring fingers travel lightly across the space at the top of the line, keeping place and gathering information about the tops of the letters. He would often interrupt his own proofreading to point out some detail his ring finger had discovered.

Unfortunately I don't think I increased speed as rapidly as Dr. Jernigan expected, but he was always optimistic and encouraging. Despite the important matters constantly demanding his attention, he regularly inquired whether I was continuing to read every day and how my speed was coming.

I can attribute many, many of the skills I use every day without thinking about them to my years of close observation of Dr. Jernigan. When I conduct a meeting efficiently and fairly, when I comfort a newly blind person or give hope to the parent of a blind child, when I write a difficult letter or quickly turn a mediocre article into one that will inspire readers, when I wend my way through political minefields to help rescue a chapter or affiliate—I recognize that I have my mentor and very dear friend to thank for these skills. But mostly I treasure the memories I have of watching him work and write so that we can all continue to share in his wisdom and commitment to helping blind people.

My work in the Federation under Dr. Jernigan's guidance and after his death included several kinds of activity. In 2000 and 2001 we devoted a good number of pages in the *Braille Monitor* to the activities of Erik Weihenmayer, the amazing blind mountain climber who finally summited Mt. Everest on May 25, 2001. The *Monitor* story that recounted the final stage of the adventure was "Weihenmayer Reaches the Top," which appeared in the July 2001 issue. I wasn't at Base Camp, but I was linked by email and satellite phone to the climbers and helped to keep them in touch with the thousands of people around the world who were following their adventure. NFB President Maurer assigned me to work with the team, the PR firm marketing the climb, and those working on the website. In my memory I can't separate the various components of that responsibility. I only know that the relief and pleasure I felt when I learned that nineteen members of the team had made it to the top and had all returned to the highest camp in safety was like nothing I have ever felt before or since.

Preparing the January/February 1999 issue of the *Monitor* was the hardest editorial work I have ever done. That was the obituary issue for my beloved friend and mentor, Kenneth Jernigan. I wanted it to capture the essence of the man, and nothing that anyone could have written could have done him justice. For me, as for many others of my generation, he represented the best in us. He embodied our highest ideals, our most determined and principled positions. He was my friend and the blind person whose good opinion has meant the most to me. He taught me to think politically and to write with clarity. I wanted that issue to represent all of that. I am certain that I fell short of my goal, but I also know that reading that issue will give anyone who did not know the man the best understanding of who he was and what he stood for.

The last letter I wrote to Dr. Jernigan, September 11, 1998, just a month before he died, contained my heartfelt promise to him and to myself. I have done my best to keep that pledge.

"We who love you will continue to nurture and build the organization you have given your life to define and strengthen. The time and thought and love you have poured into shaping me, I promise I will pass on as best I can to those who come after me. You believed in me at a time in my life when I hardly dared believe in myself. I promise you now that I will do my best to pass on what you have given me—the love, the commitment, the wisdom, the patient concern, and the dedication. To whatever degree I possess these things, I will offer them to the movement you have built and taught me to cherish."

CHAPTER 19

OF FRIENDSHIP AND FLYING

by Larry A. McKeever

Note: Larry McKeever and Kenneth Jernigan shared a close friendship that lasted thirty years. McKeever mentions several examples of how they worked together. He refers to Dr. Jernigan's feelings about air travel. Early in his career in the 1950s, Kenneth Jernigan flew on commercial airlines often to all parts of the country. After several extremely rough flights, he lost his enthusiasm for this mode of travel. Those who knew him during the 1960s and later remember that Dr. Jernigan avoided flying commercially whenever he could. Perhaps few people realized that he felt differently about flying on private planes with friends who were pilots. Larry McKeever was not the only pilot who flew Kenneth Jernigan to one place or another, but he tells of some memorable flights.

After Dr. Jernigan's death, Larry McKeever helped at NFB conventions serving as assistant to Mary Ellen Jernigan, Chairperson of Convention Organization and Activities. He continued to do this as long as he lived. He died in 2007. The account below is reprinted from the January 1999 *Braille Monitor*.

*Larry McKeever runs the sound board during
the 1989 NFB National Convention.*

I first met Kenneth Jernigan in the mid-1960s. I had been reading for the Iowa Library for several years, and when I returned from Australia, I began work at a classical music station in Des Moines.

Shortly after that Dr. Jernigan called and wondered if this off-beat station would be interested in a program of poetry. Our friendship began with the production of those programs. I was immediately impressed with his knowledge—not only of poetry but of people and the world. His dedication to the Federation was apparent from the beginning.

Later that year Jim Valliant, Dr. Jernigan's administrative assistant at the Iowa Commission for the Blind, resigned to return to Maryland. Dr. Jernigan and I discussed the possibility of my assuming that position. After an intense interview and testing I was hired and attended my first NFB convention in Washington. We eventually decided that this was not the right position for me, so I assumed another job at the Commission. Mary Ellen Anderson, now Jernigan, joined the staff at that time. That was the beginning of my friendship with both of these remarkable people, a friendship which has lasted to this day.

Early in 1968 I started a recording studio. Not too long after that Dr. Jernigan called saying that the person who had been recording the conventions was retiring. He wondered if I was interested in that job, as well as recording and producing the *Braille Monitor*. I began reading the *Monitor* and working closely with Dr. Jernigan, who usually read the articles he had written. My last *Braille Monitor* and convention recording were done just as the studio at the new NFB headquarters opened in 1988.

I remember the discussions about the difficult situation in Iowa in 1978—whether to stay and fight the naysayers or move the NFB offices. When Dr. Jernigan decided to go to Baltimore, I was saddened, but I agreed with the decision. I also remember the first time I went to Baltimore. The NFB occupied a smallish office on St. Paul Street with boxes and furniture everywhere. What a difference between that tiny space and the magnificent headquarters today at the NFB Jernigan Institute! Kenneth Jernigan was the worker, the dreamer, and always the builder.

Speaking of building, later Dr. Jernigan called me to Baltimore to discuss building a recording studio. We planned the rooms and the settings just as they exist today. Once they were built, I came again to Baltimore to equip the studio and help find someone to run it.

Everyone is familiar with Dr. Jernigan's dislike of flying. Many have heard a description of the eventful flight that Dr. Jernigan, Iowa Commission librarian Mrs. Florence Grannis, and I made to Boise, Idaho, in the early 1970s—particularly Dr. Jernigan's embellished version of that trip. In truth, we flew in rough weather across the mountains. Mrs. Grannis became ill and refused to return to Des Moines in that small plane that I was flying. After the conference in Boise, Dr. Jernigan and I flew together back to Des Moines. The weather was not quite so rough, but there are always winds above those mountains. Why Dr. Jernigan felt more confidence in me in that small plane than in a commercial pilot flying a large plane is hard for me to understand, and many simply cannot believe it. Nevertheless, the two of us shared some exciting flights together and thoroughly enjoyed them.

But fewer knew of two other flights we made in the single-engine plane I flew. Before the Idaho trip Dr. Jernigan, Mrs. Grannis, and I flew into Chicago for a meeting. After landing my back gave out. By the time their meeting was over I was not fit to fly. So we quickly went to Midway airport to get a commercial flight. It was Dr. Jernigan's ministrations that got me safely back to Des Moines. (I recovered the plane a few days later.)

Dr. Jernigan kept sufficient faith in my piloting ability to make one later trip to Tennessee. This one was uneventful. But on the way I was able to acquaint him with the operation of the airplane, the radios, and the air system. I remain convinced that, if something had happened to me on that flight, with the help of another plane to talk him down he could have landed the airplane safely if not prettily.

For the last three years of his life, I was privileged to serve as personal assistant to Dr. Jernigan at national conventions. I was with him most of the time, attending sessions, travelling between meetings, and helping wherever needed. I also helped supply the Jernigan Suite, did necessary errands, and on occasion brought dignitaries to the convention. It's impossible to describe the wide-ranging discussions we had in our walks between meetings and after the day's work was done.

By the time we reached Dallas in 1998, Dr. Jernigan had fought lung cancer for nearly a year and was tired from the illness and the treatments. But he carried on in convention sessions very nearly at the top of his form. Doing so took a great deal out of him. On the Saturday after convention, as I was leaving, he took my hand and said: "Mr. McKeever, if I don't make it to next year, find someone else to work for and tip one for me." I assured him at the time that I would tip several for him, and I did.

I feel distinctly blessed to have known Kenneth Jernigan. Tens of thousands will miss him because of the attitudes he changed. Thousands more will miss him because of the opportunities he made available. I will miss him because he was my friend.

CHAPTER 20

São Paulo and Around the World

by Lawrence F. Campbell

Note: Larry Campbell worked for thirty-five years in the education and rehabilitation of blind and visually impaired persons, twenty-five of which were international work. He worked in more than sixty countries and served as vice president and president of the International Council for Education of People with Visual Impairments (ICEVI). He was also international program administrator for the Overbrook School for the Blind which is located in Philadelphia, Pennsylvania. Dr. Jernigan regarded him as a well-connected and effective person in the international arena in work with the blind. Here Larry Campbell describes one experience they shared and includes the reaction of some in the international community to Dr. Jernigan's presentation.

AS WORD OF DR. JERNIGAN'S DEATH SPREAD throughout the world, my telephone rang off the hook, and my email basket was full—all asking the same question: what can we do to express our feelings about this great leader who so influenced thinking, not only here in the U.S. but in some of the remotest regions of the world, where equality for blind people is, in many cases, still a dream? Many fond memories of my nearly twenty years of association with Dr. Jernigan and the NFB run through my mind. Let me share with you one of the fondest.

Larry Campbell, 1999.

In 1997 ICEVI convened its tenth World Conference in São Paulo, Brazil. As chairperson of the Program Committee one of my most important tasks was to identify a keynote speaker who would deliver a thought-provoking address that would set the tone for this meeting, whose theme concerned establishing partnerships among parents, consumers, and educators. Dr. Jernigan immediately came to mind, and he graciously accepted my invitation.

Dr. and Mrs. Jernigan arrived in São Paulo a couple of days before the conference was to open, and after settling them into their hotel and giving them a very quick orientation to points of interest in the area, which included a local crafts market, I returned to the many last-minute details associated with organizing such a World Conference.

The conference was to open with Dr. Jernigan's keynote address at the State Palace on Sunday evening. Late that afternoon I stopped by the hotel to find that indeed Dr. Jernigan had fully explored the local crafts market and had purchased some onyx cordial glasses of which he was very fond. I think some of you here may have used those glasses, and I want to assure you that any and all of us who returned to Brazil after that meeting were under standing orders to scour that craft market to find more of them. After all, the NFB is a large organization, and a dozen onyx cordial glasses don't go far at an NFB function.

That afternoon Dr. Jernigan inquired as to how we would get to the State Palace. Earlier that same day Victor Siaulys, the parent of a blind child and the chairperson of the Host Committee, had suggested to me that we use his helicopter to travel to the State Palace. Ground traffic in the area is always heavy, and we were concerned it would take a long time to travel from the hotel to the State Palace. Without even checking with Dr. Jernigan, I graciously declined, knowing how he felt about being airborne.

When I told Dr. Jernigan that a car would pick us up and that I had declined the use of Victor's helicopter, he paused for a moment and said: "Well, Larry, Mrs. Jernigan has never been in a helicopter before, so why not." As you can imagine, this took me by surprise, but then again Dr. Jernigan was always full of surprises. A quick call to the pilot Sergio, and a few minutes later Dr. and Mrs. Jernigan and I were at the local heliport, boarding a 6-passenger Bell helicopter and on our way to the State Palace. While Mrs. Jernigan provided a running commentary, Dr. Jernigan, with his unquenchable curiosity, fired one question after another at the pilot Sergio, who later confided in me that he was quite certain that with a few more flights Dr. Jernigan would be asking to take the controls. I think it must have been the first time in his life that Dr. Jernigan had been airborne and thoroughly enjoyed the experience. In fact, after landing he still wanted to learn as much as he could—how helicopters were constructed and how they operated. For a while I thought the conference might open without our keynote speaker.

Upon arrival in the auditorium of the State Palace, Dr. Jernigan asked me to orient him to the room and then to walk him through the route from his seat in the front row to the podium. Two passes through these paces and he was ready to do it alone.

It will not surprise anyone here to learn that his keynote address was magnificent and extremely well received by the 1,500 delegates and local dignitaries on hand that evening. However, beyond the powerful words of his keynote address there was something else at work in the auditorium of the State Palace that evening. It is reflected in the following editorial which appeared several months later in the *Asia Appraiser*, the regional magazine of ICEVI/Asia. I think it sums up what Dr. Jernigan has represented to so many educators throughout the world. It is printed below.

"When Dr. Kenneth Jernigan of the National Federation of the Blind of the United States of America walked independently to the dais of the State Palace in São Paulo to deliver the keynote address of the tenth World Conference of the International Council for Education of People with Visual Impairment, there was thunderous applause. He was independent, elegant, and reassured the conference that visually impaired persons can come out of the social conditioning that they are inferior.

"A delegate in the back row shouted with joy, 'That is beautiful, Dr. Jernigan; why don't others emulate you?' Orientation and mobility are vital aspects of the independent living of any visually impaired person. The independent movement of Dr. Jernigan made thousands of people assembled at the Palace proud.

"The striking statement 'Leading by Example' made by Dr. Jernigan during his keynote address was relevant to what he had demonstrated. His powerful address set the trend for an excellent conference. After delivering the address, no one was needed to bring him back to his seat. He did it by himself. He, through his action, had demonstrated that he leads others by example. He also indicated how parents, teachers, administrators, and other professionals in the field should lead by example in whatever work they do.

"We can make our visually impaired children outstanding if they are led by example. Let us make them excellent in education, mobility, rehabilitation, and integration. In doing so, let us emulate Dr. Jernigan and his powerful statement, 'Leading by Example'!"

CHAPTER 21

COME RUN WITH ME
A QUALITY LIFE

by Mary Ellen Halverson

Note: Mary Ellen Halverson is a quiet woman who raised two children and then went to work as a Braille teacher for the Idaho Commission for the Blind. From the time of her training at the Commission in the 1960s, she has been one of the hundreds of students who have loved and respected Dr. Jernigan. Her father credited Dr. Jernigan with giving Mary Ellen back her freedom during college when her vision deteriorated noticeably. This feeling of love and gratitude on the part of her parents may not have been communicated to Dr. Jernigan, but his work was as important to them as it was to Mary Ellen. Here she tells of some of her experiences as a student and throughout her life. Dr. Jernigan used many of the same methods with students year after year, but they always seemed personal to each student.

IN AUGUST 1966 I ARRIVED AT THE IOWA COMMISSION for the Blind in Des Moines, Iowa, where I was to be a student in the Orientation and Adjustment Center. I was twenty-one years old and had completed my sophomore year at the University of Iowa. I had attended College Day, which was sponsored by the Commission earlier that year, and I had made a pact with my new friend Joanne that we would both enroll at the Training Center at the same time. This agreement was great moral support for both of us. We had no idea how the coming months would change our lives forever, thanks to Kenneth Jernigan and the world-renowned training program he had established.

John and Mary Ellen Halverson, 1989.

When I became a student in the center that August, I still had a little vision and wasn't sure about this term "blind" as it applied to me. I had never used a white cane and felt conspicuous with it in my hand. I had spent the years in high school and college trying to hide the fact that I could not see well—not advertise it! For example, at mealtime when I went through the cafeteria line in the dorm, I would not ask anyone what the various dishes were. I just guessed by their colors, and I did end up with surprises frequently. It seemed to me that was better than letting the cafeteria workers know I couldn't see the food. I usually sat alone to eat because I could not recognize friends. Occasionally someone would call out to me, and then I had the rare enjoyment of eating with another person.

Another memory is that in a psychology class I was taking, one could earn extra credit by going to some psych experiments in the evenings. Since I couldn't see after dark, my extra credit was limited to early fall when it stayed light longer. I tried going to one experiment when it was dark, but afterward I really could not see any curbs or steps. I finally just followed some other girls home to the dorm, but that was not pleasant. And because I couldn't see at night, dating was mostly out of the question. I made up excuses about how I had to study—which I really did. I earned very good grades as a result of studying every night; therefore I told myself I was doing quite well in college.

In classes I wrote notes with a pen but had to hurry home to rewrite them in larger print so I could actually read them. I had to put my face about two inches from the paper to see what I was reading and writing and did not want people to see this embarrassing and odd-looking position.

During my freshman year at the University of Iowa, I met two women in my dorm who were blind. They were very up-front about it. I really enjoyed going to the cafeteria with them because I too could benefit from the cafeteria workers telling them what food was on the line. I also enjoyed going other places with them as they skillfully used their long white canes wherever we went. I noticed that people were courteous and helpful to them, giving directions when asked, etc. I noticed—even envied—their freedom and the degree of independence they had. They said their canes made them more independent.

I had many long talks with my new friends Susan and Arlene during that year. I also reluctantly began attending meetings of the NFB Student Association. After the first few meetings, I hurried out as soon as the meeting was adjourned because I did not want to be caught by someone to talk about my blindness, or as I would have preferred to say "my poor sight." I did learn at these meetings that Susan and Arlene had taken training at the Commission for the Blind in Des Moines.

When I moved into the Iowa Commission for the Blind building at 524 4th Street in Des Moines that hot summer day in 1966, I did not realize that I was in for a life-changing experience. My mind, heart, and soul would be changed forever by the director of the Iowa Commission for the Blind, Mr. Kenneth Jernigan, and the training program he created.

I recently read that the Greek philosopher Plutarch, who lived centuries ago, said, "The mind is not a vessel to be filled but a fire to be kindled." I knew immediately that this is what Mr. Jernigan had done for my mind and for my whole being. One can have all of the facts and statistics about blindness, but unless there is a "fire kindled," no significant change will occur.

Kenneth Jernigan was the teacher, and I was his student. He had passion and belief in blind people, which I learned from him and began to practice in my daily life.

Mr. J., as we students fondly referred to him, led me through many different experiences in class and in other activities. One example that comes to mind occurred when I was a fairly new student. I was outside having a cane travel lesson, moving rather cautiously and slowly, and Mr. Jernigan came along and said to me, "Mary Ellen, take my arm and let's run!" We ran down the sidewalk laughing—and a spark was kindled.

Another time he took a couple of us to an NFB state convention in New York. As I understood many years later, the drive to and from New York was in itself another one of Mr. Jernigan's teaching opportunities. The many hours of driving were not wasted! As we traveled, he told us of the history and current politics of the New York NFB affiliate, taught us more about our national organization and its history, and conducted a grammar class as we rode along.

Teaching grammar was one of Mr. Jernigan's favorite ways to teach students to think clearly. He had a very specialized understanding of grammar, and he taught us to analyze sentences and parts of speech in a way that was very useful. I still remember much of what I learned. One surprise to me that I learned on that trip forty years ago was that no one word is always the same part of speech. We tried to think of examples to disprove this fact, but of course that was impossible. Mr. Jernigan greatly enjoyed the Socratic method of teaching he used in those grammar classes. I could hear the pleasure in his voice as we learned to think.

While attending the New York state convention, we went to convention sessions where we met lots of competent blind individuals, as well as many people who had never had the opportunity for training in the skills of blindness that we were learning. I was not expecting this because I was from Iowa, and I was used to seeing well-trained blind individuals who could travel competently with a white cane, read Braille, and speak with confidence.

Another aspect of our training and education on the New York trip was that Mr. Jernigan took us on a boat out to Niagara Falls. We experienced the thrill of the mist and roar of the famous falls. Although I did not know this at the time, he was teaching us that we can still enjoy touring, have a great time, and experience life to the fullest as blind people. His enjoyment of this excursion and of seeing us enjoy another new experience was infectious and endeared him to me even more.

By the fall of 1967 I was ready to return to the University of Iowa and continue working on my degree in Spanish. I walked back onto the campus with a white cane and armed with good beginning Braille reading and writing skills. Best of all I knew that it was respectable to be blind, and I no longer had to hide it. I felt free to ask questions about things I could not see and was not embarrassed about it. In fact, I was excited and proud to be a member of the National Federation of the Blind. I have been committed to help our organization work to improve the lives of blind individuals ever since. That fall, I had hope for the future and looked forward to encouraging other people who were blind or in the process of losing vision.

From that time on, I loved going back to the Commission for the Blind in Des Moines for meetings, banquets, and other projects. Many of these offered me the opportunity to see my beloved teacher and friend, Mr. Kenneth Jernigan. He always had something significant, personal, and encouraging to say. I knew without a doubt that he cared about my well-being and my success.

In 1968 Ray Halverson and I were married and graduated from college. Ray is also blind although he has a little vision; sometimes he carries a white cane, but not always. Our two children were born in 1971 and 1975. I had no doubt about my ability to raise our children as a totally blind mother. Since Ray was off at work all day, I was the one who took care of our children all day long when they were babies, preschoolers, and through elementary school. From babyhood, our kids knew that if they wanted to show me something, they had to bring it to me and let me touch or hold it.

I taught our children colors, and they could print their names by age three. I remember our daughter Holly signed her own Valentine's card at age three. When our son Mathew went to kindergarten, he came home from school one day and told me that no other kids in his class had a blind mom. He thought this was a rather amazing fact! During their early grade school years, I walked our children to school, just as all the other moms did. I went to their classes each year to talk to the kids about blindness and wrote all the students' names in Braille. This was important; blindness became an okay thing in their minds, and sometimes even cool. I was able to be a confident, normal mom because of the positive attitude about blindness I had been taught by Mr. Jernigan and his staff in the Iowa Orientation and Adjustment Center.

When Ray and I were expecting our first child, the thought never entered my mind that I would not be able to care for him because I was blind. We were living in Des Moines where Ray was employed by a large insurance company. None of our family members seemed concerned either about our caring for our baby. I realize now that was because of the confident and positive attitude Ray and I had. I believe that the key to having well-behaved children is training and disciplining them, always with respect and love. It simply has nothing to do with the parents' vision.

Our kids knew from the time they were beginning to walk that they were not allowed to play with my canes, which stood by the front and back doors. It was a serious matter that I know exactly where my canes were in case I needed to go outside in a hurry, or in case of an emergency. We now have the same rules about canes with our grandchildren. It seems that all children love to play with those long canes, but I am very firm and do not allow it.

There was a time when our kids were in junior high that they might have been a little embarrassed that we were blind parents. Ray and I understood that any difference—be it unstylish jeans or the wrong brand of shoes or blindness—was greatly magnified in the eyes of a junior high child. We were patient and respectful of their feelings, and we made it fine through that phase.

The era of grandchildren is a wonderful time, full of surprises and new experiences regarding our blindness, as well as other things. Whereas our own children grew up from day one with blind parents and accepted it as the norm, our grandchildren have parents with normal vision. As infants and toddlers, they spent much less of their time with us. Our son's four daughters probably did not understand the meaning of blindness until they were around four years old. Before that age, they would jump in my lap unexpectedly, throw a ball to me without warning, hold up something for me to look at across the room, point to a kitty outside the window thinking I could see it, ask me to read a print book, or nod their little heads yes or no when I asked a question. This has not been a big problem, just something to be aware of until they understand blindness. Some of my favorite activities with my granddaughters are telling them stories in which they can participate and playing pretend games like beauty shop and penguins on icebergs.

Fortunately there are hundreds of Twin Vision (or print/Braille) books available for us to read to our kids, from infancy up to early elementary school age. These books contain the entire printed text with pictures as well as the Braille text. At first a child may try to brush off my hand, but gradually she will "read" along with her fingers. We also enjoy acting out plays like Old West wagon train dramas, or we pretend that we live in the jungle. As our children grow older, it is easy to make many board and card games accessible with Braille or other tactile labels. My oldest granddaughter and I play Braille Scrabble. The "pretend" activities bring out wonderful creativity in our grandchildren. We love to go on nature hikes out in the yard and also pretend that our deck is a ship and that the yard is the sea. We play Mother-May-I out in the back yard too.

Our grandchildren accept that it is grandma who is fixing snacks, cooking meals, and taking care of all of their needs when they are with us for a sleepover. Often it is grandma who finds their shoes and socks when it is time to go home.

Now our daughter Holly and her husband have twin babies. They live 400 miles away, and we will not be able to see them often. But we are excited about these twins and looking forward to building close relationships with another granddaughter and our first grandson.

When Holly was in junior high, I went to work as a Braille instructor at the Idaho Commission for the Blind training center in Boise. Like many of Mr. Jernigan's students, I had always had a desire to work at a training center so I could pass along the gift of confidence I had received in Iowa. I am still teaching Braille, and I love my work. I see the changes in the students I teach, and I counsel and encourage them.

I have been an active member of the National Federation of the Blind since 1967, when I attended my first national convention in Los Angeles. At that convention, an amazing thing happened. Mr. Jernigan introduced me to our founder, Dr. Jacobus tenBroek. My brief meeting with him showed me a large man physically and intellectually, a warm firm handshake, and a strong kind voice. I knew of his accomplishments as a professor, a constitutional attorney, and author of several influential books. It was a very precious moment to me to have the privilege to be standing with these two brilliant men who had devoted their lives to changing what it means to be blind. Their work and personalities changed my life and the lives of thousands of other blind people. Dr. tenBroek died of cancer the following year.

Sometimes I wonder what life would have been like if I had not attended the Orientation Center in Des Moines. I suppose I would have struggled through college, graduated, and perhaps found a job. But would I have had the self-confidence, self-respect, and skills to be a competent wife and mother, manage a home, travel confidently around the city and the country, and generally live an active, productive, and normal life? I doubt it. I certainly could not have taught self-respect and confidence to other blind people.

I remember the day in my training at the Iowa Center when I felt a sense of freedom and happiness while out on a cane travel route. We called that the 4.7 because it was 4.7 miles long. It was a warm sunny day in late February, and I was strolling along not too far from the Capitol building on the east side of the Des Moines river. At that moment I felt in my heart that all was well and that my blindness had truly been reduced to just a nuisance. I had had six months of training by then, and I had experienced a gradual and wonderful change.

Several years ago we had a Summer Youth Program for blind kids aged fourteen to sixteen at the Idaho Training

Center. We taught the skills blind people need, and we planned activities for building confidence. On the first day I met with the students in our recreation room to read them their schedules. A couple of weeks later, a fourteen-year-old girl in my Braille class asked me a question: "Is this a twenty?" At first I wasn't sure what she meant; then I realized she was asking me about money. I had gotten to know her fairly well by then and had assumed she knew I was blind. When I realized she thought I could see, I was rather surprised. She should have heard my cane tapping as I walked down the halls and stairways. Since she was in my Braille class, she might have heard my fingers moving across the Braille pages.

Then it began to dawn on me that she associated authority with sight. I do not know if she ever had a blind teacher before. She may never have met a blind person who traveled independently before. I had taken charge of the meeting and given them their schedules. I wondered if other students were aware that I was reading from Braille. When I told her I couldn't see the bill either, she said, "But I thought you were sighted." She had learned well from society, as so many do, that the blind are not expected to lead. This incident gave me a wonderful opportunity to talk with her and to begin to help her change what she believed about blindness. And this is only one example. It takes many little incidents such as this one for blind persons to learn to present themselves as competent and "normal."

I know Mr. Jernigan took great joy in teaching students in the Iowa Orientation and Adjustment Center about self-advocacy, about the history of the organized blind, and about the beliefs and philosophy that make them competent and normal citizens. When I was a student, this instruction occurred in discussion class three times a week, in small group fireside chats, during dinners and meetings in his apartment and office, and while traveling with him and other students to other activities. Often I could hear the smile in his voice as he patiently and kindly, but persistently, taught me to think and believe in myself. It was an incredible privilege to be a student of this master teacher! When he told me that he wanted to exercise my mind, I understood that was exactly the kind of coaching I needed.

Not only do I earn a living as a blind adult, I also volunteer for the National Federation of the Blind in Idaho. As chairman of our scholarship committee, I have greatly enjoyed meeting, interviewing, and getting to know our many scholarship applicants. We always tell our finalists that, not only do we give them their scholarship money, but even more valuable is the introduction we give them to the National Federation of the Blind and to successful blind people. The idea of passing on the gifts we have received is another concept I learned from Mr. Jernigan. This time it was contained in one of his favorite books, *Magnificent Obsession* by Lloyd C. Douglas, which he recommended to me to read. Dr. Jernigan was grateful to Dr. tenBroek for guiding him and sharing knowledge. Dr. Jernigan shared his gifts with thousands, including me.

A couple of years ago I was experiencing some health problems, and after tests I was diagnosed with Parkinson's disease. Of course I began to read material about people who have Parkinsons and how to treat the disease. I found that most are very emotional and frightened by the diagnosis.

Although it is frustrating for me, I did not experience the fear that so many do. I know that the reasons are my experience with blindness and the National Federation of the Blind. And Dr. Jernigan's instruction continues to help me in ways that no one could have predicted.

When I meet a newly blind person at our training center or in the NFB, I am thankful for what I have received. I am sure that he would be pleased that we are passing along the gift of the NFB to others, just as he had received it from Dr. tenBroek many years before. When I meet a newly blind person at our training center, I realize that I take many things for granted. I know that it is respectable to be blind, but my new students do not believe that. I know that I can take care of my home and family, but new students of all ages think that is unreal. I know that I can travel confidently with my cane to and from work, attending meetings, shopping, or anywhere else I wish to go, but our students are afraid to walk down the hall or around the block when they first arrive.

It is my goal to help my students understand that, although there are inconveniences we must handle as blind people, we can and should come to enjoy our work, play, and community life. I also enjoy family gatherings, grandchildren, and vacations. In short, I am free to be, go, and do what I desire just as anyone else does. When I was a teenager, this would have sounded like a fairy tale to me, and it may still seem that way to my new students.

For me, the fairy tale has come true because of Mr. Jernigan's love and leadership.

CHAPTER 22

HE WAS A BUILDER

by John Cheadle

Note: While still a teenager, Kenneth Jernigan operated a business from his home, where he designed, built, and sold furniture. Among other items he built lamps and tables largely made of wooden thread spools, which had been saved for him by friends and relatives. While supervising the orientation center in California, he built some items in the woodworking shop there and learned techniques he had not already figured out for himself. When he moved to Iowa, he found it necessary to gather funds, design, and oversee the remodeling of a seven-story building which housed the Commission for the Blind. This occurred repeatedly during the twenty years he led the agency. When the NFB headquarters was established in Baltimore, Dr. Jernigan again found himself raising funds, planning, and overseeing numerous remodeling projects in the old buildings.

John Cheadle began his career in work with the blind in Nebraska and worked in both Missouri and Idaho. He and his wife Barbara adopted a visually impaired son, Charles, and raised him along with their other son and daughter. John

Cheadle became head of the maintenance and facilities department at NFB headquarters in 1985 and worked closely with Kenneth Jernigan on the expansions and changes that were made there. After Dr. Jernigan's death, he worked with President Maurer and Mrs. Jernigan to complete the construction of Dr. Jernigan's dream, which is now called the National Federation of the Blind Jernigan Institute.

John Cheadle, 1992.

THE FIRST TIME I ENCOUNTERED THE NAME KENNETH Jernigan was in 1973 at a family Thanksgiving gathering in Iowa. I was just beginning my career in work with the blind in Nebraska. My dad's second cousin—I guess she'd be my third cousin—listened attentively for a few minutes to my news, then said: "If you want to work for the best program for the blind in the world, you'll have to come to Iowa and work for Kenneth Jernigan." She went on to tell me how he had come to Iowa in 1958 and taken the helm of what was then regarded unequivocally as the least effective agency for the blind in the country. She said that, not only had he built the best training program for the blind, but he had also built the largest library for the blind in the country. She went on and on.

I was nearly nonplussed. I was the one with great news about work with the blind, but her revelations eclipsed my meager knowledge. How, I wondered, would she know these things? Was this Iowa program really as great as she said it was? How credible were her comments? After all, she was a housewife of modest means who lived in a very small town in Iowa named Ryan. Yet her comments seemed uniquely well informed and profoundly confident, and they kept a haunting presence in my memory as I began my new career.

Over the years, as I came to know the work of Dr. Jernigan and the National Federation of the Blind, I started to understand how profoundly our work affects the lives not just of blind people but of all people. Dr. Jernigan built programs in Iowa and in the nation. He was called a teacher, leader, colleague, and friend; and he was. And largely he was because he was also a builder—a builder of buildings, of programs for the blind, and ultimately a builder of lives.

There in rural Iowa distanced from the sophistication of federal and state programs for the blind; in rural Iowa where farmers tended the land and city folk worked mostly in industries which supported agriculture; in rural Iowa where life is close to the heart—there was a blind man who had been taught that he could neither tend the soil nor operate the machines of industry and that he was a burden to himself and to those around him. But Kenneth Jernigan came and got hold of a building and built a program, and it touched the lives of this blind man and those around him. He got training, and he got work. I learned years later that his sister-in-law, my dad's cousin, was ever grateful that Kenneth Jernigan had come to Iowa.

Shortly after I began my career, I had the opportunity to visit the programs that Dr. Jernigan had built in Iowa. Although I was mightily impressed with the programs, I believe I was equally impressed with the building. It was unlike any state-operated facility I had ever seen. Instead of the sterile coldness of bare floors and tiled walls, there was the comforting presence of wood, stone, carpeting, upholstered furniture, and even a fireplace. The warmth that pervaded the programs that he built was evident not only in the architecture and furnishings of the place but also in the staff and students. His building and his program had profound character. He had built it well.

We bought the buildings we all now know as the NFB headquarters in the spring of 1978. That summer our National Convention was held in Baltimore. Here is what Dr. Jernigan had to say: "The building, I think, offers us the possibility of doing many things. We will move from Des Moines ... [and] ...

we will establish offices here. Seminars—it is planned—will be conducted from this office. We are trying to see whether we can arrange to set up recording studios in this building and to begin to do our own recording. We will see how much training we can do of people there ... the point is that we will now have a building of our own—as a matter of fact, a whole city block." He began building on that city block in 1978, and, as you have heard, he hasn't stopped. Such was the character of Dr. Kenneth Jernigan.

In 1980, barely two years after we bought the building, I worked for a short period of time in the Job Opportunities for the Blind program at our national headquarters in Baltimore. Dr. Jernigan had already made significant changes. Mostly tenants occupied it except that the fourth floor was vacant. It was also, according to knowledgeable sources and neighborhood gossip, less than desirable, but we moved in anyway. There was about 165,000 square feet in this building, and the NFB occupied less than a fourth of it. But that was more than we had had in Des Moines. Our operations in those days were wholly contained on the fourth floor, and we didn't even use all of that.

In 1985 Dr. Jernigan offered me a full-time position in Baltimore, and I accepted. In just four years Dr. Jernigan had expanded our operations to fill all of the fourth floor and was in the process of squeezing in an additional 5,000 square feet by sandwiching a mezzanine level between a portion of the fourth floor and the roof. He had also had the exterior masonry cleaned and had installed new roofs on all of the buildings in the complex, and he kept right on building. By the time of his death, the NFB headquarters occupied more than three-fourths of the building's total square footage (plus the 5,000 square feet of mezzanine space), and it had also expanded to occupy at least 12,000 square feet in other buildings in the complex.

In 1986 we began seriously to expand our operations in the main building. Half of the first floor had become vacant. So we remodeled it and moved the aids and appliances, shipping, receiving, and storage operations from the fourth floor down to the first floor. We temporarily moved people from their fourth-floor offices in the Barney Street wing around to the Johnson Street wing. We then eliminated the dining room in order to build a sound studio and eliminated the file room to build the accounting department. It wasn't quite chaos, but it was very close.

Yet Dr. Jernigan kept the pulse of all that was going on. The Barney wing of the fourth floor was now vacant and ready to be remodeled to include a kitchen, a dining room, related storage space, a records management center to store the documentation and written history of the organization, two large work areas we call "malls," and more than twice as many offices as we had had previously. What a marvelous project that was—twenty-two thousand square feet of space to do with as we pleased, and Dr. Jernigan took great delight and pride in planning the use of every square foot.

After the contractor had laid out the floor plates for all the walls that were going up, Dr. Jernigan, the construction supervisor, and I took a tour to examine the work. It was like walking around on a blueprint that was two hundred and seventy feet wide and eighty feet deep. Everywhere there was a line on the blueprint there was a corresponding floor plate in the construction area.

Shortly after we started our tour we came to the north edge of the records management center where there were two adjacent offices. Dr. Jernigan, using his cane to follow along the floor plates, paused after we had gone nearly all of the way around one of the rooms. Tapping his cane along the edge of the floor plate, he said, "There is supposed to be a door here joining the two offices."

"No," replied the construction supervisor, "it isn't on the prints."

Dr. Jernigan turned to me and asked, "Well, Mr. Cheadle, what do you think; is it on the prints?"

"No sir," I guessed; "I don't believe it is."

Dr. Jernigan then offered us the opportunity "to increase our holdings," as he put it. He anted up a dollar to each of us, and we went and looked at the prints. He was right—and richer. I've long lost count of the number of such opportunities, but I certainly have learned a great deal at very minimal tuition.

Somewhere along the line during this phase of construction, Dr. Jernigan began asking me consistently when he greeted me, "Mr. Cheadle, how are the contractors?" I learned quickly to anticipate the salutation and tried to be prepared at all times to answer thoroughly and with precision. If I did not know, I told him I did not know; it was less expensive for all of us.

In the years since the major remodeling of the fourth floor Dr. Jernigan directed the replacement of all three elevators with modern hydraulic units that go to the roof; the addition of a new power transformer; the update of the electrical distribution systems throughout the building; and changing overall plumbing to new copper pipes. In addition, he oversaw the renovation of space in the central courtyard area to house our maintenance facility. Another building in the courtyard area was remodeled to house the first location of the International Braille and Technology Center and offices. He planned and executed the complete remodeling of the entire second floor of the main building to include more new offices with a conference center, nearly eighteen thousand square feet of space containing three miles of shelving and two thousand square feet of conditioned archival storage space.

Additionally, Dr. Jernigan directed the moving of the International Braille and Technology Center to the second floor of the main building and added offices and a conference facility. He also redesigned the front entrance to the NFB headquarters to improve the aesthetics and to make it accessible to wheelchairs. He added a sign atop our building twelve feet high and forty feet wide, topped off with a forty-foot flagpole—the sign lasted twenty years but has now been replaced with a modern digital sign, which is visible from the nearby, heavily trafficked Interstate 95.

During the last year of his life, Dr. Jernigan was still looking forward and planning. He left us with one of the biggest challenges he had ever given us—the plan for the construction of an entire new building. First we would need to find funds and manage the construction of a beautiful facility five stories tall; then fill it with dynamic programs. He had enough faith in those who would continue his work to believe that we would benefit from and complete a dream he had barely begun, a dream that would take us into a new century and far-reaching new activities.

Dr. Jernigan directed that tactile plans be made of each floor and that a model showing the proposed building's shape and location on our property be prepared. These were displayed at NFB Headquarters, and we took the model with us to the National Convention. The excitement of the people who looked at the model was palpable. They may not have known exactly what it was going to be, but they knew it would be great!

Everyone who looked at the model of the building had something to say or a question to ask about it. "Does it have a basement?" "Are we really going to move the entrance?" "How much room does it add?" "What does it look like inside?" The questions were boundless, and so were the suggestions. It often seemed that the recommendations were designed to resolve a particular concern poignant to the individual: "There needs to be enough meeting rooms." We should pre-wire the whole building for the internet." "Be sure there are enough restroom facilities." The excitement of the people who looked at the model was palpable. They may not have known exactly what it was going to be, but they knew it would be great!

By the time of his death, Dr. Jernigan had pretty much finished the design of the building. There had been weekly meetings to design the facility, and the architects applied graphic tape to the blueprints for Dr. Jernigan's study. The architects kept inviting engineers: structural engineers for steel and concrete; electrical engineers for power and alarm design; mechanical engineers for plumbing, heat, and air conditioning; and lots of others. Like honey bees to a flower garden, they kept coming to the blossoming idea.

And then it happened; Dr. Jernigan passed away. The news was not unexpected but neither was it welcomed. The dark days of October 1998 stretched through the winter and toward the spring. As they did, we kept our focus on his dream. Dr. Maurer took full leadership of the effort. He kept our regular programs running and ran the meetings with architects and engineers, committee meetings, corporate board meetings, and the fundraising meetings as well. The National Federation of the Blind has never borrowed money to accomplish its goals. We always fund our major projects ourselves; it took us two years, but we raised the cash and pledges to fund the Jernigan Institute!

Dr. Jernigan had planned well. Dr. Maurer, Mrs. Jernigan, and the rest of us who oversaw the completion of the building knew it was as he wished. But the Jernigan Institute has become more than any of us had imagined—we knew it would be, we just didn't know how.

It is an impressive building as all who see it say, but what it has enabled is the real dream. Through all of those years of planning and building, what was ethereal began to show itself against the backdrop of a beautiful building, a wonderful staff, and magnificent programs all fulminating against the rigors of old attitudes about blindness. We now host huge programs designed to better the lives of blind people. Participants come from all over the country: blind teenagers come to the youth slam; college students planning to become teachers of the blind come to our "Teachers of Tomorrow" seminars; and our own leaders, present and future, come to help hone the steps of the future for all blind people. They all take new attitudes with them when they go home, and the world will never be the same for them or those around them. The influence of Dr. Kenneth Jernigan, the builder, will march timelessly.

And, yes, the Jernigan Institute is full of wood, stone, carpeting, upholstered furniture, and a huge fireplace. I remember carrying the model design to convention in 1998 so that Federationists could examine it.

Dr. Jernigan was a builder. I will remember him for that. I will also remember him as a teacher, a leader, and a colleague; but mostly, I will remember and honor him as my friend.

CHAPTER 23

HOW I LEARNED TO TEACH

by Susan Ford

Note: Susan Ford took training at the Orientation and Adjustment Center in Iowa in 1963 and went on to study at the State University of Iowa. While teaching at a summer school for blind adults in Montana, she met her husband John. After their marriage, the two were leaders in the Montana NFB affiliate. She received a Masters degree in teaching blind children from the University of Northern Colorado. The Fords moved to St. Louis in 1982, and she was employed in work with the blind there until her retirement. After she and her husband agreed to take a blind infant into their home in the late 1970s, Susan was elected the first president of the Parents of Blind Children Division of the NFB. Below she shares some of her experiences, first as a student, and later as a teacher.

I LEARNED WHAT I KNOW OF FEDERATION PHILOSOPHY from Dr. Jernigan and others. I was a student in the Orientation and Adjustment Center of the Iowa Commission for the Blind in 1963. Dr. Jernigan taught us that blind people are worth something. He believed that they are of equal value to other people. His basic philosophy as head of the Iowa Commission for the Blind was that: with proper training and opportunity, the average blind person can do the average job in the average place of business, and do it as well as sighted neighbors or colleagues. Dr. Jernigan believed that learning alternative techniques of blindness was essential to the first statement.

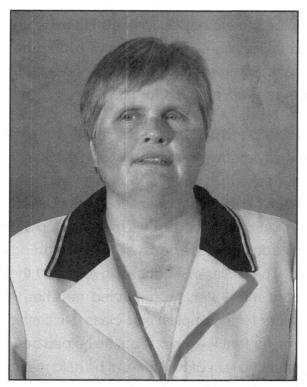

Susan Ford, 2003.

But Dr. Jernigan and Dr. tenBroek were more than philosophers. They joined their colleagues on the picket lines, in court rooms, in political presentations, in recreational activities, and in all aspects of life where you expect sighted people to be. Dr. Jernigan led us out into rural Iowa to cut down trees for burning wood in the fireplace in the recreation room at the Commission building. He would take one end of a double-cross cut-saw and invite a new student, often one who had no idea what to do, to help cut down the tree. He challenged students to do their best in all manner of things. When they doubted themselves because of physical lacks, he encouraged them with exercise classes or enticed them to run with him in the streets of Des Moines. He expected students to use their white canes effectively and overcome their fears and stay safe. When we lacked the confidence or "guts" to represent ourselves, he did it for us.

When I applied to be accepted in the College of Education at the University of Iowa in the spring of 1964, they refused my application. I asked Dr. Jernigan to come and help me plead my case. I don't know what possessed me that day, but I was afraid and didn't show up at that meeting. Dr. Jernigan was there. He pleaded my case because I wasn't strong enough to do it myself. The College of Education reversed their decision and accepted me. Later, he reminded me that we all must help each other to accomplish first-class citizenship. He never chastised me for that weakness, but he helped and supported me throughout the rest of his life. And he held me accountable to do the same for those who became my students.

Dr. Jernigan learned from Dr. tenBroek. Then he taught many students, as well. I think I never learned as well as some, but I learned a lot. I learned that I was right in thinking that I would be a teacher. In my turn, I can now show others the philosophy and strategies of the National Federation of the

Blind. I do not preach to my students or hound them. I first present myself in a positive way; then I tell my students their best will be good enough. I have taught many things over the years, and the most important is to believe in oneself and to go out and teach others to believe in each other. After we have learned the skills of blindness that are important to success, we must show the public, all kinds of people with whom we have contact what blindness is and what it isn't. We must do this in a caring way.

When I was a student teacher during my master's degree program in special education, I worked with a seventh grader. It was her first year in home economics, and she was to begin a sewing unit. Julie had chosen to make a skirt, but neither her home ec teacher nor the vision itinerant teacher knew the techniques used by the blind in sewing. I had a basic knowledge of sewing, although I did not like using a sewing machine. Julie needed to learn how to thread a simple needle and to thread the sewing machine. She needed to learn how to adjust a tape measure and to use it. She needed to know that it was possible to make a tactile line to guide the fabric to sew an even seam. Most of all, Julie needed to believe that blind people could sew, and that she could learn as well. Julie didn't know until much later how limited my sewing skills truly were. She finished the project with pride and confidence in her accomplishment. I never knew how important it was to her until she made a speech about it many years later.

During the 1970s the Federation worked on several issues pertaining to families. There were blind parents whose competence to raise their own children was challenged, and they needed help. There were prospective parents who wished to adopt and were not permitted to do so because of blindness. There were sighted parents with blind children who found difficulties getting fair acceptance for them in schools and wished some guidance.

After I got my master's degree, my husband and I moved from Colorado back to Montana, and John was employed as a rehabilitation counselor there. I worked part-time with blind seniors. Our daughter Brenda (who was sighted) was born on my birthday in 1976. We talked about adopting a blind child, thinking that as blind parents we could help that child deal with the challenges we knew he or she would face. So we applied to adopt.

We took Brenda with us to an office Christmas party when she was nine months old. Later we learned that a social worker who was there took note of the way I managed her needs: feeding her and keeping track of a very active little girl who wanted to crawl everywhere. A few months after that, the social worker participated in a meeting where the needs of a blind infant boy in foster care were addressed. The family where he was placed was moving out of state and did not wish to take this child with them. Soon we received a phone call inquiring whether we would consider taking a blind foster child. We were assured that this would be a pre-adopt placement and were urged to visit the family where he was then placed, a round trip of nearly two hundred miles. When we learned that this child's name was Brent, it seemed to us that Brenda and Brent, just a year apart in age, might complete our family.

We did visit, and John and I each separately began to notice some of his characteristics. He had light perception, because he was reaching for the windows. At twenty-six months, he did not walk or talk, so he was educationally deprived. I was eager to help him learn. He first spent a weekend in our home and came to stay at the end of May. Then I had a full-time job at home with two children both functioning at about the same one-year-old level. Brent did not eat solid food and had to be taught to chew. He was afraid of grass on bare feet and moving across open space. We knew there had been abuse because of things like scarring on his heels, and he was not accustomed to spending much time outside his crib and on the floor. His arms were very strong, and he could lower his weight from the top of a railing. These were unusual issues, but they had to be dealt with.

By August he could say about fifteen words and was beginning to chew, and in six months he had 150 words. We had to find ways to give him confidence in moving about, just as we had done with newly blind adults. By November, Brent was walking independently and acting much more like a normal toddler. We got a twin stroller which we pulled behind us, and that made it easier to take two active toddlers away from home.

When Brent was three and a half we enrolled him in Head Start. We had given him a small white cane, which he used part of the time to find obstacles and landmarks, especially outside. Inside he used pull toys for the same purpose. His teachers also had to learn to encourage Brent to explore appropriately, and he had to learn to play with other children other than his sister.

We did not talk often to Dr. Jernigan, but we were leaders in the NFB affiliate in Montana, and he knew we had Brent. Nevertheless, we were surprised to receive a phone call from him inviting us to a meeting of parents to occur in Baltimore at NFB headquarters. We were thrilled to be able to visit this new facility, and we were curious about the meeting, so off we went.

Dr. Jernigan presided at the meeting, and most of the people there were sighted parents of blind children. We decided to organize the Parents of Blind Children Division of the NFB at the next convention. This was the first time that the majority of the members in an NFB division might be sighted, but we thought that adding more activities for families would be a good thing, and it was. I was elected president of the Parents of Blind Children Division in 1982 and served for two years. Never could those of us who founded this division have dreamed how it would affect the lives of parents and blind children through the decades. Barbara Cheadle had started a newsletter for parents of blind children, and we wanted to expand it. We held a contest to find a name, which now is *Future Reflections*. Then in 1984 Barbara was elected president. By that time my family had moved to Missouri, and our children were in school. I also went back to work teaching blind adults.

Through my employment, I met another student, Stephanie, when she was twenty. She told me she couldn't read, and I asked her why that was. She said, "Because I can't see it." She had attended the school for the blind for most of ten years.

They had considered her "learning disabled;" they said she had an "intellectual deficit." They assumed she could learn neither print nor Braille. Later Stephanie learned Braille but did not have enough credits for high school graduation. She and her parents learned this only at the beginning of her last school semester. She was twenty-one and could not make up her credits. At graduation, she was presented a "Certificate of Attendance."

Stephanie went to work for a number of years replacing videos on the shelves at Blockbusters. At about thirty, she decided to get her GED and became my student again. When she began this class, her instructor discovered that Stephanie had never learned basic math skills. She could not carry in addition, borrow in subtraction, and did not know multiplication or division facts. She could not see well enough to write problems in print and had never done math in Braille. I taught Stephanie abacus procedures, multiplication and division facts, fractions, and decimals. She took her GED and passed it the first time. She went on to college and maintained a 4.0 grade point average for at least two years. After her four-year degree, she went on to earn a master's degree. She now works as a youth social worker. How could she turn her life around so completely? She came to believe that she was a capable person; that her blindness could only limit her if she let it happen. The National Federation of the Blind helped her develop that "can-do" attitude. I was the instrument. I was passing on what I received from Dr. Jernigan and others.

I met a third student, Mike, who was blinded by a gunshot wound. The first time he sought instruction, he dropped out because he thought his girlfriend would take care of him. A year later the girlfriend was gone, and he recognized that Braille and cane travel would be essential to his independence. At first, Mike thought he would never learn the Braille alphabet. But he did. Then he tackled contracted Braille and thought he couldn't learn it. But he is now reading stories and writing both with a Braillewriter and a slate and stylus. Using the white cane, he does his grocery shopping and other errands. He saved his money and bought a K-NFB reader and reads most of his mail and is in charge of the papers in his household. This spring Mike found a new apartment, purchased some new furniture, and hired help to move in. How different Mike's life and attitudes have become because of his exposure to a positive belief in himself as a blind person. This belief grew because he could see that his teachers expected it. I have reason to believe that his reading skill in print before blindness was not as great as his Braille reading skill is today.

Dr. Jernigan gave a gift to every student he taught, and in turn, to those they teach. Julie, Stephanie, and Mike are examples of how my students can change. I could not do what I do without the instruction that I received.

Some of my colleagues in the Federation are long-time members or, as Dr. Jernigan used to say, veterans who teach others, but also we continue to learn ourselves. Every time I go to a Federation seminar something that is said or done makes a difference in my life. In addition to other things I have mentioned, I have held local and state offices in Montana and Missouri, and I keep learning. Some of my colleagues are new members—not only new to the organization, but also new to the idea that it is okay to be blind. Blindness is respectable and nothing to be ashamed of.

Dr. Jernigan told a story about me that demonstrates what I mean. I was president of the Parents of Blind Children division. I said something about a little girl who "had to learn Braille." He reminded me that all children need to learn to read and write. I did not need to separate children because of how they read. The important thing is that they read. The little girl who reads Braille is just as competent and just as impressive as the little boy who sits next to her and reads print. She is more impressive than the child who doesn't apply himself or the child who plays truant from school. We must be careful not to shortchange blind people inadvertently because it affects the way our sighted friends and neighbors see us. Braille is a good way to read, just as print is, and I was fortunate to learn it well as a young child.

Along with treating our NFB colleagues with love and respect, we owe the same to others who believe differently. We can try to influence them, hoping that they will gain confidence in themselves and improve their abilities. I remember talking about older members in the Federation who never learned the skills I have. They believed they had to travel with a sighted guide. That was what society taught all of us years ago. If we can lead people to the Federation, they will learn what they can, but it is a late start for many of them. I will not go as far as the next generation. We need to find people who will fight the good fight in the future after we are gone. That is what Dr. Jernigan did when he taught me and my fellow students.

When my kids both went to fourth grade, it was the first time they were both enrolled in the same school although in different classrooms. Brent had been in a resource class for blind children, and Brenda had been in public school. The principal spoke to the children before they went to their first class, and I was there that first day. He told the children that, so far as he was concerned, every one of them had all A's that year. If they kept those A's, they would have to work at it. If they didn't work, there was a problem with their teachers, their attitudes about school, or the materials they were using. I liked what he said. It places the responsibility for learning in the hands of the teachers and the students. That's where I want it to be when I am teaching. And that's the approach I think we should take with our members: teach them what we can, encourage and support them as other leaders move forward, and then we can all move ahead together.

We have many experiences that have been written by Federation members and leaders, which can help us along the way. There are thirty Kernel books with numerous stories in each book. We will keep trying to reach the stars. We learn for ourselves, and we extend our hands to the next generation and walk with them as long as we can. We welcome them to take their places and climb with us. My students will surpass me, and that is my goal for them and for the Federation. When I was learning all of this from Dr. Jernigan, I thought little about it. Looking back over my career as a teacher and as a volunteer in the Federation, I understand more fully what I learned from him—the greatest teacher I have ever known.

CHAPTER 24

HE CONTINUES TO CHANGE THE WORLD

by Mary Symms-Pollot

Note: As a young woman, Mary Symms-Pollot was employed by Dr. Jernigan to work for the National Federation of the Blind. She held this position for only three years but feels the influence of her employer was formative in her life. She found the spirit and wisdom helpful at the time and continues to be guided by what she learned. She also has remained active in the National Federation of the Blind. She tells her story below.

I HAVE HAD TREMENDOUS OPPORTUNITIES IN MY LIFE. At the top of my list is working for the National Federation of the Blind and being taught by Dr. Kenneth Jernigan.

I always wanted to travel the world and make it a better place for as many people as possible. Thinking Washington, DC, was the place to get this done, I moved there to follow my dream. While working on Capitol Hill, I met President Reagan and many other influential world leaders. No matter how bright and beautiful the atmosphere, it seemed to me that there was a lot of talk that did not match with results. It was disappointing, and I went seeking a place that helped individuals more.

Mary Symms-Pollot, 1990.

I moved to Baltimore, and I talked to a recruiter in an employment agency. I explained that working for an organization that made a difference and kept their promises was vital for me. The recruiter seemed to understand and had a place in mind, but there were no openings. She found me a temporary job for six weeks. When there was finally an opening, I went to NFB headquarters and was interviewed by several people. I remember thinking "What a great place!," although I had no idea what an impact the Federation would have in my life. I was hired and worked at the National Center for the Blind for three years. I was changed forever.

I believe every experience in life molds each of us into the people we become. Each experience is important. I've made plenty of mistakes that have made me stronger. The first day on the job Dr. Jernigan took me to President Maurer's office and knocked on the door. Without waiting for an answer, I opened the door. I had not yet learned about company culture or the NFB's philosophy of blindness. After we talked with Dr. Maurer and went back to Dr. Jernigan's office, he asked me why I had opened the door. I was nervous about my mistake and began to talk through my thoughts about helping blind people. His frown got sterner. I yammered faster about how I realized how competent he was and how he didn't need my help. I apologized and was very embarrassed. I finally stopped talking; then he laughed and said, "I might get to like you." I was so relieved—I thought I was about to be fired! I began being more observant.

Staff members at the National Center for the Blind are hired for no specific job. They are chosen if they are considered "trainable" and have the aptitude and heart to become Federationists. People don't always fit there, but those who do may be switched to different positions from time to time. I worked as secretary for Dr. Jernigan and also for Dr. Maurer for a few days. Those positions didn't fit me. I ended up managing the Materials Center (now Independence Market). I learned to supervise people, assess their skills, and assign tasks that fit each staff member. The practice was to fit the job to the staff member using each person's strengths. Dr. Jernigan said, "We match people to positions instead of trying to change people."

One day Dr. Jernigan called me into his office. He asked me to describe the tasks assigned to one of my assistants— we'll call him Mr. Smith. I described Mr. Smith's tasks. Dr. Jernigan asked me to describe Mr. Smith's talents. I did. Dr. Jernigan asked me which tasks matched Mr. Smith's talents. I matched them up. Dr. Jernigan then asked if there were any tasks that did not match. I said yes. Dr. Jernigan asked, "What do you think you should do about that task?" I thought and responded, "Teach Mr. Smith how to do it?" There was dead silence for about a minute. Believe me it seemed way longer than that. Dr. Jernigan sternly said, "Please describe Mr. Smith's talents." I paused, thought, chuckled, and said, "Okay, I get it. Give someone else the task." He smiled and laughed. He went on to explain that supervisors often cause the failures of those they supervise.

At the Center, we each donated five dollars monthly to the "Citizens Fund" for the supplies kept in the lunchroom. Actually, it was a tax we imposed upon ourselves, and we voiced our wishes at Citizens meetings over which Dr. Jernigan presided. At one meeting we debated raising the tax because we were running out of coffee, tea, peanut butter, and bread. After what seemed to be a lengthy discussion somebody said, "I don't drink coffee, and I want my money to go toward everything but coffee." We discussed implementing a more complex accounting system. The bureaucracy was growing, and Dr. Jernigan watched with amusement. I was wondering why he didn't just end this long-winded discussion. He finally gave us a "deadline" by which we must come to a conclusion, but we couldn't agree.

Dr. Jernigan finally ended it by saying, "You have just witnessed democracy in action. It takes time. Sometimes, but not usually, people can agree. It takes negotiations and bargaining. You suggested raising taxes. You suggested adding an accounting layer to the fund. These both take more money. These are two evils of democracy. Since I run this place, I am making an executive decision. Sometimes there is need for a dictator to end conflict. In this case, I hope you will consider me a benevolent dictator. We will continue to have coffee, tea, peanut butter, and bread in smaller quantities. When it's gone, it's gone, and we can wait for the fund to be replenished from taxes. Or maybe a benefactor will donate items." It became much clearer to me that day why I had felt so strongly that I should leave Washington, DC. If I had stayed, I was afraid I would become a part of the place and the process, and I did not want to do that.

We had volunteers in the Materials Center whom I supervised. One of the tasks was to write Braille on a deck of playing cards. One volunteer was having trouble, and I didn't understand what the problem was. She started asking me what was on a card. I told her it was an ace of spades, and she asked about the next one. She kept asking through about eight cards. I then said, "You know, just like a normal deck of cards." It never occurred to me that she might not be familiar with what a deck of cards includes. I probably sounded condescending, but I had no idea what she was asking. She told me, "I don't know what is in a deck of cards." Well, I was surprised and then proceeded to explain.

Later Dr. Jernigan called me into his office. He started asking about vacations I've taken. I talked about trips to Texas, Mexico, Washington, DC, and Europe. He asked if I thought everyone had traveled like this on vacation. I said that probably most people traveled on vacation, at least to nearby places. He started talking about assumptions, and I knew I was in trouble because assuming things had been a downfall of mine. He talked about people who had never traveled outside of Baltimore. He said many people don't have bank accounts and have never flown on an aircraft. He said many people had not learned to read and might not know what is in a deck of cards. I then understood why this discussion was taking place. Our volunteers are very important to us at the NFB, not just at the national headquarters but nationwide in all the chapters. I knew this and felt bad that I had hurt the woman's feelings. I realized that I had not been listening to her reactions or questions. I still remember this talk and have tried to ask more questions and apply this lesson. I hope I have become more humble and sensitive.

The spirit of the Federation is one of family. While living in Baltimore, I felt a part of the family, grew to love the people, and learned to embrace change. I had truly found a place where I was making a difference. I had never really analyzed my philosophy about disabled people. The National Federation of the Blind taught that disabilities only get in the way if people let them.

Part of my training was to travel with a long white cane. My cane travel teacher, Mr. Cobb, gave me a pair of sleep shades to cover my eyes so I could not see. He instructed me how to hold the cane at a comfortable height and move it from side to side in front of me to cover the width of my body. Although scared when starting, I found the cane gave me plenty of warning of what was in front of me. People were generally noisy, and desks were big and easy to find with the cane. I learned to navigate inside the building walking up and down the hallways. I felt as though I was getting the hang of it. Then Mr. Cobb said, "Let's go outside." What? I didn't like this idea, but I was persistent and implemented our family motto of "never, never, never give up."

So outside we went into the streets of Baltimore. I seemed to do well traveling around the block. Of course, it was familiar to me from parking my car every day. Then Mr. Cobb taught me how to cross the street. We discussed keeping track of directions: north, south, east, and west. We walked through the edge of a park, and I only ran into a couple branches on a tree but was not mortally wounded. Then he requested we head west to the street where city buses ran. Yikes! I was sure death was inevitable, but off I went with only a little whining.

We worked for a bit that day and again the next day. Then I felt something shift inside me. All of a sudden it was clear to me that I could do this! I could travel this way, just as blind people do. I finally understood the emotional strength that blind people have while traveling around the city and world. This caused my confidence and spirits to soar. The blind didn't need my help in the way that I formerly thought. What they needed was the kind of training that I was getting. I had read it: With proper training and opportunity, a blind person can compete with a sighted person in the same situation with the same credentials. Now I felt it. My opinion on training, opportunity, and advocacy was changed. The blind had been working together for over fifty years in a collective group, advocating for independence and respect. They have respect from me!

Teaching was a constant at the Center. Dr. Jernigan asked if I would like to learn to drive the NFB bus. That was an adventure, and I realized that I could learn all sorts of things. One day Dr. Jernigan greeted me with "How are you," and I proceeded to tell him my troubles. Later he called me to his office and explained he had asked me how I was as a courtesy. A greeting, he told me, is to share pleasantness and not an appropriate time to hear a lengthy explanation.

After leaving the National Federation of the Blind in 1991, my brother and I backpacked in Africa and South America for four months. It was a fabulous experience I had dreamed about but never dared to do. I learned to adjust to circumstances with cockroaches and dirty bathrooms, appreciate people and cultures, and drive a motorcycle. I went back to school and studied Spanish and earned my international MBA.

While growing up on a farm, dad told us that hard work builds character. You can imagine how I felt about that when I was hoeing weeds or picking cherries. Dr. Jernigan helped to build character too. My dad and Dr. Jernigan met in 1989; they were fond of each other and kindred spirits, and they had a common project that they loved—me. Dad said, "I did my best to raise her, but you have finished the job. Thank you Dr. Jernigan." Dr. Jernigan laughed and said, "You made a good start and gave me good raw materials." At my MBA graduation, I received the Barton Kyle Yount award for "Outstanding Scholarship, Accomplishment and Character." I laughed and said to my dad, "Look, I have an award that says I have character. May I stop all those character-building lessons?" He chuckled and said that I was just getting started. Dr. Jernigan would have enjoyed that moment, too. I think he would have said the same thing.

I worked internationally for ten years selling and promoting Idaho agricultural products, providing food for people worldwide and helping Idaho farmers sell their products. While building a distribution network, training hundreds in frozen food handling, and traveling alone as a woman in Latin America, at times I could hear Dr. Jernigan's voice: Don't assume; be aware; assess people's skills; train for positive outcomes; be flexible; be strong; be humble; be smart; be careful; be persistent; adversity builds character. These are valuable principles he taught me.

I met and married a wonderful man, Mark, and we now have three children: Christopher, Katherine, and McLeod. Friends often ask why I continue work with the blind. I explain that my heart and mind grew and were nurtured by the NFB. We have a wonderful NFB family here in Idaho, and my children are learning about giving as they help with projects. Yet before 2001, I had wondered if the training and knowledge I learned from NFB members would apply directly to my life.

McLeod arrived in May of 2001 at two pounds, fourteen ounces. The placenta had not worked correctly before birth. My new baby faced problems! During the past twelve years, he has had fifteen surgeries and has made wonderful progress. My husband and I are his primary advocates, and it is not always easy with twenty-four doctors and many providers. McLeod has nerve damage that is slowing his visual processing for reading and writing, but luckily I have lots of friends who know alternative techniques for reading. My experience with the NFB has been invaluable as we strive to help him reach his full potential. He has progressed farther than we were told he could. One doctor said he didn't expect McLeod ever to walk or talk. We laugh at that because McLeod is a VERY active boy. My husband and I believe in our son.

When McLeod was five, he came in the house to inform me that he had started my car. I was not sure what he meant, so I asked him to show me. He got the keys and then led me to the car. He chose the correct key, unlocked the door, climbed in, put the key in the ignition, and turned it on! We had to find a way to prevent this behavior, yet it showed progress. Discipline did not work as well as we would have hoped; therefore, we made an agreement with him. If McLeod asked permission when we went somewhere in the car, he could turn it on after the driver was seated, then go to his own seat and put on his seatbelt. If he ever started the car under any other circumstances, he was deprived of this privilege indefinitely. He understood the terms and abided by them. We had to be creative, just as most parents, and McLeod was as good as

Katherine (twenty months older) at testing his parents and others.

Training changes lives. I learned the value from Dr. Jernigan, Dr. Maurer, and the NFB. There are times when I think it might be easier to deal with blindness than some of McLeod's issues. Our situation is different, but I am better prepared than I would have been because I was mentored by Dr. Jernigan and Dr. Maurer, so I forge on. McLeod will become more of who he already is: a considerate, sweet, strong boy. I cannot change his nature, and I don't want to. I could ruin him if I baby him and do too much for him, so I will push him to succeed. My goal is to get every possible opportunity for him while he is young. With training and therapy, McLeod and his huge team of family, friends, and professionals—he calls them "Care Bears" will progress toward independence. McLeod will find his niche and become a contributing member of society.

My life is full and fulfilling. I do my best to give back what I have received to the NFB, my children's schools, my church, PEO, Lions, and other organizations. I am putting into practice lessons learned from my parents, and I continue to benefit from the direction instilled by the NFB and Dr. Jernigan. Building leaders is what he did best. I am so grateful for all that he taught me. He changed my life forever. I learned more about loving, and I continue to share his wisdom. He continues to change the world every day, through me and through the thousands of other people he touched.

CHAPTER 25

A CLOSE WORKING FRIENDSHIP

by Frank Kurt Cylke

Note: Frank Kurt Cylke served for more than thirty-five years as the director of the National Library Service for the Blind and Physically Handicapped in the Library of Congress. In 2011 the NFB Board of Directors created an award in memory of Kenneth Jernigan. Kurt Cylke was the first to receive this award at the time of his retirement. It reads:

Kenneth Jernigan Award
National Federation of the Blind
For your dedication to the highest ideals
For your commitment to extraordinary service
For your imaginative leadership in
bringing information to the blind
We, the organized blind movement, confer upon
Frank Kurt Cylke,
The Kenneth Jernigan Award
Your hand assisted in every challenge
Your heart responded to every need
You're a trusted colleague and a valued friend
July 8, 2011

Mr. Cylke participated in NFB conventions every year from 1974 through 2011. He also met with Dr. Jernigan several times a year in Washington, DC, Baltimore, and other places around the world. Although the quotes below perhaps understate the close friendship that developed between Kurt Cylke and Kenneth Jernigan, those who knew them best know how valuable this relationship was to both of them. During the last year of Dr. Jernigan's life, Kurt Cylke sent brief handwritten messages to him almost weekly.

Below are printed excerpts from the *Braille Monitor*, including the brief remarks delivered at the December 1998 memorial service for Dr. Jernigan.

Kenneth Jernigan and Frank Curt Cylke together at the convention podium, 1991.

WORKING WITH THE BLIND HAS BEEN A GREAT pleasure. Everyone is familiar with the book, *All I Really Need to Know I Learned in Kindergarten* by Robert Fulghum. Well everything I learned, I learned at the NFB. I appreciate every member, and I appreciate the critical questions. I can't count the members of the Federation with whom I have worked and become friends.

Kenneth Jernigan and I came to be very, very close friends. It wasn't that way when I started. It was that way through the years. I appreciated Dr. and Mrs. Jernigan's cooperation and Dr. and Mrs. Maurer's cooperation. For years I sat at the head table at the banquet with Mrs. tenBroek. Like me, she was a librarian, and you can't imagine what that was like for me. Jim Gashel and Dr. Zaborowski, etc., etc. It's been a wonderful experience. I believe the experience was a very synergistic one among the Library of Congress, National Library Service (NLS), and the NFB.

I fronted for the NLS Division for the Blind and Physically Handicapped, but behind me was and is perhaps the most talented group of people I believe I have ever experienced …

I came to the NLS in the early 1970s and stayed for thirty-nine plus years. I knew nothing about libraries for the blind at that time. The Library of Congress, NLS, was experiencing an awkward patch with the NFB. The Librarian of Congress sent me to NLS—I did not solicit it—but part of my personal philosophy is "His food I eat; his song I sing." When I got there I said to myself "I know nothing about this, but let me throw myself into it because this ought to be interesting."

Shortly after I got there, I found that from my perspective the Library's position had been the wrong one and untenable. They had committed a serious social and political breach, and it was up to me to correct it. I worked very hard to do so, and fortunately Dr. Jernigan was of a similar mind. He was more than ready for a rapprochement if the Library would just admit that it had made an error.

A young employee was scheduled to speak to the full NFB convention in 1971 and did not attend or call to say he was not attending. This was an affront to the organization, and Dr. Jernigan took it that way. In retrospect I believe he had a right to. My predecessor chose to defend his staff member's actions, and that's what initiated the problem. It was an affront to the NFB to have a national conference with a featured speaker and not to have that speaker call to excuse his absence. Anybody is rational enough to understand that there could be a crisis in your life, but not to tell the NFB was a problem—anyone can make a phone call.

When I arrived in 1974, it was time to put all of this behind us. Thankfully our relationship got better and better as the years went by, and after almost four decades, being the Director was the most interesting thing I have ever done. I had never met a blind person before. That's why I was put there—the library perceived I would be a neutral person without an ax to grind.

I'm not being patronizing here, but I think the highlight of my service was making a rapprochement with the organized blind community, understanding how important the library program was and is for information and recreation to the community, and turning the program into a consumer-oriented program. We have set up various committees—the Collection Development Committee, the Machine Committee, and others. We based our whole program on what the consumer wishes, blending that with the obvious professionalism of the library side in selecting the appropriate books, magazines, and delivery services. I also established a new staff position, a point of consumer liaisons, held from the very beginning by Judy Dixon as it still is. That position is set aside specifically for a member of the user community to make sure that there is involvement in all of the decisions at NLS and that a consumer voice is heard.

I had two other interesting experiences I would identify as highlights. One was introducing the four-track cassette in the 1970s. The NLS staff worked many years toward introducing the digital-talking Book. We learned a great deal between these two changes in technology: from the disk to cassette and from the cassette to the digital. I believe the digital has gone so well because we learned a lesson, which was inculcated in us by the NFB, of listening to the consumer. When we designed the digital machine, we had the full involvement of two consumer organizations. We tested it in fourteen different locations, and the test involved a representative from the NFB as well as from an organization for the physically handicapped in Wisconsin. We tested with all sorts of users: bright and slow, young and old, those without physical handicaps and those with physical handicaps, those with perfect listening and those without. The reception of the machine has proven this to be an ideal way to go about it. Batelle was doing the hardware, HumanWare was doing the software, and the NFB was working on testing.

Everything is a compromise. The machine could be a little smaller, could be a little bigger, but I think it came out pretty well. This machine is for a broad population and most people are happy with it. Of course it could not have been done without a fine engineering group at NLS. So far we have produced 330,000 machines, and we have had 110 problems. That's fantastic. I have mentioned that I always feel awkward as the head of the organization because I get all the attention. Obviously a great deal of the work is done by the staff. They deserve most of the credit.

Through my career, there have been bad times—the NFB was there with me—and there will be bad times again. But the good times predominate. I remember the *Playboy* situation. The interesting thing was that it was a member of the press corps, on a hot July day, who went to a Congressman from Ohio (now deceased) and showed him a Braille copy of *Playboy*. The Congressman said, "This is horrendous that government money should be spent on this." Therein started the tale. It got to the point where the Library's budget was brought up on the floor of the House of Representatives. When that specific point was made, they deducted the cost of the production of that magazine from the budget. Blind people have the right to read what sighted people do. The government does not want to produce pornography, and it doesn't, but the NFB has always insisted that blind people want to read as big a variety of material as they can get their hands on. When the case went to court, Congressman Jerry Lewis and Congressman

Vic Fazio, both of Ohio, came to testify as friends of the court on behalf of the Library and had the money restored. My perspective was that, once they called for a roll call vote, nobody, regardless of their political view, wanted to vote for *Playboy* in Braille, but they didn't really oppose it because we got the money back and continued to do it.

In my almost forty years of running the program, Congress has been very generous to the library for the blind program. We never asked for money that we didn't need, and we never asked for money that couldn't be justified. In every case we received the money that we asked for. Now in some cases it became a public discussion when we were asking for a big shot of money (seventy-five-million dollars) to execute the digital program. Unsolicited, the NFB served the NLS very well. Members told the Congress why the books are important to the blind and why the change to digital books had to be immediate. Although I worked with many NFB leaders, my closest and most constant contact was Kenneth Jernigan.

Some people have asked about the Joint Organizational Effort Committee during the 1990s. I'm not trying to be humble, but the JOE Committee—that was really Dr. Jernigan's idea, and he brought together all in one room the NFB, NLS, American Council of the Blind (ACB), the Canadian National Institute for the Blind (CNIB), and American Foundation for the Blind (AFB). At that time there was a lot of friction among the groups. Dr. Jernigan brought them together very well, and there were several projects where we all worked together. We had different ideas about our user base. One project that members of the Committee funded was a contract with the Census Bureau to get us some numbers. There were other projects, but as for JOE, Dr. Jernigan gets the credit for bringing the organizations together, for starting the committee, and for supporting it. When you look at all that Dr. Jernigan accomplished, it is really amazing. I think that relationships in the field of work with the blind have been better ever since.

Looking back again, I was there when Ray Kurzweil brought the concept of his reading machine to Dr. Jernigan at the 1975 convention. I consider that one of the highpoints of my life. Ray was a young kid—a PhD student at MIT, I think—and he was selling Dr. Jernigan on the concept. Just to observe Ray selling it and Dr. Jernigan coming from zero to grasping it to embracing it was amazing. Now there's this little machine that you can hold in your hand—a cell phone which can read called the KNFB Reader Mobile—that's something.

The Library is being computerized just as much as the rest of the world. Users can now download books from a restricted website BARD (Braille and Recorded Downloads). Like the rest of the population, blind users who are under forty find this as normal and easy as the internet is to most college students. More and more people over sixty are also beginning to download books. I think everybody agrees that this trend will continue and accelerate. I know NLS will do its best to keep up. This is no longer my work.

I think of things I have learned about blindness during the last 4 decades and where we are today. The situation of the blind community is not widely and publicly known and accepted. I wound up with library services for the blind and physically handicapped, and everybody in this blindness world is aware of it, but the general public isn't. I think the NFB is making a lot of difference. The NFB's effort of having Mark Riccobono drive around in that automobile was wonderful because it will cause people to say, "Oh, a blind person driving a car," and the students from Virginia Tech working on this are saying, "Wow, we're going to help blind people drive a car." It's amazing.

I can remember sitting at a dinner in Kenneth Jernigan's home when this topic first came up. I will admit that I said, "My goodness, is this man reasonable?" I didn't say this to him, but I had it in my head. I'm confessing that I was saying in my head that "I just don't understand this; how could that ever be?" That was maybe fifteen years ago; now I've seen it on the *Today Show* and I've read about it in the paper. Ford is working on the same thing. I look at that and I remember, and I think that this is an amazing world we live in.

(Dr. Jernigan announced his serious illness early in December of 1997. From that time until his death, Mr. Cylke frequently sent him handwritten notes such as the following:)

December 5, 1997:

> A note to let you know your friends are thinking of you and praying for an intercession. I have not phoned as I did not wish to become a bother. If you feel up to a conversation at any time, do feel free to call me either at the office or at home. With continuing best regards to you and Mrs. Jernigan, I remain your friend, Kurt Cylke

July 31, 1998:

> It appears we will meet again on September 14. I expect it will be a joyous affair—I know it will be. This Sunday I am off for a few days to Newport, Rhode Island, to sail with my son and a few other friends. I will be thinking of you and praying, of course. Your Friend …

(Dr. Jernigan made his last public remarks at the Canadian Embassy in Washington, DC, after he was presented the Winston Gordon Award by the Canadian National Institute for the Blind. Immediately afterward Mr. Cylke sent another note.)

September 16, 1998:

> Yesterday certainly was special. More than the recognition your remarks carried the day. We are indeed in a new world where together agencies of and for the blind will reduce problems significantly. I trust that the effort did not tire you completely. There is more to do that requires your special talent …

September 25, 1998:

> A note to let you know your friends are thinking of you and praying for your situation. You were missed at our recent visit to Baltimore. Marc Maurer held up his end, but it was not the same. With fraternal love, I wish you a painless time …

(The following was presented at the memorial service for Dr. Jernigan:)

I have the greatest respect for Dr. Maurer, Jim Gashel, and others as I have said. But my friendship with Kenneth Jernigan was a very special relationship. Only once in a generation, perhaps only once in a lifetime, does an individual enter into our sphere with power and drive to change humankind for the best. We are all fortunate that Kenneth Jernigan was with us for the time that he had here on earth. An intellectual; an educator; a leader; a guider; an administrator; and, yes, a book man.

While Kenneth Jernigan held no library degree and indeed never served as a librarian, he may be considered the librarian of all times—for blind and physically handicapped individuals. Under his direction, the State of Iowa built a magnificent library with a superb collection and outstanding service pattern. As President of Friends of Libraries for Blind and Physically Handicapped Individuals in North America, Kenneth Jernigan advised and consulted with the National Library Service and other library and information services in the United States as well as in other countries.

Kenneth Jernigan loved books, Kenneth Jernigan wrote books, Kenneth Jernigan edited books, Kenneth Jernigan published books, Kenneth Jernigan recommended books, and Kenneth Jernigan distributed books. Not once, to my knowledge, did he ever suggest removing or not adding an item from any collection. He believed only in building the store of materials available to the blind and physically handicapped community.

He and I shared a love of poetry. He quoted many poems on many occasions, and they were always insightful and to the point. The poem below was a comfort to me when he died.

> God saw you were getting tired,
> And a cure was not to be,
> So He put his arms around you
> And whispered, "Come to me."
> With tearful eyes we watched you,
> And saw you pass away.
> Although we loved you dearly,
> We could not make you stay.
> A golden heart stopped beating,
> Hard-working hands at rest.
> God broke our hearts to prove to us,
> He only takes the best.

Kenneth Jernigan believed that knowledge would set the blind free. It has and will continue to do so.

CHAPTER 26

KENNETH JERNIGAN'S PROPHETIC VISION

by Ray Kurzweil

Note: Dr. Raymond Kurzweil is one of the foremost inventors and thinkers in the world today. He has written numerous books regarding his unique understandings and approaches. He credits Kenneth Jernigan with being a key influence on his life. Currently, Ray Kurzweil is director of engineering at Google. He continues to work with the National Federation of the Blind in the development of pioneering technological devices, and each year provides substantial funding to the National Federation of the Blind scholarship program.

IT STARTED IN 1975 WHEN I MET JIM GASHEL, AND HE introduced me to Dr. Jernigan. We had this little project of a reading machine for the blind, which we were trying to interest people in, and a lot of people were interested in it and wished us well. But Dr. Jernigan, being the visionary and entrepreneurial person that he was, wanted to get involved and help us—help us in ways we hadn't expected, including helping us design the reading machine. We didn't realize we needed that help, but we did. Dr. Jernigan and Mr. Gashel organized a whole team of blind engineers and helped insure that the reading machine would be really useful to blind people.

Raymond Kurzweil, 2015.

In my first session with Dr. Jernigan I didn't know a lot about blindness—I'm still learning, though I know more than I did forty years ago. He said that blindness could be just a characteristic, just a minor inconvenience, and that blind people could accomplish anything they wanted to, just like sighted people. At the time I wondered to myself to what extent that was really true—was this a goal or a political statement, or was it a reality.

I think technology has one small part to play in realizing Dr. Jernigan's vision. I very quickly came to recognize that Dr. Jernigan's statement was a plain, realistic assessment, provided that you had an organization like the National Federation of the Blind to make some prerequisites of the vision a reality. Those prerequisites include training in the skills and knowledge to accomplish the things desired.

The right attitudes about what blind people can accomplish are important for blind and sighted people alike. And information accessibility in all forms must be encouraged at every level. Technology has one role to play, but the technology needs to be useful to blind people. It needs to have the right features. Blind people must be involved in its development. The technology and the skills needed to use it effectively must be available.

One lesson I have learned is the difference between the words "disability" and "handicap." Visual impairment, blindness, is a disability. It may or may not be a handicap, depending on whether that person has the right set of skills and access to the right kind of technology. That's why organizations like the National Federation of the Blind and the World Blind Union are vital, so that the power of this technology is applied to overcoming those handicaps.

One handicap is the inability to access ordinary print for material that isn't readily available in Braille or Talking Book form. Reading machines had the potential of overcoming that. They had to be designed in the right way, and people had to have access to them, to be able to afford them, and high quality training had to be offered. That's true for all technology including the internet. Overcoming handicaps is not necessarily an issue of technology. Sometimes simple technical solutions such, as the fiberglass cane, can overcome limitations in travel. But that's a matter of having the right set of skills, and again we need organizations like the NFB to make sure they are available.

My orientation is technology, and it is my hope and belief that I can help solve some problems. The KNFB Reader Mobile and the BLIO software are exciting tools for me and for the blind.

Let me share some recollections. I grew up in Queens, New York, and had a unique religious upbringing. Although my parents were Jewish immigrants who had fled Hitler, I had a religious education at a Unitarian Church, where the philosophy was "many paths to the truth." So we would spend six months studying Judaism, then six months Buddhism, and so on. The unifying theme was tolerance and the idea that everyone can contribute. There was an emphasis on social consciousness and being part of the greater struggle for equality and justice in society. So we played an active role in the Civil Rights movement at that time and took part in Civil Rights marches.

I remember thinking how fortunate I was to live in the time of Martin Luther King Jr. Even from afar I felt inspired and grateful to be able to play a small role in that historic drama. I felt at the time, and continue to feel, that Dr. King was one of the great leaders in American history.

Well, that's how I feel about Dr. Jernigan, and I believe that Dr. Jernigan's impact and legacy are at least as significant and profound. And like Dr. King the benefits of Dr. Jernigan's work go far beyond the immediate issues that each of these two remarkable leaders fought for.

Let me go back to 1975. We had developed a prototype of the Kurzweil Reading Machine but needed support to perfect it and launch this technology as a product. We showed our work to many of the organizations in this field, and the people were friendly and supportive. But words of encouragement don't exactly pay the rent. When we met Dr. Jernigan and Jim Gashel our luck changed.

Literally within hours came the reply that Dr. Jernigan was most excited about what we had demonstrated and wanted to work with us immediately to raise funds, to perfect the machine technically, and to get the word out.

Now that's what I call responsiveness. That was just one small example of Dr. Jernigan's leadership: bold, decisive, knowledgeable, confident, insightful, and effective. That particular collaboration resulted in significant funds being raised and a group of blind scientists and engineers from the NFB working closely with us to perfect the reading machine. I do recall at the time thinking it unusual that so many of them came from the state of Iowa.

And that was the beginning of a friendship that lasted the next quarter of a century. As fortunate as I felt as a child growing up in Queens, New York, to participate from afar in a movement led by a great American such as Dr. King, imagine how blessed I have felt to have had the opportunity over the past quarter century to work closely with Dr. Jernigan and to get to know him as a friend and colleague.

Raymond Kurzweil and Kenneth Jernigan with the original Kurzweil Reading Machine at the Iowa Commission for the Blind, 1977.

Dr. Jernigan was as exceptional a person as he was a leader. I cannot think of anyone in my life more gracious. To be welcomed into the home of Dr. and Mrs. Jernigan was always a special pleasure. He had a terrific sense of humor and was a great storyteller, a wonderful host, and a remarkably attentive friend. Despite his many responsibilities he always had time thoughtfully to relate to everyone he met as a unique and distinctive human being.

As a leader he had a simple and profound vision of how things could be, of how things should be, and a rare ability to translate that vision into effective action in the complex world we live in. He was, of course, a great orator. I will always remember his NFB convention banquet addresses, the grand cadence of his words, and the soulful rhythm of his delivery.

I feel joy to have had the privilege of knowing Dr. Jernigan during his lifetime and gratification for knowing that he was able to taste the fruits of his labor. Unlike Moses, he got to walk on the Promised Land. While there is much left to be done, Dr. Jernigan has left behind a great movement and many talented people who continue to be inspired by his legacy. We can take pleasure in the satisfaction he expressed near the end of his life in what had been accomplished and in his confidence in the leadership he left in place.

Dr. Jernigan is with us today. He wants us to be joyful and optimistic about the world that lies ahead. It is a world made richer by Dr. Jernigan's having been part of our lives.

In his last year of life, Dr. Jernigan articulated a vision that he knew he would never get to see: the world's first world-class research and training institute for the blind. It was a prophetic vision. Unlike many other leaders, Dr. Jernigan knew he was a mortal man and prepared for new leadership long before it appeared to be necessary. He nurtured Marc Maurer's leadership skills and was as successful in this endeavor as in everything else he did. When Dr. Jernigan passed from the scene, the vision of the research and training institute was just that: a vision and a daunting challenge that many doubted would ever come to fruition. It is a fitting testament to Dr. Jernigan's lifetime of leadership, and a reflection of the dedication of its membership and the continuation of inspired leadership in the person of Dr. Maurer, that this institute now rises like a sphinx in the outskirts of Baltimore.

Let me share with you why I think Dr. Jernigan's vision came at a propitious time. Technology has always been important, but we are now standing on the precipice of an inflection point in human history. Technology is reaching what I call the knee of the curve, a point at which its inherently exponential growth is taking off at a nearly vertical slope. I've studied technology trends for several decades and developed mathematical models of its progression. The most important insight that I've gained from this study is that the pace of progress is itself accelerating. While people are quick to agree with this assessment, few observers have truly internalized the profound implications of this acceleration. It means that the past is not a reliable guide to the future. We're doubling what I call the paradigm shift rate every decade. So the twentieth century was not one hundred years of progress at today's rate of progress because we've been accelerating up to this point. The last one hundred years was akin to twenty years of progress at today's rate of progress. And we'll make another twenty years of progress at today's rate of progress, equal to all of the twentieth century, in the next fourteen years. And then we'll do it again in another seven years. Because of the power of exponential growth, the twenty-first century will be like twenty thousand years of progress at today's rate of progress, which is a thousand times more change than what we witnessed in the twentieth century.

The other insight I've had is that technology is a mixed blessing. It brings both promise and peril. If we could magically go back two hundred years and describe the dangers of today's world to the people back then (as just one example, enough nuclear weapons to destroy all mammalian life on Earth) they would think it crazy to take such risks. On the other hand, how many of us today would want to go back to the world of two hundred years ago? Before you raise your hands, consider this. If it wasn't for the progress of the past two centuries, most of us here tonight wouldn't be here. Average life expectancy in the year 1800 was only thirty-seven years. And most people on Earth lived lives filled with poverty, hard labor, disease, and disaster, not to mention the ignorance and prejudice that were rampant with regard to the capabilities of the blind.

So we've come a long way through both promise and peril. And few of us would want to go back. As Dr. Jernigan said many times, we'll never go back, certainly not to the lack of opportunity that was the rule for blind people a half century ago.

We also see the promise and peril of technology in its impact on the blind. The digitization of information has brought many opportunities as blind people have led the world in rates of computer literacy. Reading machines; screen readers; voice-based news services such as NFB-NEWSLINE®; and Braille translators, printers, and note takers have all provided greater opportunity. But the downside of technology has also been evident. With the great profusion of electronic displays, access for the blind is often an afterthought if it is thought of at all. The moment that text-based screen readers were perfected, the graphical user interface was introduced. It then took at least a decade for Windows-based screen readers to become workable, at which time a new set of challenges emerged from a profusion of new Web-based protocols, such as Flash and JAVA, that are once again creating barriers.

This intertwined promise and peril is going to accelerate. Will this represent a great enabler for blind students and workers? Or will it represent a new set of obstructions? To assure the former, we'll need new technology breakthroughs, public accessibility standards, and a panoply of programs for training and availability. This is why Dr. Jernigan's initiative was prophetic.

It looks like we have the NFB's National Research and Training Institute for the Blind just in the nick of time. It is now known as the Jernigan Institute for Research and Training. Dr. Jernigan clearly perceived that a prerequisite of valid research regarding blindness was and is the participation and leadership of the blind themselves. As the Jernigan Institute has become a reality, President Maurer has insisted on this and continues to work with me and others to find the cutting edge of new ideas and technology to insure that the blind are not left behind. Despite his illness Dr. Jernigan realized he did not have a moment to spare in articulating his vision. And this is why I believe that Dr. Jernigan's foresight was a prophecy.

CHAPTER 27

HE DIED AS HE LIVED

by Mary Ellen Jernigan

Note: Here is the presentation Mary Ellen Jernigan gave at the memorial service for her husband in December 1998; it is both moving and informative.

IN THE MONTHS, THE WEEKS, THE DAYS BEFORE HIS death, Dr. Jernigan and I talked of many things—one of which was that this gathering which has brought us together today would soon occur and that this time it would be I not he standing before you at the microphone. So we talked about what to do. I made a suggestion or two, which he vetoed. "Let others do that, or you do it later. What you must try to do on this day—what people will want you to do; what I want you to do is to talk about me—me as you knew me." At the time it seemed a fairly simple directive. It seemed less so as I began to think about carrying it out.

For I was not yet twenty-one when I first met Dr. Jernigan, and the whole of my adult life is his creation. My very first

348

encounter came in the form of a vibrant booming voice on the other end of a telephone line: "I understand you have just been initiated into Phi Beta Kappa. That tells me one of two things—you've either got some brains, or you're very good at bluffing people into believing you do. If you've got the time and inclination to find out which, I do." Well I had the time and inclination, and I was hooked. Thirty-three years have passed—years in which I had the good fortune to share in a special way the life and work of this unusual man.

I will leave it to others to recite the facts and accomplishment of five decades of inspired service and leadership—to chronicle, to evaluate, to place in historical perspective.

My task is something else, and I would frame it like this:

In the all too brief year that has passed since Dr. Jernigan's illness first became apparent, there has been an enormous outpouring of sentiment. It has come from across this country and from abroad. It has come from blind people, yes. But it has come from an astonishingly large number of sighted people also. And the message—sometimes expressed with supremely literate eloquence; sometimes with elegant simplicity; sometimes with halting difficulty—has been essentially the same and very basic: this man made a real difference in my life; the world is a better place for his having lived in it. So what I have been asking myself is why—why did this man have such a universally profound effect upon so many?

First I thought, well, it's obvious. You look at how he lived. Next I thought, No! It's obvious. You look at how he died.

And finally I said, Wait! It's the same thing. It was when that thought crystallized that the answers began to come. When a man knows he has but a year to live, how he chooses to spend that year tells you something. And if it happens that he chooses to spend that year as he spent the rest of his years, it tells you even more.

So let us look together at Dr. Jernigan's last year.

When we do, we see a man who spent his birthday, Christmas Eve, Christmas Day, and Valentine's Day in the hospital and made them joyous occasions for all; a man who, having been told in the morning to expect to die within the year, spent the afternoon comforting and reassuring those around him; who on that same day brought together the delegates of the North America/Caribbean Region of the World Blind Union by conference telephone to arrange an orderly transition to a new President; and who later that same evening initiated a vast exploration of all possible alternative therapies—facing the future with hope and belief and insisting that the rest of us do so also.

Over the next two weeks he assembled the collective leadership of the organized blind movement and began making far-ranging, long-term plans for the years to come. Immediately he began a grueling regimen to fight the disease—facing with resolute discipline each day's conglomeration of needles, pills, vitamins, supplements, intravenous tubing, breathing machines, detoxification procedures, and of course the ever-present nausea. He did what he had to do and took care to shield others from knowing the physical agony of it all.

With the construction of three levels of magnificent sky decks, he brought to final completion the twenty-year-long transformation of a once dilapidated South Baltimore factory building into the sparkling facility we now know as the National Center for the Blind and then startled us all with a bold new vision to undertake the construction of the National Research and Training Institute for the Blind—a 175,000-square-foot, five-story building which will position us to take full advantage of the opportunities which will abound in the coming millennium.

He summoned the strength to cause the first million dollars to be committed to the capital campaign and to oversee preparation of the detailed architectural plan for the new facility. He commissioned construction of the three-dimensional model you will see on display today. He examined the model with his own hands, making final adjustments to the plans as he did so.

He fought his way back from a nearly fatal bacterial infection, donned his tuxedo, selected and served to good friends the finest wines from his cellar, and returned the next day for another round at the North Carolina clinic. He edited two final Kernel Books—volume number 14, *Gray Pancakes and Gold Horses*, and volume 15, *To Touch the Untouchable Dream*.

Not wanting any part of our home ever to become inaccessible to him, he added an elevator, taking great delight in designing it to appear as if it had always been part of the 154-year-old structure. Since he could now reach the roof by the new elevator, he built a deck there. And while he was at it, he revamped the heating and air conditioning system and installed for me a restaurant-capacity stove complete with an indoor gas grill.

He added to his collections: wines, liqueurs, coins, music boxes, old time radio tapes, and most especially his carved onyx glasses. He negotiated and signed contracts at first-class hotels for the year 2000 and 2001 National Conventions—keeping the single room rates still under $60.

He served as National Convention Chairman at his forty-seventh consecutive National Federation of the Blind convention—a convention he described as very nearly perfect and during which he spoke to the Parents Seminar, the Scholarship Class, the Engineers Division, the Cultural Exchange and International Program Committee, and the Resolutions Committee; roamed the Exhibit Hall; delivered a major address; gave an award at the Banquet; presented the audit and financial reports; and was moved to tears by Lloyd Rasmussen's singing of the Technology Song.

He re-examined his relationship with God, a process which led us both to the Catholic Church, and more specifically to St. Joseph's Monastery Parish and to Father Gregory Paul.

Then, with the fading of summer into early fall, came also the fading of any reasonable hope for survival. As the weakness and pain increased, he accepted what was to come with dignity and grace and with the utmost care and concern for those around him, for the organization he had spent his life serving, and for the broader field whose unity and advancement he had done so much to promote. He pulled forth reserves of strength to complete the things he wanted to finish:

He saw to the final details of the construction project at our home, organizing a massive top-to-bottom, inside-and-out cleaning project, taking particular delight in learning that the front steps, which had always been thought to be a nondescript, blackish stone, were really gleaming white marble underneath, and insisting that they be shown off to all.

Kenneth Jernigan grills steaks for his friends, 1995.

He visited with friends and colleagues who came to say good-bye, and as always he fed people—in our dining room, in our yard, on our roof, at the National Center, at his favorite restaurants when he could manage the strength to go out and with carry-out from those same restaurants when he became unable to leave home. He took enormous pleasure in serving his most prized wines and feeding his friends.

He hosted a twenty-fifth wedding anniversary celebration for Dr. and Mrs. Maurer though he himself was too weak to attend. He spent a last night at the National Center for the Blind, conducted a seminar for leaders of the National Council of State Agencies for the Blind, and the next morning took one final walk on the new Skydeck.

When, through a fluke in the medical system, he learned that the cancer had spread throughout his bones before his own physician received the report, he found himself gently breaking the news to the doctor and offering consolation. Upon learning that the sculptor who had been commissioned to create a bronze bust of him had (out of concern for his failing strength) been told he must work entirely from photographs, he insisted on dressing in full regalia and sitting for him in person.

He sent Dr. Maurer and me to Atlanta to make preparations for next summer's convention, giving us detailed instructions as to what to do. He selected and had wrapped the presents he wanted to give this Christmas. He called Ernie Imhoff to thank him for a beautifully perceptive article in *The Baltimore Sun*.

He inquired daily about the well-being of his kittens and gave instructions for their care. He moved both of our birthdays forward so as not to miss them. He talked and planned with me and Dr. and Mrs. Maurer about what he hoped for David and Dianna in the years to come.

He spent large blocks of time with his brother Lloyd, with whom he shared an ever-stronger bond and for whose character, accomplishments, and integrity he had a deep and abiding respect. He shared a last precious evening with his daughter Marie (Toinette as he always called her) and her husband Tony Cobb.

He had long, unhurried conversations with our President, Marc Maurer, in whom he had total, complete, and absolute trust; and in whose development and emergence as the widely-respected leader of the organized blind movement he took an unremitting joy—believing to the very depth of his being that whatever part he himself had played in that development and emergence was his own most cherished achievement.

He willed himself the strength to travel to the Canadian Embassy in Washington, D.C., to receive the Winston Gordon Award. There, in that beautiful setting, surrounded by family, friends, and colleagues, he made what he knew and we all knew would be his last public appearance. Though weak and in visible pain, he strode to the podium, where with a touch of humor, with elegance and simplicity, he spoke to us as he always did—of the brightness of the future.

This was Dr. Jernigan's last year. Do we find in it an answer? Why the great impact of this man? This man who had the supreme confidence and grace to die exactly as he had lived?

Yes! I think we do. We find it in hope and belief, energy and intellect, planning and purpose, discipline and drudgery, care and compassion, loyalty and love. But above all we find it in an infectious joy that took each and every moment of life and made of it a treasure to be shared with others.

To the question, "Do you miss him?" the answer is of course, excruciatingly so. Every minute. Every day. But the answer also is, how can I? He taught me to think, and he is present in every thought I have. He taught me to love, and he is present in everything I love. Under God's guidance he formed and shaped and molded the world I live in and those who live in it, and it and they are all around me—vibrant and alive—as is he in each of us and in the work he left us to finish.

As for those treasured moments: here is one for us all to share. Near death, in a voice weak, but clear with conviction Dr. Jernigan said these things:

I have lived to see the plans for our new building far enough along to know that it will be done.

I have lived to see unity on our own terms in the blindness field in North America.

I have lived to see Marc Maurer come into the full maturity of leadership.

As I draw to the end, I don't feel I've left any loose ends.

I am content. I am at peace.

But what about us? Can we be at peace about this? Perhaps not all of the time and not just yet. But neither can we fail to carry forward the legacy he left us—to live with joy, to make of life's moments treasures to be shared. He would expect us to do no less.

And so I close with the words of this verse someone sent to us—one we read together and found of comfort:

> Do not stand at my grave and weep.
> I am not there. I do not sleep.
> I am a thousand winds that blow.
> I am the diamond glints on snow.
> I am the sunlight on the ripened grain.
> I am the gentle autumn rain.
> When you awaken in the morning's hush
> I am the swift uplifting rush
> Of quiet birds in circled flight.
> I am the soft stars that shine at night.
> Do not stand at my grave and cry;
> I am not there. I did not die.

CHAPTER 28

TEN YEARS OF PROGRESS IN THE JERNIGAN INSTITUTE A LETTER TO THE FRIEND I NEVER MET

by Mark A. Riccobono

Note: Sixteen years after the death of Dr. Jernigan, Marc Maurer chose not to run for reelection as President of the National Federation of the Blind. Instead, he supported Mark Riccobono. We have every reason to believe that Mark Riccobono has the ability and understanding to lead the Federation forward in as exciting, loving, and farsighted a manner as those who held this office before him. Below is the report he gave to the convention in 2014, just before he was elected. One year after he became NFB President, his leadership continues to be strong and exciting.

TODAY WE COME TO ACKNOWLEDGE A MILESTONE IN our movement: ten years of progress in the Jernigan Institute of the National Federation of the Blind. One of the last projects Kenneth Jernigan undertook in his life was dreaming and planning for a research and training institute—a place where we could bring together our collective hopes, test our life experiences, and build new patterns of education that would be dramatically different from anything that had previously existed.

From left to right: Oriana, Melissa with guide dog, Austin, Elizabeth, and Mark Riccobono stroll through the park, 2015.

I never met Dr. Jernigan in the flesh. I came into the Federation as a college student in 1996, and in the two years that I had before his death, there were probably half a dozen times I should have taken the opportunity to introduce myself. I foolishly thought that I was not worth his time or that he had more pressing things to do than talk to me. Today I recognize the tremendous opportunity I lost, and I have tried not to repeat that mistake with others. Although I did not have the benefit of receiving Dr. Jernigan's mentorship firsthand, I have been educated by his writing, inspired by his voice, and influenced by his life's work.

In reflecting on the past ten years, I find myself wondering what he would think of what we have done and what I might say to him personally if I had that opportunity. Then it came to me that, while I might never know what he would say about the Institute that bears his name, I certainly could tell him what we have done and what we dream of doing in the decades ahead. And so I have written him a letter that I would like to share with you this afternoon because it reflects the tremendous progress we have made and points to the work ahead on our journey together.

Dear Dr. Jernigan,

I wanted to write to you on the occasion of the tenth anniversary of the National Federation of the Blind Jernigan Institute. I have had the honor of working there since day one, and for the past seven years I have served as executive director. I have felt the love, hope, and determination that have come out of our innovative programs—I have always thought of it as carrying your spirit forward to a new generation. I want to share with you what we have been doing in our Jernigan Institute and tell you how the work continues to shape my own development as a member of the National Federation of the Blind.

My first assignment at our Jernigan Institute was to build a new, dynamic, hands-on brand of science education for blind youth and have it ready for our first summer. I know that you loved science fiction, and you would have delighted in joining these young blind people in touring the Goddard Space Flight Center, talking to NASA engineers, and building and launching a rocket from Wallops Island. The significance of that first summer was, like your Iowa experiment, the way we put the Federation model to the test. We started with our own experience, which, for many of us, meant the experience of having been shut out of science. True to your example, we chose not to be victims with sad stories of exclusion, but rather victors, determined that what we were denied would serve as our inspiration to improve conditions for the next generation. We gathered outstanding blind educators, skilled blind scientists and engineers, subject matter experts in the areas we wanted to teach, and all of us dreamed about what we would do with our combined talents. This created a beautiful model for collaboration and innovation. We often had to teach ourselves before we could teach the blind teens. A number of dogfish sharks were dissected by blind mentors developing and perfecting their nonvisual techniques. That first summer was critical in educating the blind teachers that we did not have to be bound by the traditional models of education and that we could create something new and unprecedented. We knew immediately that the next task would be to use that experience to teach others how to do the same thing.

You made a commitment to Mrs. tenBroek to have a special space in our building to house Dr. tenBroek's personal and professional papers. We have dedicated over 17,000 square feet to our Jacobus tenBroek Research Library on Blindness. Dr. tenBroek's papers are well preserved, and we have developed tools for researchers to use so that they can discover his significant contributions to society. The library also contains your own papers, as well as the hundreds of books and periodicals that the organization has collected over the decades. We have digitized our print books and magazines, and we continue to grow our unique collection of the history and achievements of the blind. We are now focusing more energy on capturing and telling the story of blind people in writing, on video, and through other emerging media. Blind people are more a part of society than ever before, yet most people do not know a blind person. The walls of our institute are filled with pictures of blind people living the lives they want. We now need to take those images beyond our walls and use today's technology to distribute them around the world in order to create greater awareness about our organization and demonstrate the power of the blind in action.

In the early days of our institute, the majority of our time and resources were spent on specialized products for the blind. While we are still collecting and testing these, today a majority of our time and resources are spent on the same products our sighted friends are buying. This shift reflects both the higher expectations we have for our participation in the mainstream and our advanced experience with technology. We have set a new standard that demands that technology be built from the beginning with nonvisual access as one of the design considerations. Through our implementation of a web accessibility certification program, participation in the establishment of standards for digital content, and collaboration with key experts around the world, our NFB Jernigan Institute has been pivotal in bringing leadership and expertise to the technology industry.

A cornerstone of our technology program over the past decade has been our continued relationship with Ray Kurzweil. We jointly developed and commercialized a reading machine that could fit in a pocket and pioneered accessible ebook reading platforms that contributed significantly to the current revolution in ebooks. Ray Kurzweil is now the director of engineering at Google, and this has created an opportunity for us to work together on a new front—deeply embedding accessibility into the culture of one of the world's cutting-edge information technology companies, and facilitating dialogue about how we might combine our expertise to develop new accessible products that would be available to blind people at the same time they become available to the general public. This is just one of many technology partnerships we are pursuing.

I have heard you had a preference for traveling by car rather than by air. Well, we have now built technology that would allow you to be in the driver's seat. And the science fiction stories of vehicles that drive themselves are quickly becoming fact—some speculating that they may be on the market within five or six years. When we opened our institute, we began sharing the dream that, with the right combination of imaginative partners, we could create a car that a blind person could drive. We hoped that the challenge of building this technology would get people to think about blindness in new ways and motivate them to work on innovative approaches to nonvisual access that would go far beyond the act of driving a car safely. While it has done that, the most enriching part of this project has been what it has done to shape our own attitudes and expectations for ourselves as blind people. Our Blind Driver Challenge® has also given us the tools and increased credibility to sit at the same table with the engineers working on driverless vehicles so that we now can have influence in the nonvisual interfaces that will be built into these new modes of transportation.

We are capitalizing on the interfaces we built for driving a car by imagining how we might use them on a bicycle. As you well know, it is not the physical riding of the bike that is the problem for blind people, but rather avoiding all the obstacles in the way. Access to reliable and affordable transportation systems is still a significant barrier for the blind, and accessible bicycle technology may play a significant role in increasing our options to travel independently. Getting technology onto a bicycle is just one of the many dreams that have been circulating throughout our convention that we are now actively working to fulfill. Some things in the Federation do not change—we gather together, dream together, and work on transforming our dreams into reality.

Our organization is about changing the lives of blind people, and it has most certainly changed mine. I never thought of myself as a driver until I was called to lead the blind driver project for the Federation. In every way that matters, the Federation has taught me to be a driver rather than a passenger in my own life. The blind driver experience has totally transformed my approach to our work. I no longer know what the limits are for us, and I carry this sense of wonder, adventure, and limitless possibility to every new assignment that comes my way.

I should share just a few more things about education, since that is one of the primary assignments in which I have focused my energy and something in which you so deeply believed. During the summer of 2007, we decided we needed to take our programs for young people to the next level by bringing two hundred blind high school students to Baltimore and giving them the opportunity to work with blind mentors and instructors. Imagine taking the feeling you get when you walk into the convention hall and packing it into an entire week on a university campus. We put on the largest and most dynamic education program in the history of the blind—the NFB Youth Slam—and we have now done it several times. During the past decade, through our National Center for Blind Youth in Science initiative, we have taught: aerospace engineering, agriculture, architecture, art, biology, chemistry, civil engineering, computer science, cyber security, earth science, electrical engineering, forensics, genetics, geology, geoscience, human physiology, journalism, kinesiology, marine biology, mechanical engineering, mineralogy, nanoscience, neurolinguistics, paleontology, physics, psychology, recreational math, robotics, shark dissection, simple/complex machines, space science, and video description. In the process we have developed hundreds of future blind leaders and dozens of outstanding new partners.

Many of our programs have grown out of the work of our affiliates. In Maryland we started an initiative to teach Braille to blind children, and we coined the phrase "if they will not teach them, we will teach them ourselves." Since 2009 we have built that affiliate project into a national movement— Braille Enrichment for Literacy and Learning, or NFB BELL. This summer we will have thirty-four programs in twenty-three of our affiliates. That means that more than 150 blind children will receive direct Braille instruction this summer—and this is just one of a dozen Braille-related programs we conduct. We have also made substantial investments in the future of Braille- related technologies and tools to bring about the creation, editing, and dissemination of tactile and three-dimensional learning objects. With our continued leadership, imagination, and innovation, the next ten years are going to produce some of the most powerful Braille and tactile learning experiences in the history of the blind.

Dr. Jernigan, I know that much of your work was made possible because of your ability to effectively read and write. Your eloquent and concise description of the attitudes educators in your time held about Braille still ring true: "Jenny can read print, but Johnny must read Braille." To combat the bias against Braille, we have developed the only research- based assessment tool for determining the appropriate reading medium for blind children, and I can give personal testimony to its validity and importance. My daughter Oriana—who just turned four years old—is getting ready to go into pre-K in the

Baltimore Public Schools. My wife Melissa and I were a little nervous about what type of reading and writing instruction would be recommended for her. A local teacher used the National Reading Media Assessment and determined that our daughter should be learning both Braille and print in school. We were already prepared to press for this instruction, but it was a relief to have evidence from the field to support our experience. I did not learn Braille when I was young, and my vision was worse than Oriana's when I was her age. Her path will be better than the one I took because of the progress made possible by the National Federation of the Blind, and for that I will always be grateful. Oriana is just one example of the many young people of this generation who will be shaped by and benefit from the programs built and disseminated from our Jernigan Institute.

It is my dream, but more than that, it is my commitment that the education programs of the Federation become so widespread that they touch every blind child as soon as their parents know their child is blind. What adventures will those children dream of pursuing when they never live a day without knowing the determination, the power, and the love of the National Federation of the Blind in their lives? This is what we are working on in our education programs, and I believe it is achievable during our next ten years.

Dr. Jernigan, there is much more to tell you, but I recognize that you probably already know what I have said to you and more. After all, your spirit has been part of our work this whole time, and your contributions to our movement continue to ring in the hearts of Federationists across the country. I am curious what you would say about our movement today. From my perspective the details of what we do have changed, the scope of our influence and program has grown, and the complexity of our work has increased, but, at its core, the heartbeat of the organization is the same as it has been since the founding of our movement. Recently, we have been expressing this core Federation feeling in these words: I am filled with hope, energy, and love by participating in the National Federation of the Blind because my expectations are raised, my contributions make a difference to me and to others, and I can celebrate the realization of my dreams with my Federation family.

There is one more thing I want to thank you for, and that is your recommendation that Marc Maurer, your friend and mentee, my friend and mentor, be the president of the National Federation of the Blind. He has been everything you expected him to be, and he has risen to every demand the Federation has placed on its president during the past twenty-eight years. Every day he exemplifies what it is to be a dreamer, a visionary, a leader. He has kept and has strengthened the bond of faith that we in the Federation have with one another. His energy and imagination have been given in full measure, but it is his demonstrated love for the Federation and the members who give it vitality that has forever sealed his place in our hearts. That we have made such tremendous progress through our Jernigan Institute is just one shining example of his leadership and his effort to build leadership in others.

Mark Riccobono and Marc Maurer celebrate
Riccobono's election to NFB Presidency at the 2014
NFB National Convention in Orlando, Florida.

Lately we have been talking a lot about transition and about Dr. Maurer's plan to focus his energy on passing the torch to a new generation of leaders—a generation of leaders who have benefited from the great joy he takes in building the National Federation of the Blind. We are now prepared to serve as his teachers wherever knowledge needs to be shared, his innovators when a new idea needs wings, his engineers when there are programs to develop, and his friends in the movement, always and forever. Although transition and change always create uncertainty, I believe we are ready to hold tight to that bond of faith and carry it forward in a way that will be worthy of the love that Dr. Maurer has put into his service to our movement. I know that I do not intend to let him down, and I am confident I can find thousands of other Federationists who feel the same way.

That is my report. I am sorry I did not take the opportunity to meet you in person, but my gratitude for what you have done for me and those I love knows no bounds. I hope that my own actions in our Federation are ones that you are proud to have happen in a building that carries your name. I close my letter with a quote from one of your speeches, a quote that I now reflect back to you as my recommitment to the mission of the National Federation of the Blind: "Yesterday and tomorrow meet in this present time, and we are the ones who have the responsibility. Our final climb up the stairs will not be easy, but we must make it. The stakes are too high and the alternatives too terrible to allow it to be otherwise ... We will continue to climb. Our heritage demands it; our faith confirms it; our humanity requires it. Whatever the sacrifice, we will make it. Whatever the price, we will pay it."

Yours in the movement,
Mark A. Riccobono, Executive Director, Jernigan Institute
National Federation of the Blind

Those are some of my reflections on my ten years at the Jernigan Institute, and I hope that I have contributed as much to our movement during the past decade as the movement has contributed to my own development as a blind person. I know with certainty that what we have built, we have built together, and there are many great milestones yet to be achieved on our journey. In celebration of the tenth anniversary of our institute and the coming seventy-fifth anniversary of our movement, we reflect on the past with gratitude, we come to the present with firm resolve, and we prepare to build our own future with the determination, joy, and unbreakable bond of trust and love that will always mark the spirit of the National Federation of the Blind.

CHAPTER 29

BLINDNESS: THE FEDERATION AT FIFTY

by Kenneth Jernigan

Note: Kenneth Jernigan was an outstanding writer and speaker. He probed and analyzed ideas and facts, both those that were widely accepted and those hardly considered before. His delivery showed mastery of cadence, melody, conviction, and warmth. People loved to hear him speak. Fortunately, we have recordings of many of his speeches, and the NFB has filed and organized most of his written work. Here, we are including the address he delivered at the NFB Convention banquet in 1990, which was the fiftieth anniversary of the organization. This will offer the reader a glimpse of the man as he spoke for himself. A recording of this presentation is also available at https://nfb.org/Images/nfb/Audio/BanqSpeech/BSP-1990.mp3. Other speeches and articles are included on the nfb.org website. A partial list of these materials will be shown in the Fifth Extra.

Dr. Kenneth Jernigan laughs while at the microphone, 1975.

IF THE ENGINEERS OF 1800 HAD POSSESSED COMPLETE drawings for a transistor radio (one that could be bought today for $10), they couldn't have built it, not even if they had had billions or trillions of dollars. They lacked the infrastructure— the tools, the tools to build the tools, and the tools to build those; the plastics, the machines to make the plastics, and the machines to make the machines; the skilled work force, the teachers to train the work force, and the teachers to train the teachers; the transportation network to assemble the materials, the vehicles to use the network, and the sources of supply. All of this is generally recognized, but it is far less well understood that what is true of material objects is also true of ideas and attitudes. In the absence of a supporting social infrastructure of knowledge and beliefs, a new idea simply cannot exist.

So far as I can tell, there are only three possible reasons for studying history—to get inspiration, to gain perspective, or to acquire a basis for predicting the future.

In 1965 Dr. Jacobus tenBroek, the founder and leader of our movement, spoke at our twenty-fifth banquet, reviewing the first quarter century and charting the road ahead. We were meeting in Washington, and more than a hundred members of Congress were present. I was master of ceremonies, and some of the rest of you were also there. Tonight (twenty-five years later) we celebrate our Golden Anniversary, and the time has once again come to take stock. Where are we, where have we been, and where are we going?

In a sense the history of our movement begins in the distant past—in the medieval guilds and brotherhoods of the blind in Europe, in the tentative stirrings of organization in China, and even earlier—but the National Federation of the Blind is essentially an American product. Its genesis is native. Although (as we all know) Dr. Jacobus tenBroek presided at the founding of the National Federation of the Blind in 1940 at Wilkes-Barre, Pennsylvania, he had a teacher (Dr. Newel Perry), who laid the foundations and served as precursor. And Dr. Perry, in turn, had a teacher, Warring Wilkinson.

Most of what we know about Wilkinson is contained in the eulogy which Dr. tenBroek delivered at the time of Dr. Perry's death in 1961[1], but our knowledge is sufficient to tell us that

Wilkinson was a worthy teacher of the teacher of our founder. He was the first principal of the California School for the Deaf and Blind. He served in that capacity for forty-four years, from 1865 to 1909. He not only loved his students but also did what he could to move them toward the main channels of social and economic participation. Particularly, he saw the potential in young Perry, sending him from the California School for the Blind to Berkeley High to complete his secondary education. To do this Wilkinson (who was ahead of his time both in his understanding of education and the needs of the blind) had to overcome numerous obstacles.

I was fortunate enough to know Dr. Perry, meeting him when I moved to California in 1953. He was then eighty, and he spent many hours with me reminiscing about what conditions for the blind were like when he was a boy. He came to the California School for the Blind when he was ten—"penniless, blind, his father dead, his home dissolved. Two years earlier he had lost his sight and nearly his life as the result of a case of poison oak, which caused his eyeballs to swell until they burst and which held him in a coma for a month." It was at the School, of course, that he first met Warring Wilkinson.

While going to high school (from which he graduated in 1892) he lived at the California School for the Blind. He also lived there while attending the University of California from 1892 to 1896. His admission to the University (as had been the case with high school) had to be secured over strong resistance. Again, Wilkinson was the pathfinder, young Perry his willing and anxious instrument. "Wilkinson's role in Perry's life as a youth can hardly be overestimated: father, teacher, guide, supporter—in Perry's own words, 'dear Governor.'"

After graduating from the University, Dr. Perry devoted himself to further education and to the search for an academic job. "He took graduate work at the University of California, meanwhile serving successively as an unpaid teaching fellow, a paid assistant, and finally as an instructor in the department of mathematics. In 1900, following a general custom of that day, he went to Europe to continue his studies. He did this for a time at the University of Zurich in Switzerland and then at the University of Munich in Germany. From the latter he secured in 1901 the degree of Doctor of Philosophy in Mathematics, with highest honors.

"He returned to the United States in 1902, landing in New York, where he was to remain until 1912. He had about eighty dollars in capital, a first-class and highly specialized education, and all of the physical, mental, and personal prerequisites for a productive career—except one, eyesight.

"During this period he supported himself precariously as a private coach of university mathematics students. He also applied himself to the search for a university position. He displayed the most relentless energy. He employed every imaginable technique. He wrote letters in profusion. In 1905 he wrote to 500 institutions of every size and character. He distributed his dissertation and his published article on mathematics. He haunted meetings of mathematicians. He visited his friends in the profession. He enlisted the aid of his

THE POWER OF LOVE | 377

teachers. He called on everybody and anybody having the remotest connection with his goal.

"Everywhere the outcome was the same. Only the form varied. Some expressed astonishment at what he had accomplished. Some expressed interest. One of these seemed genuine—he had a blind brother-in-law, he said, who was a whiz at math. Some showed indifference, now and then masked behind polite phrases. Some said there were no vacancies. Some said his application would be filed for future reference. One said ironically: 'For what—as an encouragement to men who labor under disadvantages and who may learn from it how much may be accomplished through resolution and industry?' Some averred that he probably could succeed in teaching at somebody else's college. Many said outright that they believed a blind person could not teach mathematics.

"Many of these rejections may, of course, have been perfectly proper. Many were not. Their authors candidly gave the reason as blindness."

Dr. Perry failed not because of lack of energy or qualification but because the necessary infrastructure of attitudes and beliefs did not exist to allow it to be otherwise—so he did not find a job in a university. Perhaps it was better for the blind (for those of us gathered here tonight) that he did not—but for him what pain! What absolute desolation and misery! And he had to face it alone—no family, no supporting organization of the blind—only himself and the bleak wall of continuing rejection year after year. He might have quit in despair. He might have become embittered. But he did not. Instead, he returned to

California and settled down to build for the future. If he could not have first-class treatment for himself, he was absolutely determined that at least the next generation of the blind would not be denied.

He taught at the California School for the Blind from 1912 to 1947—and day after day, month after month, season after season he exhorted and indoctrinated, preached and prepared. He was building the necessary infrastructure of ideas and beliefs. Those who were his students went on to become his colleagues, and as the number grew, the faith was kept. There would be a state-wide organization of the blind in California. It did not happen until 1934, but when it came, it was built on a solid foundation. And there would also be a National Federation of the Blind—but not yet.

Dr. Perry was to that generation what Warring Wilkinson had been to him. In the words of Jacobus tenBroek, his most brilliant student and the man who would lead the blind in the founding of their national movement: "We were his students, his family, his intimates, his comrades on a thousand battlefronts of a social movement. We slept in his house, ate at his table, learned geometry at his desk, walked the streets interminably by his side, moved forward on the strength of his optimism and confidence."

Dr. tenBroek graduated from Berkeley High School in 1930 with, as he said, "plenty of ambition but no money." He was prepared to enter the University of California but was denied state aid to the blind, a program then newly instituted as a result of Dr. Perry's efforts in sponsoring a constitutional amendment, which had been adopted by the voters of California in 1928. In Dr. tenBroek's words, "The reason for the denial was not that my need was not great. It was that I intended to pursue a higher education while I was being supported by the state. That was too much for the administrative officials. Almost without discussion, Dr. Perry immediately filled the gap. Just as Warring Wilkinson had earlier done for him," said Dr. tenBroek, "he supplied me with tuition and living expenses out of his own pocket for a semester while we all fought to reverse the decision of the state aid officials.

"It was," Dr. tenBroek said, "ever thus with Dr. Perry. The key to his great influence with blind students was, first of all, the fact that he was blind and therefore understood their problems; and second, that he believed in them and made his faith manifest. He provided the only sure foundation of true rapport: knowledge on our part that he was genuinely interested in our welfare."

So the new generation came to maturity, and Jacobus tenBroek was to be its leader. Born in 1911 on the prairies of Alberta, Canada, he was blinded by an arrow in a childhood game and moved to California to enter the school for the blind. He went on to earn five academic degrees—from the University of California at Berkeley a bachelor's in 1934, a master's in 1935, a law degree in 1938, and a Doctorate in Jurisprudence in 1940; and from the Harvard Law School a Doctorate in Jurisprudence in 1947. There is no need for me to talk to this audience about Dr. tenBroek's brilliance—his learned articles and books, his chairmanship of the California Board of Social Welfare, his scholarly pre-eminence and national acclaim, his writings on constitutional law that are still the authoritative works in the field. Rather, I would speak of the man—the warm human being who fought for acceptance, led our movement, and served as my mentor and role model—the man who was my closest friend and spiritual father.

When Dr. tenBroek was first trying to get a teaching position in the 1930s, the climate of public opinion was better than it had been a generation earlier, but he faced many of the same problems which had confronted Dr. Perry—and sometimes with identical letters from the same institutions. "It was," he said, "almost as if a secretary had been set to copying Dr. Perry's file, only changing the signatures and the name of the addressee."

Here is what Dr. tenBroek wrote to Dr. Perry in March of 1940. At the time he was studying at Harvard:

"Last November a large Midwestern university was looking for a man to teach public law. Having read my published articles but knowing nothing else about me, the head of the department in question wrote a letter to the University of California inquiring whether I would be available for the position. Cal. replied that I would and accompanied the answer with a considerable collection of supporting material. However, when the department head learned that I was blind, the deal was off although none of the competing applicants had as good a paper showing.

"This incident seems to me of particular interest because, although I have been refused other jobs, this was the first instance in which blindness could be traced as the sole explanation for rejection. Of course, in other cases blindness was also the determining factor, but the fact could not be demonstrated as well."

There were other letters and other rejections—but on June 8, 1940, Dr. tenBroek was able to write to Dr. Perry:

"We have justification for hanging out the flags and ringing the bells. I have been offered and have accepted a job at Chicago University Law School. The job pays $1,800, is denominated a half-time position, and lasts for only a year. But it is a job nevertheless. And the Harvard people, who exerted no end of pressure to get it for me, regard it as an excellent opportunity. The position is designated `tutorial fellowship' and consists in supervising the research of the first- and second-year law students. It involves no actual classroom teaching, except possibly by way of an occasional fill-in job."

This was how Dr. tenBroek (the man who fifteen years later was to win the Woodrow Wilson Award for the outstanding book of the year in political science and who was always the most sought-after professor at the University of California) was to begin his teaching career. Yet, even today there are sighted people (and also some of the blind—people who ought to know better) who tell me that the blind are not victims of discrimination. Yes, the tenBroek job search was fifty years ago, but you know and I know that we have not yet come to first-class status and equal treatment in society. The framework of ideas and beliefs to make it possible, though long in the building, is still not complete. Warring Wilkinson, Newel Perry and his students, Jacobus tenBroek and the founders of our movement, and the Federationists of succeeding decades have worked year after year to improve the climate of public acceptance and make opportunity available for the blind, but the job is not yet finished. Each generation has built on the work of the one before it. Each has fought and hoped, dreamed and drudged for the one to follow—and also for the blind then alive.

What we have done must be seen in perspective; for no act of the past (no gain or denial) is irrelevant, and no present behavior of ours can be divorced from tomorrow. We are close to freedom, and we must finish the journey.

1940 was notable for something else besides Dr. tenBroek's debut at the University of Chicago. It was also the year of the founding of this organization. With the passage of the Social Security Act in 1935 the federal government had supplanted the states in providing assistance to the blind. In 1939 Congress and the Social Security Board combined to pressure the states having the most forward looking programs (chief among them California but also Pennsylvania, Missouri, and Wisconsin) to repeal their progressive laws. This supplied the immediate impetus for the formation of the Federation, but of course the momentum had been building for a generation. The event occurred at Wilkes-Barre on November 15 and 16, 1940, coincident with the convention of the Pennsylvania Federation of the Blind.

In a letter to Dr. Perry dated November 19, 1940, Dr. tenBroek said in part: "The confab at Wilkes-Barre gave birth to an organization, the National Federation of the Blind—of which you, vicariously through me, are president. The long-range aims of the organization are the promotion of the economic and social welfare of the blind, and its immediate and specific aims are the sponsorship of the principle of Senate Bill 1766 and an amendment of the Social Security Act.

"Seven states were represented at the organizational meeting—Minnesota, Wisconsin, Illinois, Missouri, Ohio, Pennsylvania, and California. We arrived in Wilkes-Barre in the middle of Friday afternoon. ...

"On Saturday morning, while the Pennsylvania state meeting was going on, I had several back-of-the-scenes conversations with Pennsylvania leaders. ... In the afternoon ... we drew up a skeleton constitution, which we presented to a meeting of all of the delegates to the national meeting, beginning about four o'clock and ending about the same time twelve hours later. ... The meeting was interrupted at 5:30 in the afternoon long enough to give the other delegates a chance to eat dinner, and the Pennsylvania leader (Gayle Burlingame) and me a chance to appear on the local radio, where we lambasted hell out of the Social Security Board."

On January 4, 1941, Dr. tenBroek wrote to Dr. Perry concerning the details of getting the new organization started. "With the National Federation of the Blind not yet two months old," he said, "its permanence is definitely assured. The factor guaranteeing that permanence is the closely knit nucleus composed of Minnesota, Pennsylvania, and California. We three have now had enough experience with each other to know that we can make a go of it. ... We can add to this trilogy the state of Wisconsin.

"I had a letter from Minnesota yesterday to the effect that they are ready to pay their assessment but that they wish assurance that Pennsylvania and California are also ready before they mail their check. I also had a letter from Pennsylvania stating that it is ready but wishes assurance that Minnesota and California are ready. I have written to both of these states requesting them to make out their checks, payable to the Treasurer of the National Federation, and to send them to me, with the stipulation that I shall not forward them to the Treasurer until I have the dues from each of the states of California, Pennsylvania, and Minnesota. Consequently, if California is ready, I suggest that you follow the same procedure ..."

But the new president did not limit himself to procedural matters. The Federation immediately assumed its present-day role of working to improve the quality of life for the nation's blind. In a letter to Dr. Perry dated March 15, 1941, President tenBroek described the efforts he had been making to get changes in the administration of public assistance to the blind. Here, in part, is what he said:

"After a week in Washington I have more unsocial exchange to report than specific accomplishment. ... Gradually working our way upward, Gayle Burlingame and I first presented our case to Jane Hoey, director of the Bureau of Public Assistance, and her associate, a lawyer named Cassius. Next we went to Oscar Powell, executive director of the Social Security Board; and finally to Paul V. McNutt, administrator of the Federal

Security Agency. Hoey is simply another social worker of the familiar type but with a higher salary than most. Cassius has lost none of his qualities since Shakespeare described him, except that his wit has been sharpened by a little legal training. Powell is a very high caliber man with a fine sense of argumentative values, a considerable store of good nature, and unusual perception. He simply is not a believer in our fundamental assumptions. McNutt, on the other hand, is a lesser Hitler by disposition and makes our California social workers look like angels by comparison.

"Hoey and Powell had argued that the new ruling of the Board did not necessarily result in a reduction of a recipient's grant by the amount of his earnings or other income. McNutt took the position that it did and, moreover, that it should. 'Are you saying to us,' I asked McNutt, 'that blind people should have their grants reduced no matter how small their private income and no matter how great their actual need?' His answer was that he was saying precisely that. I formulated the question in several other ways, only to get the same reply. I can't say that I wasn't glad to get this official declaration from McNutt since it provides us with an official declaration by the highest administrator of them all that ought to be of immense propagandistic value to us. Moreover, McNutt's conduct during the conference has provided us with the most perfect example of the arbitrary and tyrannical methods of the Board that we could hope to have.

"In the remaining week that I shall stay in Washington, we shall attempt to carry our appeal to the last administrative step. Senator Downey of California and Senator Hughes of

Delaware are attempting to secure for us appointments with Mrs. and President Roosevelt.

"As things stand, the only course open to the blind of California is to urge the legislature to retain the blind aid act in its present form and tell the federal government to go to hell. Even if we can get a favorable amendment to the Social Security Act, it certainly will not be until after the California legislature adjourns."

This is what Dr. tenBroek wrote in 1941, and although we have often said in this organization that the first task which the Federation faced after its founding was to help the blind of the nation get enough money for bare survival, I sometimes wonder if we have made the point with sufficient clarity to convey the desperation of it. The report which was prepared following the 1941 convention of the Federation in Milwaukee says in part:

"Mr. Stephen Stanislevic of New York City reported as follows: 'The blind population of New York State is roughly estimated at 13,000. Of these, more than half are in New York City. A very small number of our people, a few hundred in all, are at present employed in sheltered industries, on government projects, at newsstands, or in miscellaneous enterprises. The majority depend for sustenance either upon private bounty or upon Social Security grants. The average monthly grant per individual is $27 in New York City and $23 in the up-state counties. This is the paltry pittance which the wealthiest state in our Union sees fit to dole out to those of its citizens who are blind.'

"Mr. Hugh McGuire explained that in Indiana there are approximately 2,600 blind and that between 2,200 and 2,300 are drawing assistance with the monthly average of $20."

That was forty-nine years ago, and much has happened in the interim. Not that it happened by chance, of course. Mostly we made it happen. How many times since 1940 has the National Federation of the Blind led the way in social reform in this country, not only for the blind but also for others? To mention only three examples, we pioneered exempt earnings for the recipients of public assistance; we pioneered fair hearing procedures in rehabilitation and other public programs; and we pioneered jobs for the disabled in government service.

As I have already said, our first task as an organization was to initiate programs to enable the blind to get enough to eat. In 1940 and the decades immediately following, most of the blind of this country were desperately poor, and there were almost no government programs to help. When people are hungry, little else matters. Later (although many of us were still in poverty—and, for that matter, are now) we worked on rehabilitation and employment, and today we emphasize civil rights and equal participation in society. But essentially our role is what it has always been—seeing that blind people get equal treatment and a fair shake.

It is not only in basics but also in detail that our operation today is often much the same as it was in past decades. Let me give you a rather specialized example. I have made a lot of banquet speeches at these conventions, and certain key ideas are central to them all. I can sum up the essentials in a few sentences. The real problem of blindness is not the blindness itself but what the members of the general public think about it. Since the agencies doing work with the blind are part of that general public, they are likely to possess the same misconceptions that are held by the broader society. The blind, too, are part of that broader society, and if we are not careful, we will accept the public view of our limitations and thus do much to make those limitations a reality. The blind are not psychologically or mentally different from the sighted. We are neither especially blessed nor especially cursed. We need jobs, opportunity, social acceptance, and equal treatment—not pity and custody. Only those elected by the blind can speak for the blind. This is not only a prime requisite of democracy but also the only way we can ever achieve first-class status.

These are the essential points of every banquet speech I have ever made. The banquet speeches are meant to be widely circulated. They have the purpose of convincing those in work with the blind and the public at large that they should rethink their notions about blindness. They also have the purpose of stimulating our own members to increased activity and added vigor. Hopefully the speech will be sufficiently inspiring, entertaining, and literate to make people want to listen to it—and later (when it is distributed) to read it. The difficulty is that just about the same thing needs to be said every year, but it has to be restated so that the listeners (and ultimately the readers) will feel that it is different—and maybe even new. After a while, putting it all together becomes quite a problem.

I don't think I ever talked about this matter with Dr. tenBroek, and I certainly did not attend the 1949 convention at Denver.

With this background let me share some correspondence with you. Kingsley Price was a Californian, who became a college professor and was living in New York in the 1940s. In a letter dated April 8, 1949, Dr. tenBroek wrote to urge him to attend the Denver convention. "The problem does not arise," Dr. tenBroek said, "out of an unmixed desire to enjoy your company. I would like to get you to give the principal banquet address. This is something that I have not been able to dodge very often in the seven conventions that we have had. [Conventions were not held in the war years of 1943 and 1945.] The banquet address," Dr. tenBroek continued, "is a kind of focal point in which the problems of the blind, their peculiar needs with respect to public assistance, employment, and equal opportunity are formulated and presented both with an eye to rededicating and stimulating the blind persons present and an eye to enlightening and possibly converting the many sighted persons who have been invited to attend. For me, this has always been a job of rehashing and repeating certain central ideas. My imagination and new methods of statement have long since petered out. The next alternative is to get a new 'stater.' This is what I would like you to be.

"We would, of course, introduce you as a New Yorker since there are far too many Californians in the limelight as it is. We also, if we thought hard, could find one or two other chores about the convention for you to do.

"Please think this matter over as long as you want, but let me have an immediate answer."

Among other things, Dr. tenBroek obviously wanted to get Price to become more active in the movement, and he probably thought the banquet speech might be a way to do it. There has always been a tendency for the successful members of a minority to try to avoid involvement. The only trouble with this behavior is that it won't work. At an earlier period many blacks tried to straighten their hair and hide in white society, but then they realized that it was better to make it respectable to be black. The corollary, if I need to say it, (and every one of us had better know and understand it) is that it is respectable to be blind. That's what the National Federation of the Blind is all about.

No blind person in this country is untouched by our successes or, for that matter, our failures, and no blind person can avoid identification with the rest of us. This is true regardless of how the blind person feels about it and regardless of how we feel about it. Blindness is a visible characteristic, and all of us are judged by each other whether we like it or not. The feeling I have toward those blind persons who try to hide in sighted society is not anger but pity—and, yes, I am talking about those who are regarded (and who regard themselves) as highly successful.

When Professor Price replied to Dr. tenBroek, he said that he might be able to come but would probably do a bad job making the banquet speech. He should not have been deceived by the light tone of Dr. tenBroek's letter of invitation, for Federation presidents take banquet speeches seriously. In a letter dated April 21, 1949, Dr. tenBroek set him straight:

Dear Kingsley:

I am not now, nor on June 20th shall I be, in the least inclined to accept a bad job in the banquet address. If I were willing to accept a bad job, I can think of at least a hundred persons of assured competence to satisfy the requirement.

The banquet address is the focal point of the whole meeting. It has come to be regarded as the most important thing that is done at a convention. Many people of influence in the community are invited to hear it. The Governor of the State often is present, and the occasion is used to give him instructions as to what his policy should be towards the blind. The address is expected to be of such a character that it can be published and circulated the nation over with some advantage to the blind.

The address must be on the subject of the nature of the problems of blindness, and the discussion should be frank and forthright. Amplification of points by way of personal experience is always helpful and attractive. One conclusion that must always be reached is that the blind should speak for themselves because they are the only persons qualified to do so.

I enclose a copy of my Baltimore address, which may give you an idea of what needs to be said. The same truths have to be retold, but the hope is that they will be dressed up in a new and fresh style, even to the point of appearing to be different truths.

One further word: It may be that the address will be broadcast direct from the banquet hall. Consequently, both speech and delivery need to be well in hand.

I hope these admonitions are solemn enough to convince you of the importance of doing a good job and yet not so solemn as to scare you away. We are desperately in need of a new voice and a new brain to do this job, and a man from New York has geographical advantages as well.

Cordially yours,

In considering our past I am mindful of the fact that except for inspiration, perspective, and prediction, there is no purpose to the study of history. Certainly we can find inspiration in the lives of Warring Wilkinson, Newel Perry, and Jacobus tenBroek. Often in lonely isolation they worked for a distant future which they knew they would never see but which is our present. Using meager resources that they could ill-afford to spare, they fought to build a framework of opportunities and benefits which constitute the underpinning and foundation of what we have today. How can we be unmoved by their story? It speaks to us across the years—calling us to conscience, giving us strength for the battles ahead, reminding us of our heritage, and underscoring our duty to those who will follow.

Yes, there is inspiration in our history, and it also gives us perspective. Otherwise we might become discouraged. Even today, with all of our work, more often than not when we come to one of these conventions and talk to the press, they assign their medical reporters to deal with us. They want to write stories about our guide dogs, the causes of blindness, and how capable we are because we can do the ordinary tasks of daily living, like cutting our food or finding our way.

But the balances are shifting. Each year a few more reporters are beginning to understand that our story is not one of physical loss, or courage in the face of deprivation, but lack of opportunity and denial of civil rights. A perfect example is the recent story in the *Wall Street Journal* about the blind who are running their own businesses. It contains not a scrap of pity, nor a wasted word about those who (though blind) are valiantly struggling to earn a living. Of course, it contains drama—but it is the drama of a people fighting to rise to first-class status in a society which treats them like children and wonders why they object.

Recently I went to the White House and talked with the President of the United States about the problems we are having with the airlines and the Federal Aviation Administration. We are being excluded from exit row seats on airplanes, but year after year the Federal Aviation Administration has said that there is no issue of safety in our sitting there. Now (because of pressure by the airlines) they have changed their minds. As we have become painfully aware, the issue of seating is only one tiny part of an overall pattern of bullying and harassment which blind persons face today in air travel. The difficulty which always confronts us when we try to discuss this issue is the talk we get about compassion and how commendable it is that we are trying to be independent—all of which is a bunch of nonsense. If we pose a hazard in exit row seats, we shouldn't sit there—and we wouldn't want to. If we don't pose a hazard in exit row seats, then we have as much right to sit there as anybody else, and to try to make us move is an infringement of our civil rights. In either case compassion has nothing to do with it.

Dr. Kenneth Jernigan, circa mid-1990s.

When I tried to convey these ideas to President Bush, his response made it clear that he had been thoroughly briefed— and by somebody who hadn't the faintest idea about the issues. In answer to my question the President said that if there was no evidence that we constituted a greater hazard than others in exit row seats, he would put an end to the rule if he had the power to do so—which, of course, he has. I wasn't very hopeful about the outcome because of two things. President Bush kept avoiding the word blind, gingerly referring to us as the non-sighted, and he said that Secretary of Transportation Skinner had personally tested an airplane door to see whether an individual without sight could open it—which is comparable to my going (with my lack of experience) to a hospital to see what can be done with surgical instruments.

The President assigned his lawyer, Boyden Gray, to look into the matter and get back to me. The results were what might have been expected. Mr. Gray did not talk to us, nor did he look at the video tape of our test evacuation of an airplane. Instead, he talked with Secretary of Transportation Skinner, who told him that we constituted a safety hazard—which data he ceremonially transmitted to me.

So was it just an exercise in futility? Not at all. This is where perspective helps. In 1940 Dr. tenBroek was not able even to get a hearing from President Roosevelt even though two United States senators tried to help him do it. Moreover, my talk with President Bush was only one brief skirmish in our long airline fight, and the history of our past efforts tells us that we will ultimately win. It is true that Dr. tenBroek did not get to talk with President Roosevelt, but it is also true that most of the Social Security reforms for which he fought have been adopted—and mostly they have been adopted through the efforts of the National Federation of the Blind.

Likewise, we lost the recent motion to cut off debate on our airline bill in the United States Senate, but we had fifty-six votes. And when has any other group in the blindness field ever been able to bring a bill of its own to the floor of the United States Senate and have it be the pending business of that body for several days? Never—and never with the number of votes we mustered. Again, this was only a single skirmish in an individual battle in a long war—a war which has been going on for more than a century, a war which we are winning, and a war which we intend to finish.

Yes, our history provides us with both inspiration and perspective—and it also gives us the basis for prediction. Of course, no individual can be sure of what will happen tomorrow, but I feel absolutely certain that this organization will continue to grow and lead the way in improving the quality of life for the blind. The outward appearance of the issues may shift, but the basics will not change—not until we have achieved equal treatment and first-class status in society. And we will achieve it.

In examining our past I have not attempted to assess my own role and contributions. How could I? I have been too close, loved too deeply, put too much of my life into the process. All I can say is this: When Dr. tenBroek was dying, I made certain pledges to him. I have tried to keep those pledges. I shall always try to keep them. And when in 1986 I thought the time had come that the movement would best be served by my leaving the presidency, I did it. The decision was not easy, but I think it was right. I believe that President Maurer was the best person we could have chosen for the position and that he will lead this organization into the twenty-first century—stronger, more vibrant, and more committed than it has ever been. And there is something more: I think the new generation that is on the horizon will provide leaders and members who will be present fifty years from now when we meet for our hundredth anniversary. We must never forget our history; we must never dishonor our heritage; we must never abandon our mission. With love for each other and faith in our hearts we must go the rest of the way to equal status and first-class membership in society. Let us march together to meet the future.

Footnote:

1. All of the material concerning Dr. Perry except what I got from my own discussions with him is taken from "Newel Perry: Teacher of Youth and Leader of Men," by Jacobus tenBroek, *Braille Monitor*, February 1976. The quotes from Dr. tenBroek are taken from letters in the files of the National Federation of the Blind.

You Can Help

The National Federation of the Blind has special giving opportunities that will benefit the giver as well as the NFB. Of course the largest benefit to the donor is the satisfaction of knowing that the gift is leaving a legacy of opportunity. Gifts may be structured to provide tax benefits for either current donations or estate planning.

At the time of Dr. Jernigan's death, a fund was established in his memory to assist blind individuals and families with blind children to meet other blind people and learn about opportunities at national conferences for that purpose. A donation made payable to the National Federation of the Blind can be made in his honor and designated for the Kenneth Jernigan Fund.

Your gift makes you a partner in the NFB dream. For further information or assistance, go to our website www.nfb.org or contact the NFB.

FIRST EXTRA

Congressional Record
Wednesday, October 14, 1998
Delivered by Senator Paul Sarbanes
Democrat of Maryland

A Tribute to Dr. Kenneth Jernigan, President Emeritus of the National Federation of the Blind [page S-12572, 54 lines]

Mr. Sarbanes: Mr. President, today I rise to pay tribute to a man who has dedicated his life to improving opportunities for others. He is Dr. Kenneth Jernigan, who served as President of the National Federation of the Blind from 1968 to 1986 and as the Federation's President Emeritus until his death on October 12, 1998. In these capacities Dr. Jernigan has become widely recognized and highly respected as the principal leader of the organized blind movement in the United States.

On September 14, 1998, Mr. President, I was privileged to attend an especially moving ceremony to recognize Dr. Jernigan for worldwide leadership in the development of technology to assist blind people. The award, consisting of $15,000 Canadian and a two-ounce gold medallion, was given by the Canadian National Institute for the Blind, and the event was held at the Canadian Embassy here in Washington.

This recognition by our neighbors to the north was a tangible expression, Mr. President, of the respect which Dr. Jernigan has earned throughout his lifetime of service on behalf of blind people in the United States and around the world. Through his grit, determination, and skill Dr. Jernigan achieved personal success. But more important than that, as a lifetime teacher and mentor he gave others the chance for success as well.

Born blind in 1926, Kenneth Jernigan grew up on a small Tennessee farm with little hope and little opportunity. But, Mr. President, in the story of Kenneth Jernigan, from his humble beginning in the hills of Tennessee to his stature as a national—and even an international—leader, the story of what is right with America is told.

Dr. Jernigan may have been blind in the physical sense, Mr. President, but he was a man of vision nonetheless. In his leadership of the National Federation of the Blind, he taught all of us to understand that eyesight and insight are not related to each other in any way. Although he did not have eyesight, his insight on life, learning, and leading has no equal.

Mr. President, for those who knew him and loved him, for the blind of this country and beyond, and for the National Federation of the Blind—the organization that he loved and built—the world without Kenneth Jernigan will be difficult. But the world he has left in death is a far better world because of his life.

The legacy which Dr. Jernigan has left is shown in the hundreds of thousands of lives that he touched and the lives that will still be touched by his example and the continuing power of his teaching. This will be the case for many generations to come. Mr. President, Kenneth Jernigan will be missed most by his family and friends, but his loss will be shared by all of us because he cared for all of us. He cared enough to give of himself. With the strength of his voice and the power of his intellect, he brought equality and freedom to the blind. As he did so, Mr. President, Kenneth Jernigan taught us all to love one another and live with dignity. That is the real and lasting legacy of Kenneth Jernigan ...

Second Extra

Remarks delivered by Fredric K. Schroeder at NCSAB

Perhaps the comments of Fredric K. Schroeder, federal commissioner of the Rehabilitation Services Administration, upon the occasion of the presentation of the National Council of State Agencies for the Blind Lifetime Achievement Award to Kenneth Jernigan on April 22, 1998, best characterize the transformative effect of Kenneth Jernigan's half-century of work on behalf of the blind. Here are Dr. Schroeder's remarks:

"Dr. Jernigan's selection as the first-ever recipient of the National Council of State Agencies for the Blind's Lifetime Achievement Award represents an historic moment in the affairs of blind people in America.

Not so very long ago blind people and agencies for the blind found themselves on opposite sides of many, perhaps most, major issues.

But that was twenty years ago, and that time is past. A transformation has occurred in work with the blind, and that transformation is due in no small part to Dr. Jernigan's leadership in bringing cohesive, focused action to formerly disparate elements in the blindness field.

Much of what is central to rehabilitation philosophy today is ideas (often unpopular at the time) which he pioneered decades ago. Indeed it is very nearly impossible to overstate the key role Dr. Jernigan has played in our field. His influence has been and continues to be immeasurable.

I know that it must have touched Dr. Jernigan very deeply to know that his many years of service, of pressing the system to do more, of faithful determination to fight for the rights of blind people (even when his views were unpopular) have resulted today in unprecedented harmony and cooperation in the blindness field.

By honoring Dr. Jernigan, you have honored the individual, and you have recognized the emergence of a new day, full of promise, in the lives of blind people everywhere."

THIRD EXTRA

AN INTIMATE GLANCE

The writing below is included to give the reader just a taste of what it was like to know Kenneth Jernigan—unpredictable, whimsical, delightful, dead serious—all in one lovable package.

Quoted from the *Braille Monitor* dated June 1998:

On the Nature of Mental Discipline and Sonnets
by Kenneth Jernigan

Recently in North Carolina, when I was undergoing cancer treatment and having a restless night, I put together a piece for the *Monitor* that I have been intending to do for more than thirty years. I doubt that I will ever write such an article again, but at least for once here goes.

From time to time I am asked what technique I use in writing speeches and articles, and I always give a general or cursory response. It is not a question of keeping secrets but of wondering whether the person (even though making the inquiry) would really want a full explanation if one were offered. Of course, I could (and usually do) say that writing requires a lot of time and hard work, but that is a platitude.

Let's get right to the meat of it. If I am to talk about how I write speeches and articles, I must discuss the sonnet, which is the most demanding verse form in the English language. It requires great mental effort while appearing to be amazingly simple. As a starter, a sonnet must have fourteen lines—not thirteen, not fifteen, fourteen. And each line must have exactly ten syllables—not nine, not eleven, ten. But wait! We are not through. Each syllable must be precisely placed.

To explain, I must leave the world of common sense and go to the rarified esoterica of graduate school literary classes. And more precisely I must talk about poetic feet. A poetic foot is a stressed and all associated unstressed syllables, much like a measure of music.

But there is more, much more! There are several kinds of poetic feet, but for our purposes we will deal only with the iambic. An iambic foot is an unstressed syllable followed by a stressed syllable. If a line consists of two feet, we call it dimeter. If it has three feet, we call it trimeter. If it has four feet, we call it tetrameter. If it has five feet, we call it pentameter. There is more, but for these purposes that is sufficient.

And now we can deal with the sonnet. As I have already said, it must have fourteen lines of iambic pentameter—not more, not less.

And if you think I have finished, be patient. I have only begun. The sonnet must have a particular rhyme scheme. The last part of the first line is called "a"—and so is everything that rhymes with it. Thus, if the first line ends with the word "cat," then "that," "hat," "mat," and anything of similar ilk will be called "a."

The last part of the first line that is not "a" will be called "b." Thus, if the line ends with the word "dog," then "log," "hog," "frog," etc. will be called "b." The next line that is not "a" or "b" will be called "c"; the next "d"; etc. And there you have the rhyme scheme for poetry.

In the English language there are two main kinds of sonnets—the Petrarchan, which came first and was named for the Italian who popularized it, and the Shakespearean, which is of obvious origin. Each has its own particular and demanding rhyme scheme, but both require fourteen lines of iambic pentameter.

The Petrarchan sonnet has a little (but only a little) flexibility. Its rhyme scheme is "abbaabba, cdecde." The "cde" lines may vary somewhat in placement, but the first eight lines may not. Thus, you may have "cc," "dd," "ee." Or you may have "cd," "cd," "ee." Or you may have any other arrangement you like for the "cde" lines—so long as you leave the first eight alone.

As to the Shakespearean sonnet, forget about flexibility. It isn't there. The rhyme scheme is "abab," "cdcd," "efef," "gg." Nothing more, nothing less. Take it or leave it.

Do you think I have finished? Not on your life. There is more. The first eight lines (I won't bother you with the technicality of their name) must pose a question or problem. And the last six (and again I won't bother you with their name) must give the answer or solution.

I first tried to write a Shakespearean sonnet in late 1944 or early 1945 when I was a senior in high school. You will observe that the language is romantic and the sentiment commensurate. Here it is:

From out the distant realm of higher grace
Your passing glance illumines all my thought,
And I do dream of how 'twould be, your face
With all its wondrous gleams of beauty wrought,

If could I but ascend the filmy clouds
That do obscure you from my closer view,
And pierce each vestige of the mist that shrouds
Each soft and perfect tint, each paling hue;

But could I breach the veil of clinging haze
That doth impair my vision's clearer sweep,
Perhaps 'twould serve but to reveal a maze
Of hidden flaws unseen across the deep.

Tis better thus to worship from afar,
Where naught but beauty gleams from out the star.

It was not until I was a sophomore in college that I undertook to write a Petrarchan sonnet. You will observe that by that time my language had become more down to earth. In fact, my journalism professor accused me of being a cynic. (I might insert here that—even though Freud would doubtless disagree—my sonnets have not primarily been written for philosophical but disciplinary purposes.) In any case, here is my first Petrarchan attempt:

Often when I hear a great hero praised
For some marvelous deed which he has done,
And I see him basking in the warm sun
Of fame, his name by all so fondly phrased,
Or when I see some honest fellow, dazed
By jeering insult, slandered, loved by none,
Because of failure, or some goal not won,
I muse upon the sad prospect amazed.

Cannot mankind this truth of truths perceive,
This one mighty immortal lesson learn,
That what we have is ours by circumstance,
That fate says who shall fail and who achieve,
And even Solomon's glory did turn
Upon a trick of near inheritance?

In recent times I have written only Petrarchan sonnets. A few years back, Mrs. Jernigan and I were driving home from one or another of the state conventions, and I suddenly heard her say to me: "Are you singing?"

"No," I said "I guess I was thinking out loud and trying to compose a sonnet." Here is what I wrote:

There is no slightest way to comprehend
The farther reaches of the stream of time,
Which is not stream but myth that birthed the slime
Which coalesced to form the thought I send
To probe the afterwhere of logic's blend
To seek to find some underlying rhyme
Or reason as a universal prime

To answer Einstein's search for means and end.

But if I cannot find the why and how
Of distant first and just as distant past—
Or, equal chance, of neither then nor now,
But circling stream that makes the future past,
Still must I seek and probe and try to know,
Because there is no other way to go.

My last effort at writing a sonnet was at least a year or two ago. Here it is. You will observe that I even went so far as to give it a name:

To Heisenberg

Perhaps my final breath will gently go
In restful sleep or age or other way,
As uneventful as the close of day
When only soft and quiet breezes blow
To mark the undramatic ebb and flow
Of all that lives and turns again to clay.
But just as like, my life may end in fray.
We dream and speculate but cannot know.

Yet, if the veil that hides what is to be
Could lift to show us at a single glance
The full procession of our future time,
The knowledge got would rob us of romance,
Would trade our will for one compelling prime.
We would be slaves, unable to be free.

There are two sonnets by American authors that I regard as outstanding. They are "Nature" by Longfellow and "Tears" by Reese. And even the Longfellow poem is flawed since two syllables have to be run together to make it scan. However, the sonnet that I have taken as my model of excellence was written by a Britisher. I committed it to memory when I was in high school and have referred to it ever since. It is "Remember" by Christina Rossetti:

> Remember me when I am gone away,
> Gone far away into the silent land;
> When you can no more hold me by the hand,
> Nor I half turn to go yet turning stay.
> Remember me when no more day by day
> You tell me of our future that you planned:
> Only remember me; you understand
> It will be late to counsel then or pray.
>
> Yet, if you should forget me for a while
> And afterwards remember, do not grieve:
> For if the darkness and corruption leave
> A vestige of the thoughts that once I had,
> Better by far you should forget and smile
> Than that you should remember and be sad.

So there you have my favorite sonnet and also some of my techniques for writing. Of course, there is much more to be said to round out the picture. I could, for instance, talk about dactylic, trochaic, and anapestic rhythms; about tercets and sestets; or about hexameters and other such. But I think I have said enough to make the point.

So what does all of this have to do with mental discipline and writing speeches and articles? If I have to tell you, it probably won't do any good. To those who say that I have gone over the edge and lost touch with reality, I reply that I have not forgotten how to engage in combat or street fighting and that I still know how to relate to the members at the National Convention. It can be put to the test. To those who say that madness is indicated, I respond that everybody has (or probably should have) at least a touch of insanity. If (assuming you choose to do so) you want to remember me in the future, think of the sonnet, for of such is the stuff of life—at least, of my life.

As A. E. Housman said:

> Oh, when I was in love with you,
> Then I was clean and brave;
> And miles around the wonder grew
> How well did I behave.
> And now the fancy passes by,
> And nothing will remain,
> And miles around they'll say that I
> Am quite myself again.

FOURTH EXTRA

BIOGRAPHICAL DATA
KENNETH JERNIGAN

Born in Detroit, Michigan, November 13, 1926. Blind since birth. Died October 12, 1998, Baltimore, Maryland

Education: High school diploma, Tennessee School for the Blind, Nashville, 1945. B.S. with Honors, Social Science, Tennessee Technological University, Cookeville, 1948. M.A., English, Peabody College (now Vanderbilt University), Nashville, 1949. Member, editorial staff school newspaper, and co-founder of independent literary magazine. Post-graduate work, Peabody College, 1949-51.

Honorary Degrees: H.D., Coe College, Cedar Rapids, Iowa, 1968. LL.D., Seton Hall University, South Orange, New Jersey, 1974. H.D., Drake University, Des Moines, Iowa, 1975. Doctor of Public Service, MacMurray College, Jacksonville, Illinois, 1997.

Employment: After graduation from high school, operated furniture shop in Beech Grove, Tennessee, building furniture and managing business. English teacher, Tennessee School for the Blind, Nashville, 1949-53. Faculty member,

California Training Center for the Blind, Oakland, 1953-58. Director, Iowa Commission for the Blind, Des Moines, 1958-78. Executive Director, American Action Fund for Blind Children and Adults, Baltimore, 1978-97.

Honors: Received Newel Perry Award, given by the National Federation of the Blind to the person judged to have made the greatest contribution to the welfare of the blind during the year, 1960. Received Francis Joseph Campbell Award, from American Library Association in recognition of imaginative and constructive leadership in developing outstanding library service for the blind, 1967. Received special award for pioneering work in rehabilitation of the blind from the President of the United States, 1968. Received Tennessee Technological University Distinguished Alumni Award, 1975. Designated President Emeritus, National Federation of the Blind, 1986-1998. Received Distinguished Service Award from the President of the United States, 1990. Received Lifetime Achievement Award from the National Council of State Agencies for the Blind, 1998. Received International Leadership Award from the American Foundation for the Blind, 1998. Received the Winston Gordon Award from the Canadian National Institute for the Blind, 1998.

Professional Activities:

- President, Tennessee Federation of the Blind, 1951-53. Member, Board of Directors, National Federation of the Blind, 1952-86. First Vice President, National Federation of the Blind, 1958-68. President, National Federation of the Blind, 1968-86. Director, National Center for the

Blind, 1978-1998. President, North America/Caribbean Region, World Blind Union, 1987-1997.

- Appointed to National Advisory Committee on Services for the Blind and Visually Handicapped by the Secretary of Health, Education, and Welfare, 1972. Appointed as a Special Consultant on Services for the Blind by the Federal Commissioner of Rehabilitation, 1975. Delivered speech (broadcast live nationwide on National Public Radio) to National Press Club in Washington, DC, 1975. Appointed special consultant to Executive Director of the White House Conference on the Handicapped, 1976. Appointed consultant to the Smithsonian Institution, advising on museum programs for blind visitors, 1976. Appointed to the Advisory Committee of the White House Conference on Library and Informational Services by the President of the United States, 1977. Delivered 60th anniversary commencement address, Tennessee Technological University, 1989.

FIFTH EXTRA

SELECTED SPEECHES AND ARTICLES BY KENNETH JERNIGAN

CONVENTION SPEECHES:

- *Blindness: Handicap or Characteristic? – 1963*
- *Blindness: Concepts and Misconceptions – 1965*
- *Blindness: Milestones and Millstones – 1968*
- *Blindness: New Insights on Old Outlooks – 1969*
- *Blindness: The Myth and the Image – 1970*
- *To Man the Barricades – 1971*
- *Blindness: The New Generation – 1972*
- *Blindness: A Left-Handed Dissertation – 1973*
- *Blindness: Is History Against Us? – 1973*
- *Blindness: Is Literature Against Us? – 1974*
- *Blindness: Is the Public Against Us? – 1975*
- *Blindness: Of Visions and Vultures – 1976*
- *To Everything There Is a Season – 1977*
- *Blindness: That's How It Is at the Top of the Stairs – 1979*
- *Blindness: The Lessons of History – 1980*
- *Blindness: The Corner of Time – 1981*
- *Blindness: Simplicity, Complexity, and the Public Mind – 1982*

- *Blindness: The Other Half of Inertia* – 1983
- *Blindness: The Circle of Sophistry* – 1984
- *Blindness: The Pattern of Freedom* – 1985
- *Blindness: The Coming of the Third Generation* – 1986
- *The Federation at Fifty* – 1990
- *Shifting Balances in the Blindness Field* – 1992
- *The Nature of Independence* – 1993
- *Of Braille and Honeybees* – 1994
- *The Day after Civil Rights* – 1997

KERNEL BOOK STORIES:

- "Growing Up Blind in Tennessee during the Depression" (*What Color Is the Sun*)
- "Competing on Terms of Equality" (*The Freedom Bell*)
- "To Park or Not to Park" (*As the Twig Is Bent*)
- "Making Hay" (*Making Hay*)
- "The Value of Planning" (*The Journey*)
- "Standing on One Foot" (*Standing on One Foot*)
- "The Hook on the Doctor's Door" (*When the Blizzard Blows*)
- "Of Toothpaste and Shaving Cream" (*Toothpaste and Railroad Tracks*)
- "Tapping the Charcoal" (*Tapping the Charcoal*)
- "Old Dogs and New Tricks" (*Old Dogs and New Tricks*)
- "Beginnings and Blueprints" (*Beginnings and Blueprints*)
- "The Smells and Sounds of Sixty Years" (*Like Cats and Dogs*)
- "Please Don't Throw the Nickel" (*Wall-to-Wall Thanksgiving*)
- "The Barrier of the Visible Difference" (*Gray Pancakes and Gold Horses*)
- "Even I" (*To Touch the Untouchable Dream*)

OTHER:

- *Fighting Discrimination and Promoting Equality of Opportunity*, delivered by Kenneth Jernigan, President, North America/Caribbean Region, World Blind Union, at the Second General Assembly of the World Blind Union, Madrid, Spain, September 21, 1988

- *Reflections of a Lifetime Reader*, delivered by Kenneth Jernigan to the Conference of Librarians Serving Blind and Physically Handicapped Individuals, Louisville, Kentucky, May 7, 1990

- *The Pitfalls of Political Correctness: Euphemisms Excoriated, Braille Monitor*, August 1993

- *Changing What It Means to be Blind: The World Blind Union and the Twenty-first Century*, Keynote Address delivered by Kenneth Jernigan at the Fourth General Assembly of the World Blind Union, Toronto, Ontario, August 26, 1996

- *Partnership Between Consumers and Professionals in the Education of Blind Children*, Keynote Address delivered by Kenneth Jernigan at the 10th World Conference of the International Council for Education of People with Visual Impairment, São Paulo, Brazil, August 3-8, 1997

ACKNOWLEDGEMENTS

It has taken several years and the help of many people for this book to reach the form you see today. My heartfelt thanks goes to all, especially the twenty-eight people who wrote of their experiences. Those who sent suggestions and material that were unused also offered important insights. I thank all of you for your cooperation, patience, and flexibility through the editing process.

Further, I wish to thank all of those who helped by reading and rereading chapters, those who helped with date entry, proofreading, and page layout and other suggestions for presentation for this project. I shall not attempt to name everyone, but you know who you are, and so do I. Without your help, the book could not exist.

The two people who finally helped to bring the book together with many hours of work and creativity are Mary Ellen Jernigan and Marsha Dyer. To you I am especially grateful. Together, I hope and believe we have brought to the reader a picture of a man and a movement which will inspire and educate as Kenneth Jernigan taught us to do.

Ramona Walhof
September, 2015

Printed in the United States
By Bookmasters